Pray and Grow Rich

Catherine Ponder

Pray and Grow Rich

Parker Publishing Company, Inc.   West Nyack, N.Y.

Reward Edition .... July, 1973
Fifth Printing .... November, 1976

PRINTED IN THE UNITED STATES OF AMERICA

Prayer is receiving more consideration today than at any time during the past thousand years!

This Book Is Dedicated to

My various prayer partners of the last twenty years—a Negro maid, an elderly matron, a childhood friend, a businessman, and several housewives—whose prayers helped me do all the things "they said couldn't be done":—Become a minister, write successful books, establish a church, become an international lecturer, bring up my young son alone when I became widowed, and make a comeback from the sudden death of loved ones. Together, my prayer partners and I have found that the poet and prophet was right when he promised, "More things are wrought by prayer than this world dreams of."

What This Book Can Do for You

A young man with a grave problem was asked by his minister, "Have you prayed about it?" He answered, *"Prayed?* This is no time to pray. It's time to *do* something!"

To pray is to *do* something—the most important "something" you can first do about any problem.

Why?

Because prayer is where the true action is! Prayer is the only action you can take that truly makes things different—from the inside out.

This is true because physical action releases the weakest form of energy, whereas mental and spiritual action releases the highest form of energy.

Prayer deals primarily with the states of mind and laws of mental activity that rule your world. Prayer changes your mentality; prayer first changes your thinking as it calms, uplifts and renews you. This is one of the purposes of prayer—to change your thinking, which in turn changes your world.

But prayer goes further. There is another reason for all the shouting about the "power of prayer."

Prayer releases the highest form of energy in the universe, as it links you with a God energy, which is your source. When this happens, prayer "turns you on!"

How?

When you pray, you stir into action an atomic force. You release a potent spiritual vibration that can be released in no other way.

Through prayer you unleash and loose a God energy within and around you that gets busy working for you and through you, producing right attitudes, reactions and results. It is your prayers that recognize and release that God power.

You may not feel the force of prayer because it operates at a higher vibration than that ordinarily felt by man. In fact, prayer releases an energy that is usually too fine to be recorded physically.

Nevertheless, as you pray you expand mentally and spiritually so as to become big enough in consciousness to *receive* a larger flow of the divine energy generated through prayer. Prayer is not only asking and communing. *Prayer is also receiving.*

A skeptic once insisted that he did not believe in the power of prayer. When asked if he had ever prayed, he replied that he had once. His explanation was that on that occasion he was lost in a deep forest and could not find his way out. He had been there several days and was beginning to feel the pangs of starvation. He said that in his "weakness" he prayed.

"Then God *did* answer your prayer, or you would not be here," exclaimed his acquaintance.

"No," replied the skeptic, "God did not answer my prayer. A couple of hunters came along soon afterward and showed me the way out."

This man did not understand that his prayer had been answered, and that the hunters were the human agency through which God's work had been done. Nevertheless, through the act of prayer, he had for a moment recognized the God power within and around him, and had thereby contacted and released it to produce results for him. He had not only asked; he had also received.

ONE PRAYS WITH THE MIND

In recent times we've heard much about "the power of thought" as well as about "the power of prayer." These two terms are linked. They are twin powers. The mind is the connecting link between God and man. Prayer is a method of thought that links God and man. One prays with the mind.

Some authorities claim that what it usually takes a person six hours to do could easily be accomplished in only one hour by a person who knew how to pray and meditate first!

A man who practices daily meditation recently proved it, as he often has. He had been given three writing assignments which he was expected to complete in a single day. At first, he was tempted to panic just thinking about the task before him—one that would take the average journalist several days at best to complete.

Then he quieted his mind, prayed and meditated for an entire hour. During this meditation time, ideas for all three writing assignments quietly flowed into his conscious mind. He then proceeded with the tasks and completed them in a few hours without the usual "blood, sweat and tears."

An engineer with grave responsibilities on a large project had only one method for solving his engineering problems. When they arose, he always retired to his private office and sat quietly behind his desk, meditating and praying for guidance. Always the answer came as the right ideas or the perfect solution cropped up.

One day one of his employees, a young "jet set" engineer right out of college, asked the secret of this engineer's phenomenal success. When informed, this young man replied incredulously, "You mean you *just* pray and meditate and the answer comes?"

The root meaning of the word "man" is "one who looks up." Some psychologists claim that man uses only about 1/10 of 1 percent of his energies and powers, because he does not live up to the root meaning of his name: He does not look up, nor does he look within, often enough. It is sad to realize that perhaps all but 1/10 of 1 percent of man's forces are wasted because they are expressed outwardly instead of inwardly. But something can be done about it!

WHY PRAYER HAS MIRACLE POWER

Scientists tell us there are no miracles—only the working of higher laws not commonly understood. Actually there seems to be one set of natural laws for the physical world and another set for the invisible world of mind and spirit. The laws of mind and spirit are so much stronger that they can be used to accentuate, neutralize, or even reverse the laws of the physical world. *Prayer is the one power in the world that seems to set off the working of those higher laws.*

Prayer can get the job done—when nothing else has.

Why is prayer so powerful? Why can prayer accentuate, neutralize or even reverse the laws of the physical world?

Because *through prayer, you tap the operation of higher laws of supreme mind and spirit. Through prayer you release a spiritual force which shatters fixed states of mind that have caused so much havoc in your world.* Your imprisoned thoughts and pent-up negative emotions go free and dissolve, as a higher energy floods your being and your world.

Indeed, *the energy and power released in prayer help you to "crash through" the negative thought strata that had previously bound you to all kinds of problems.* Thereafter, the impossible becomes possible. Your ships come in. So-called miracles occur. It is then that you realize that prayer *did* overcome the usual "laws of nature" and did what they said couldn't be done!

If prayer were commonly understood and practiced by mankind universally, the dreaded things of this world—crime, disease, poverty and war—could become ancient history. You can begin helping to eradicate these universal ills, as well as a score of personal ones, as you begin deliberately developing your prayer powers described in this book.

PRAYER MAKES YOU IRRESISTIBLE
FOR RECEIVING RICHES

Perhaps you are thinking that prayer has not yet made your dreams come true or your "ships of gold" come in. That is because the art and science of prayer are not accomplished in one giant step nor in one dramatic act. Prayer is a continuous practice which should be applied to the little as well as to the big things in your life.

Does this sound dull? Well, it isn't! If you have thought so, you do not know what you've missed.

Prayer can be supremely exciting. Once, when I was trying to get guidance about my teenage son's future, as I prayed Air Force planes flew overhead so low that they interrupted my prayer time. When this happened on two separate occasions in a row, I realized that apparently was the answer. Within a matter of weeks, my son had decided to delay attending college and had enlisted in the United States Air Force.

Prayer also has a sense of humor at times. Once when I was trying to get guidance about whether to accept a lecture invitation in the State of Indiana, a college band near my apartment suddenly started playing, "Back Home Again In Indiana" so loudly that it roused me from my prayer period, and I took that as intuitive guidance to go to Indiana to lecture. It proved to be one of the most thrilling lecture experiences I have ever had.

Dr. Billy Graham once said, "The man who has never discovered the power of prayer in a spiritual sense has never really lived." I believe it! You will too!

Once you get the workings of it, there is a certain indescribable fascination about prayer; an unforgettable, irresistible quality, an exuberating and exulting feeling that draws you back to it again and again. As you turn within to its power more and more, you discover you are carrying within your own being a portable paradise which you can contact anytime anywhere, regardless of what is happening around you.

There is a quaint saying among the Pennsylvania Dutch, "The hurrieder I go, the behinder I get!" Prayer slows you down to get real traction. Prayer gets you in the mood to receive your good. Prayer gives you a taste of heaven, and it tastes good! (The word "heaven" means "expansion" and the practice of prayer expands both you and your good.) St. Francis of Assisi, who loved to pray in a cave, described prayer as "a heavenly sweetness."

Your soul gets twisted out of shape when you battle life, people, circumstances. Prayer takes away your spirit of fuss, gives you a gentleness of pace. One of the most obvious signs of the person who prays is the quiet way he is able to maintain his equilibrium in the grip of circumstances, until those circumstances finally lose their grip on him!

One cynic has said there is nothing so unattractive as a prayer-less woman. I am even more cynical: There is nothing so unattractive as a prayer-less person, because his prayer-less-ness has demagnetized him to the blessings of life.

When you pray you quiet your mind, body, emotions, vibrations. Prayer gives you a sense of peace and tranquillity that are attracting powers. In one way or another, prayer first makes you more attractive, and then gets busy attracting your good to you. *Prayer makes you irresistible to your good!* And, most certainly, to all the riches of confident living, including adequate financial supply.

NOTHING DULL ABOUT RIGHT PRAYER

A lot of dull things have been written about prayer, but you will not find any of them in this book!

If prayer has seemed a dull practice to you in the past—a practice that you regarded as fine for sweet ol' ladies and innocent children but one that just did not work for you—it was probably because you simply did not know how to pray. There's more to prayer than mumbling a few self-conscious words that you know never reach the ceiling!

In his book, *Prayer Can Change Your Life,*° Dr. William R. Parker points out that among the people who participated in his prayer experiments at Redlands University, those who prayed at home on their own without benefit of psychological insight or spiritual instruction got no results. Their prayers brought absolutely no improvements, because they knew not what effective prayer demanded of them.

When you pray with your conscious mind only, just a fraction of your total mind prays, and you get only a fraction of the results due you through prayer.

The purpose of this book is to acquaint you with all the fascinating ways you can pray: through relaxation, denials, affirmations, concentration, meditation, the silence, realization, thanksgiving. Regardless of your life situation, you will find there is al-

---

° William R. Parker and Elaine St. Johns, *Prayer Can Change Your Life* (West Nyack, N.Y.: Parker Publishing Company, Inc., 1957).

ways a way you can pray—to suit your mood and circumstances—
a method that gets the job done. There is no better way to secure
all the riches of life you so earnestly desire.

After studying the favorable effects prayer had on his patients,
world famous doctor and scientist Alexis Carrel, M.D., promised:
"If you make a habit of *sincere* prayer, your life will be very
noticeably and profoundly altered." But you must be sincere in
prayer. You should pray the way you make love—*with everything
you've got!* One plain spoken theologian has described this method
as "passionate praying." Truly, as you study the laws of prayer
hereinafter described, you will find yourself getting into the act
—the act of prayer—more and more and getting richer—more and
more—without tensions or fears.

Prayer will then turn on the action of God's goodness within
and around you. As you persist in developing your various prayer
powers, *it will dawn on you that prayer is where the action is;*
that prayer *has* "turned you on" and you will undoubtedly have
the results to prove it! But whether or not the sure-fire answers
to prayer have come through yet, you will be convinced of its
necessity in your life from the peace of mind and deep soul satisfaction you are experiencing—which, in turn, lead to every outer
blessing, and I do mean richer blessings and more of them.

When this happens, you will no longer complain, "Why all the
shouting about the richness and power of prayer?"

You will be one of the enriched "shouters"!

CATHERINE PONDER

Contents

7. The Prayer for Miracles (Continued)

How to activate your miracle consciousness. The Christ mind. The power of the phrase "Jesus Christ." Call on the name Jesus Christ. Write out Jesus Christ prayers. Picture Jesus Christ. Behold the Christ in others. How to behold the Christ in yourself. How inviting the Christ within heals one. How to invoke the peace of Jesus Christ. How to affirm the finished works of Jesus Christ. Ways to invite the universal Christ presence. How a sophisticated woman was healed. How to be blessed with the forgiving power of Jesus Christ. The miraculous word power of Christ Jesus. The white miracle light of the Christ. How to invoke Christ consciousness through words of Jesus. How to release your miracle energy power.

The history of concentration. The incredible power of concentration. A housewife's experience. The necessity of concentration in prayer development. How to induce concentration through list-making. Your first list. How a businessman made a special list. Your list of choice—the second list. A healer's secret formula of success. Top executives prove value of list-making to themselves. Your third list. How to induce concentration through imaging. The grand results of modern prayer wheels. How a businesswoman worked out a happier life. My own experience in completing an assignment. How a prayer wheel served a college professor. How a tenement family "graduated" from their tenement. Imaging creates and

How a complex human relations problem was cleared up. How to identify with the prayer of realization. Healing of breast accomplished through realization in prayer. Spiritual prediction for this century coming true. Holy telepathy: How to get true realization through prayer. How to ask for inner assurance of answered prayer. How to receive guidance by dwelling on subject. How to affirm guidance most effectively. Your inner sensing and feeling is the secret of effective prayer. Many prayer methods can bring realization. How the author attained realization in prayer of concentration and meditation. Realization through group participation. How prayer was tested in scientific experiments. Some examples of how realization was received through prayer telepathy. After realization, then what?

How to prepare rather than despair. Get ready for surprises! After prayer comes the never-failing light.

Pray and Grow Rich

1

The Shocking Truth About Prayer

Once when there was a storm at sea, a distressed passenger on a great ocean liner rushed up to the ship's captain and asked, "How serious is this storm?"

"It is so serious, madam, that only prayer can save us."

"My gracious!" gasped the woman. "Has it come to *that?*"

The shocking truth about prayer is that most people are afraid of it. They would rather go down with the storms of life than pray their way out of them.

Why?

Probably because of their *sheer ignorance* of the most fascinating force in the world.

Prayer *is* such a fascinating power that once it gets your attention, it will not let you go. Because of its fascination, the spirit of prayer is easier caught than taught. Once you've tapped this power it becomes a steady pressure, demanding attention and expression in your life.

You may even find yourself becoming a "prayer addict," because you will find you have to have it for real victories. Prayer will sustain, uplift and renew you as nothing else will. Prayer will calm, satisfy and fulfill you as nothing else can.

The shocking truth about prayer is that as a spiritual being, made in the image of God, a little lower than the angels, *you have dynamic prayer powers within you!* Through developing these prayer powers, you renew your mind and body, calm the storms of daily living, and you may even completely transform your life for unexpected good.

1

An additional shocking truth about prayer is that there is nothing complicated about it. There are simple ways in which you can begin to employ and *enjoy* the power of prayer. Indeed, there are far more ways to pray than you've dreamed possible, each of which is a delight.

The word "dynamic" has the same root as the word "dynamite." That which is dynamic is powerful, forceful, filled with energy, and leads to change. That which is dynamic tends to blast you out of a rut!

A "law" is a principle that works. The word "law" also suggests a desire for order in one's life. And the word "prayer" means "communion" with God and His goodness.

Thus, *the dynamic laws of prayer* are dynamic principles *that work;* they are laws of mind and spirit that are powerful, forceful, filled with energy, and that lead to vast improvement in your life as they help you make common union with God and His goodness. Furthermore, they are far more easily contacted and executed than most folks realize. Emerson went so far as to say we are already "begirt" with these laws *which execute themselves!* In his Essay on "Spiritual Laws" he declares:

> The lesson is forcibly taught . . . that our life might be much easier and simpler than we make it; that the world might be a happier place than it is; that there is no need of struggles, convulsions, and despairs, of the wringing of the hands and the gnashing of the teeth; that we miscreate our own evils. We interfere with the optimism of nature. . . . We are begirt with laws which execute themselves.

How wonderful to have this awareness of good come effortlessly into our lives! That as we make contact with these powerful laws of mind and spirit, they execute themselves!

How a Businesswoman Got Out of a Deep Rut in Her Life

A businesswoman felt she had gotten in a rut in both her business and personal life. Though she was busy, she was also bored. Finally she talked about her problems with a friend, who said, "Prayer is the one thing that can blast you out of the rut you are in." The friend then asked her to begin decreeing for five minutes every day: "OF MYSELF I CANNOT DO IT, BUT THE CHRIST WITHIN ME CAN AND IS PERFORMING MIRACLES IN MY MIND, BODY AND AFFAIRS HERE AND NOW."

Within a week, electrifying changes began taking place. Old conditions and relationships quickly faded away. Suddenly new doors opened in her career which soon led to a happy new personal life as well. The miracle power of prayer had worked.

You will discover, with this busy career woman, that developing your dynamic prayer powers is the most important thing you can do, regardless of what else is on your agenda. A well-developed prayer consciousness will lead you to everything else: peace of mind, health of body, success in your affairs, and all-round happiness.

Prayer is the "package deal" to new and successful living! A schoolteacher once declared, "As I develop my prayer powers I've got it made, because everything else in life will then come." Prayer is the one supreme instrument given to man by God for all attainment.

NOTHING EVER DULL NOR COMPLEX ABOUT DYNAMIC PRAYER

A shocking truth about prayer is that there is nothing complex about it. There is nothing "ho hum" about prayer. It is just the opposite—the most soul-satisfying experience in which you will ever get involved. Instead of being dull, it becomes an exciting process.

The history of prayer shows that man has always prayed. One of the first things primitive man did was to pray for food and for protection. Even primitive, unevolved man realized the necessity for, as well as the naturalness of, prayer.

It has only been since man has become more "civilized" that he has decided he was too sophisticated to pray; thus he has named prayer a mysterious, complex process. (Quite contrary to popular opinion, the really sophisticated people of this world *do* pray. They even get sophisticated results! I was recently guest at a dinner party given in an exclusive club by the widow of a Texas oilman. The main conversation at dinner was how this elegant, world-traveled woman had recently experienced a marvelous spiritual healing through using definite prayer techniques. Her prayer method was discussed in detail over dinner among a gathering of "highbrow" guests. And so I repeat: The really sophisticated people of this world do pray and they even get sophisticated results!)

Prayer can again become a simple, satisfying experience of renewal and enlightenment for you as you realize the various ways you can pray effectively for the riches of life, and all that goes with them.

Many people hesitate to pray because they do not understand the nature of God. Since the word "prayer" means "communion," the purpose of prayer is to commune with God, whose nature is supreme good. To pray is to make common union with all good.

If you think of God as a stern, spiteful, puritanical old man sitting off in the sky, severely judging you, then why pray? Why complicate matters further by trying to make contact with that kind of being? If you still think of God as having a split personality of good and evil, then it is understandable why you would have little desire to make common union with such a being in prayer.

The sign in front of a church recently read: "Our God is not dead. Too bad about yours!" Of course, God is not dead. God as love, God as spirit, God as supreme good, cannot die. But let's hope the limited concepts of Him are dying out of man's consciousness.

YOUR UNIVERSAL GOD POWER IS WITHIN YOUR GRASP

Theology has long taught that God is both immanent (within) and transcendent (universal), though mankind has usually thought of God only as transcendent—out there somewhere far away. One theologian has described the people who believe in God-immanent as the "God-withiners," and of the people who believe in God-transcendent as the "God-beyonders."

God as transcendent is the universal God presence that is everywhere evenly present. You become attuned to God's universal presence when you affirm, "THERE IS ONLY ONE PRESENCE AND ONE POWER IN THE UNIVERSE, GOD THE GOOD, OMNIPOTENT." You can bring that universal presence into your life by affirming: "THERE IS ONLY ONE PRESENCE AND ONE POWER IN MY LIFE (or IN THIS SITUATION, DIAGNOSIS, PERSONALITY, OR APPEARANCE) GOD THE GOOD, OMNIPOTENT."

Does such a prayer sound rather high-flung for producing practical results in your life? Well, it isn't as you will see by the following cases.

A businessman once overcame ill health, financial failure and family difficulties by daily dwelling upon the prayer, "THERE IS ONLY ONE PRESENCE AND ONE POWER IN MY LIFE—GOD THE GOOD, OMNIPOTENT." At the time he began making this prayer statement, both he and his wife were in ill health. They had spent much money on various treatments, but still suffered. This man had gone from one job to another, and had never found his true work. Their only child had been a problem.

As this man began to affirm only God's goodness in his life, things began to improve. Nothing spectacular happened, but he could see that omnipotent good was becoming more evident. This encouraged him and gave him courage to persevere in claiming God's blessings.

First, his wife's health improved. Soon they were both able to give up the expensive drugs and health treatments so long prescribed. As he continued affirming the good, he was offered the kind of job he had long desired. The way opened later for him to buy this business, which had been his dream. His business prospered in ways he could not have foreseen. Their child matured and found work that challenged and satisfied him. He later married and settled down to a harmonious, successful way of life.

This businessman still keeps this prayer statement where he can see and use it daily: "THERE IS ONLY ONE PRESENCE AND ONE POWER IN MY LIFE—GOD THE GOOD, OMNIPOTENT."

The late F. L. Rawson, famous London metaphysician who had

such success in protecting men in war, did so through dwelling upon the universal God presence. Often he would decree, "THERE IS NOTHING BUT GOD." His explanation for his success in prayer was this: "Instead of praying for or spiritually treating the persons, I spiritually treat myself; that is, I try to get out of my own mind the false ideas of God and man that have been ingrained therein by years of false training. If I can get my realization of God clear, the person is healed (or protected) instantly."

Spiritual healer H. B. Jeffery used a similar technique, as pointed out in his book *The Principles of Healing*.[1] The prayer statement he often gave those seeking healing was, "I LIVE, MOVE AND HAVE MY BEING IN GOD, AND HE WORKS IN ME TO WILL AND TO DO HIS GOOD PLEASURE." Dwelling upon the universal God nature has often healed the sick and troubled.

A writer named Mary Austin developed cancer and was given a year to live. She chose to go to Rome to spend the time studying early documents of Christianity. She became so absorbed in her studies that she lost all fear of cancer. One day she realized the cancer was gone. By her study of the nature of God and other religious themes, healing had come. In another instance, a person was healed after praying over and over, "THERE IS NOTHING BUT GOD."

YOUR INDWELLING GOD POWER

God is also immanent or within you. This is the God-nature which Jesus tried to point out to all mankind. It was to this indwelling spiritual nature that Paul referred as man's "hope of glory." (Col. 1:27) Job described it as a "spirit in man." (Job 32:8)

When you realize that God is not only the universal spirit of good filling all the universe—but that God is also within you—and that it is this indwelling God-nature you are contacting, developing and bringing alive in prayer—then you can see that there is no need to strain or reach out.

---

[1] H. B. Jeffery, *The Principles of Healing* (Fort Worth, Texas: Christ Truth League, 1939).

You have your own indwelling Lord who longs to help, inspire and guide you. This indwelling Lord is interested in every detail of your life. You can pray to this indwelling Lord about everything that concerns you—from finding a parking place on a busy street to the healing of a supposedly incurable disease.

Why Many People's Prayers Go Unanswered

Many peoples' prayers are not answered because they do not know about this indwelling Lord. They are straining to try to get the attention of a supposedly far-off God, who may or may not be interested in their problems (or so they believe). It can be frustrating to try to pray to that kind of God, and it is little wonder that many people don't even try.

The shocking truth about prayer is that there is no strain or frustration in true prayer because when you pray you are making common union with the God-nature of supreme good *within* you. *In true prayer you turn within, not without!*

A grandmother told her grandson that God was within him. The little boy wanted to believe this, but it was a new idea to him, so he doubtfully mused, "If God is within me, what is He doing? Is He just lying down in there?"

It often seems that our indwelling God-nature has been lying down on the job because we have not known how to make common union with this innate goodness. *Actually God is far more willing to give than we are to receive. A loving Father wants our prayers answered. He wants our dreams (which are really His dreams for us!) to come true. He has no higher way of expressing Himself than through His own image and likeness— man. The problem has not been that God didn't want to give man greater good. The problem has been that man did not know how to receive it. Prayer is the missing link. Through prayer man opens his consciousness to receive the fullness of God's blessings. Prayer is receiving.*

The ancients knew the age-old secret—that God is within. In the original Sanskrit the word for "prayer" was "pal-al," meaning "judging oneself as wondrously made." This is among the highest forms of prayer, to recognize yourself as being a wondrous expression of God, and then to commune with that inner God-nature. (Later chapters instruct you how to do this.)

What a thrill it is to realize that God is within. A six-year-old girl attended a church for the first time. When her father, a doctor, met her after Sunday School to escort her to the church service, she seemed to be on "Cloud Nine." When her father asked how she had liked it, she replied dreamily, "It was wonderful!"

"Honey, what was so wonderful about it?"

"Daddy, I found out where God is! He's out there in the trees, grass, animals, and world just as I've always known. But Daddy, God is also *within* me and I can talk with Him there any time I want to!"

The turning point came in George Fox's life in 17th Century England when he made this same discovery: that God is a living spiritual presence, revealed within the soul. Having learned this, he developed such spiritual power that his very presence caused his followers to "quake" and tremble. Thus began the Quaker religion. George Fox often described God as "the teacher within."

Sixteen centuries ago the Roman monk, Augustine, declared he was amazed that men should go abroad to gaze upon wonders while passing by the greatest wonder of all—their own God-given divinity—which he described as a "crowning wonder." St. Augustine's advice was: "Retire into thyself, for Truth dwells in the inner man."

PRAY FIRST INSTEAD OF LAST

The shocking truth about prayer is that when you have a need, you can always be shown how to meet that need, if you pray about it first instead of last; whereas you can do many things on the human level and still the need will not be met when you have neglected to pray about it.

A businesswoman had a severe sore throat which drugs had not cleared up. One night she attended a small prayer group and asked the group to pray for the healing of her throat. Their prayer for her spoken in unison was this: "YOU ARE NOT POWERLESS TO CLAIM YOUR GOOD. NOTHING CAN HOLD YOU IN BONDAGE. YOU ARE FREE WITH THE FREEDOM OF SPIRIT. YOU FREELY CLAIM YOUR GOOD NOW."

The businesswoman spoke these words aloud too. Within twenty-four hours, her throat was completely healed. (For an explanation of health problems in the throat area, see the chapter on "Power" in my book, *The Healing Secret of the Ages*.)

Prayer is the most practical thing in the world. Pray first instead of last!

A Case of Power of Prayer in Finance

During the depression years, a businessman who knew about the power of prosperous thinking as well as about the power of prayer, took a bankrupt business in Los Angeles and made a fortune from it. Years later he sold the business and retired. But the man who bought this thriving business was not a prosperous-thinking-nor-praying man, and in a few years was losing money.

Several of the salesmen and employees who had worked with the first man and had watched him build the business into a million-dollar one finally asked the new owner to invite the former owner to show him how he had built the business through spiritual methods. In sheer desperation, the new owner agreed to do so.

The retired millionaire set to work by coming into town and renting a room at a downtown hotel, for the sole purpose of being left alone to do intensive prayer work about the situation.

He soon learned that several hundred thousand dollars had to be raised quickly or the business would close. Every morning he called in the owner and salesmen to talk with them about the power of prosperous thinking. (See my book, *The Dynamic Laws of Prosperity*, for simple techniques in developing prosperous thinking.) When they mentioned the need for several hundred thousand dollars, he would quietly say, "It will come, and in time."

For nine days he remained in his hotel room praying for guidance, affirming prosperity, instructing the employees in prosperous thinking, and generally *building a spiritual consciousness through which his prayers for this business could be answered.*

Finally, on the ninth day, when he went into the hotel dining room for dinner, he felt guided to chat with a man he found sitting alone at a nearby table. Though strangers, they discovered that they had mutual friends in New York and Los Angeles. They had read many of the same books, and used many of the same ideas through prayer and prosperous thinking to build successful businesses. Before they parted that first night, the man from the East asked the millionaire if he knew of a good place to invest some money, explaining that he had a son-in-law who wanted to come West, and he was looking around for him.

In a few days it was all settled. The rich man from the East brought not only his son-in-law and money into the previously failing business, but also brought his own wealth of spiritual knowledge and experience. The owner who had let the business go down willingly sold his own interest at a profit and got out. The salesmen kept their jobs and the business was once again in the hands of prosperous-minded, praying people. Of course it again prospered.

As for the practical results that prayer wrought in this situation, the man from the East explained he had intended to go to San Francisco to look around, but that he had suddenly felt guided to go to Los Angeles. He had also intended to look leisurely for a business in which to invest, perhaps taking months to decide upon one. But while in prayer, he had gotten the feeling he should get to Los Angeles at once. He had planned to go to a certain hotel upon arrival in town, but on the plane he had talked with a man who had strongly recommended he check into the hotel where, unknown to him, the millionaire was praying.

Furthermore, he had made all these decisions only after the millionaire had checked into the hotel and during the nine days he was holed up in his room praying. As he had prayerfully looked to a rich, loving Father for guidance, and had made rich affirmations, they had literally brought to him a rich man and rich results.

During the nine-day stay in the hotel one of the prosperity affirmations he had declared daily was this: "THE INFINITE MIND IS MY REAL RESOURCE AND I AM UNLIMITED BECAUSE GOD IS UNLIMITED." An equally powerful prayer when confronted with desperate circumstances is this: "I AM SPIRIT, WORKING WITH MIGHTY, POWERFUL, SPIRITUAL FORCES. THE DEMANDS OF SPIRIT MUST AND ARE BEING MET NOW."

This man proved that prayer is the most practical thing in the world. Pray first instead of last! If it's good in the last place, it's certainly as good for first place!

THE PATH TO RICHES OF INSTANT GOOD

Many people doubt that their prayers have any powers, so their idea of prayer is to pray only in an emergency—the prayer of desperation. The pilot of a large trainer plane radioed his ground control station as follows:

"One wing sheared off; landing gear gone; visibility fifty feet; cargo dynamite. What are your instructions."

Quickly from the radio tower came this message:

"Now repeat after me, 'Our Father who art in heaven, Hallowed be Thy Name. Thy kingdom come.'"

Many people are like that man in the radio tower; they think prayer is only for emergencies.

Whereas, if people prayed more there would be fewer emergencies to meet, and those would be met victoriously.

Prayer is an art and a science. The dictionary describes an "art" as "a skill"; also as "human ability to make things happen." The dictionary describes "science" as "knowledge which is gained by systematic study and practice."

Prayer, then, is a skill or ability to cause good things to happen in one's life through contact with one's own indwelling Lord, when this skill is studied and practiced to experience a richer life.

This explains why some people seem to have prayer-power and others do not. Those who do not, pray only in an emergency, if at all. They wait until they are coming in for a crash landing before it occurs to them to ask God's help.

It is good to practice the presence of God just as you would practice music. Practice makes perfect in the art of prayer, just as in developing any other skill. It is easy to do this because the more you practice the art of prayer, the more enjoyable and satisfying it becomes, and the more fascinated you become with both its mystical and practical value. After a while, you find yourself "going within" on a moment's notice any time, anywhere— making contact with your own indwelling Lord, which then brings peace, renewal and right results.

Prayer is the path to instant good! Your health good, your family good, all good you can think of—for greater riches in your life.

PRAYER IS SOUL-STRETCHING

Has prayer sometimes led you down a dead-end street of no results, rather than up the glowing path of instant good?

Prayer is soul-stretching.

When your prayers have not been answered, perhaps it is because your soul was being stretched big enough to accept that answer.

Maybe you've heard the story about the young minister who went home to visit his parents for the first time after having taken his first church. His parents expected glowing reports of his work. When his mother asked, "Son, has your ministry grown much since you took it over?" he honestly replied, "No, but I have! I have had to grow to try to make it grow." That young man was getting his soul stretched.

When your prayers seem not to be answered, it is often because the answer is going to be bigger and better than you had anticipated. So keep on praying, in order that you will be big enough in consciousness to be able to accept the rich blessings when they come!

This is the time to affirm: "I AM OPEN AND RECEPTIVE TO GOD'S GOOD IN EVERY PHASE OF MY LIFE NOW. I AM OPEN AND RECEPTIVE TO GOD'S GOOD AS IT MANIFESTS IN EVERY PHASE OF MY LIFE NOW." Do it now, affirm it confidently, expecting surprising new riches in your experience!

I recently asked a famous minister, who enjoys all the blessings of life in abundance, the secret of his success. He replied that early in his career he began daily declaring: "I AM OPEN AND RECEPTIVE TO GOD'S BLESSINGS IN EVERY PHASE OF MY LIFE NOW." He has continued this prayer practice over the years with abundant results of health, wealth and wisdom.

At times when you pray you may not get what you pray for; yet you pray not in vain. Though things do not always change as you wish them to when you pray, one thing is sure: *You change!* Always some change is wrought in the invisible that is needed and that leads to life's answers.

When your prayers are not immediately answered, it is often because you have been trying to limit God's good in your life.

You have probably been unconsciously saying, "Not Thy will, but mine be done. Put it here, Lord." Your prayers thus go unanswered until you unconditionally surrender and say, "Lord, you know best. I know Your will for me is greater good than I can possibly imagine. I now let go and let this prayer be answered in Your highest and best way. I now let go and let Your unlimited good flow its riches into this situation or condition."

You may be sure that under all conditions, irrespective of your seeming needs and desires, lasting good will come to you when you ask only that God's good will manifest in your life. *If each of us abandoned ourselves fully to God's good will, the world would again become a Garden of Eden.*

The shocking truth about prayer is that all prayers are answered by our loving Father. Whenever a prayer seems to remain unanswered, you can be sure that somewhere there is a closed door between you and the Infinite Giver. *Always, desire in the heart is God tapping at the door of your consciousness, trying to get you to accept greater good in your life.* Instead of pushing aside your desire as impossible of fulfillment, declare: "I AM

RECEIVING. I AM RECEIVING NOW. I AM RECEIVING ALL THE GOOD GOD
HAS FOR ME NOW, AND GOD HAS UNLIMITED GOOD FOR ME!"

When your prayers have not been answered, look within and
ask to be shown how to remove the block.

NO FRUSTRATING STRAIN IN PRAYER

People often become discouraged in prayer because they
struggle to pray in certain ways for which they are not yet ready.
Often they feel that unless they are able to pray as some advanced soul prays, their prayers cannot have power.

How foolish. *The simplest prayer can be answered.* A little
eight-year-old girl heard a lecture I gave on prayer and said
afterward: "I know all about the power of prayer and it works.
Last week my dog left home and was gone two days. He had
never done that before and I was afraid he would never return—
until I remembered the power of prayer. Then I went out, sat in
my swing and prayed for him to come home. In a few minutes my
dog came running into the yard and was very glad to see me."

*You unfold in prayer power gradually, normally, naturally as
you are ready for it. You do not have to strain.* In fact, strain
defeats prayer. Even though your growth sometimes seems
gradual, even slow, that is the normal way. Forced growth can
bring a negative reaction. All spiritual advancement comes in
phases of normality.

There is nothing strange, odd or abnormal about prayer power.
It is an easy, natural, normal process. You can always get results,
right where you are, at your present level of understanding
through prayer. *You have all the prayer power you need right
now to meet life victoriously!*

A troubled housewife was nervous and sleepless. Upon tele-
phoning her minister she was asked to affirm, "THE PEACE OF JESUS
CHRIST IS POURED OUT UPON ME NOW, AND I AM RELAXED IN MIND
AND BODY." As the minister declared these words for her over the
telephone, this tense woman relaxed and peace came. But hours
later she again became nervous and frightened.

Though she had never had any faith in her own prayer power,
she now felt forced to depend upon it. Groping for the right

method, she finally just gave up and said, "Not my will but Thine be done, dear Father." A great sense of peace again enfolded her and she relaxed into a deep sleep.

Through this experience she learned a great truth: *You already have all the prayer power you need to meet life victoriously right now, regardless of the problem. It's just a matter of getting down to business and using the prayer power you already have.*

WHEN YOU THINK YOUR PRAYERS GROW STALE

As you develop your prayer consciousness, if your prayer powers seem to grow stale—if you have periods when you do not seem to be able to pray effectively or even pray at all—do not be discouraged. These are often periods when your prayer consciousness is changing and expanding. A digestive process, a purification, is taking place. You may feel uncomfortable, with an indescribable feeling of being "crowded" deep within your being, so that it is hard to make inner contact. A cleansing process is at work, crowding out and dissolving old negative emotions.

As your prayer powers come alive within you, they cleanse the deeper levels of your subconscious mind. As those old thoughts and feelings rise to the surface of your conscious mind, that is when you feel a "crowded" sensation because a deep change, a deep healing is taking place.

After this purification process is over, you will again be able to pray effectively, but perhaps in a different way, on a deeper level. *There are degrees and levels of prayer to meet your needs at the various levels of your life experiences.* The 16th Century mystic, St. Teresa, described this progressive unfoldment in prayer in her celebrated book, *Interior Castle*,[2] with each degree or level of prayer being compared to a separate room in the house of the soul. She compared the soul's growth through prayer to that of a silkworm that becomes a butterfly.

Thus, as you develop your prayer powers, you go through various degrees and levels of prayer to other degrees and levels of prayer. That is why one type of prayer does not always satisfy

---

[2] E. Allison Peers (trans. and ed.), *Interior Castle* by St. Teresa of Avila (Garden City, New York: Image Books, Doubleday & Co., 1961).

you; nor will it always work for you. That is why you need to know the various methods of prayer described in this book and how to invoke them.

If prayer has not proved so triumphant in your life as you feel it might, perhaps it is because you have not realized all the various ways you can pray. At times one method of prayer seems right. At other times, this same prayer method just doesn't work. When your prayer methods seem to have lost their power, that can be a good sign! It may indicate that you are growing spiritually, mentally, emotionally, and that you are ready to "try your wings" through another type of praying.

THE VARIETY OF PRAYER

The shocking truth is that no two people pray exactly alike. Prayer is personal. Prayer is individual. You should not be alarmed if your prayer methods are completely different from those of your family or friends. Often a husband and wife pray completely differently, yet each is satisfied, each makes spiritual contact.

A businessman told me that he prays verbal prayers of denial and affirmation. These are his methods of prayer and he has experienced marvelous results in health and prosperity from them; his wife, on the other hand, practices prayers of meditation and the silence. These methods have been equally effective for her.

There are many levels and degrees of prayer to meet the spiritual needs of many types of people, all in various levels of spiritual understanding. *The saints and mystics of old were very powerful in prayer, yet no two described their prayer experiences in the same way. Neither do we!*

ORIENTAL AND WESTERN PRAYER
METHODS REVERSED

The Oriental method of prayer teaches that relaxation and control of the body, purity or cleansing of thought and emotions, deep breathing, followed by turning inward and practicing concentration, meditation and ecstatic union with one's divine self are all steps of prayer that must come first. And that only in the advanced phases of one's prayer development—after one has mastered all these phases—is then included the ability to manifest things or the ability immediately to realize one's desires.

Jesus' method was just the opposite: Ask, seek, knock, and results shall come. He constantly prayed and manifested immediate results of healing and prosperity for his followers, though He emphasized praying for spiritual blessings too.

In a sense, both views are right. It seems normal that the Orientals, with their detachment from things and materiality and with their slowness of pace, would place more emphasis upon developing the deeper phases of prayer first. Yet most beginners in prayer would find it bewildering to try! Certainly if someone had informed me years ago when I began my quest into the power of prayer that I had to learn to relax and control my body, cleanse my thoughts and breathe properly, control my thinking, then learn to concentrate, meditate and practice the silence *before* getting my prayers answered, I would have said, "Forget it."

So Jesus' method of showing people how to pray and manifest things, or get outer results, right away is surely a fine method for interesting one in the power of prayer and convincing one that prayer works.

Perhaps Jesus knew that once one gets things through prayer, or that prayers regarding people and things have power, one becomes so awakened to the prayer powers within him that the fascination then grows and he wants to go deeper into prayers of concentration, meditation, the silence and realization. However, our materialistic western mind somehow likes to be convinced and shown the power of prayer first with things, people and events.

Thus the prayer methods described herein begin with the western approach to prayer: how to get immediate results. The first eight chapters describe prayer methods through which you reach God, and through which your prayers have beneficial influence upon yourself, as well as upon things, people and events, as you learn prayers of relaxation, cleansing, decree and concentration. The last chapters of the book describe prayer methods through which God reaches you in the deeper phases of prayers of meditation, the silence, and realization.

The shocking truth about prayer is that it will teach you its own amazing secrets as you study the various methods described herein. As you practice the types of prayer given early in the book, this will prepare you for the deeper methods of prayer that will unfold naturally within you and which are described later in the book.

Knowing the various methods of prayer hereinafter described will give you a whole new perspective on the subject. You will realize there are yet ways and methods through which your prayers can be answered!

You will discover that you have more dynamic prayer powers than you had previously dreamed possible. Perhaps this is the most shocking truth of all about prayer—and about you!

SUMMARY OF CHAPTER 1

The shocking truth about prayer is that:

1. Most people discount the power of prayer because they are afraid of prayer due to their sheer ignorance about the most fascinating force in the universe.
2. You have dynamic prayer powers *within* you because you are a spiritual being made in the image of God, and prayer is simply making union with your God-nature.
3. There is nothing complicated about it! Prayer is natural to man.
4. God is immanent or within, and God is transcendent or universal. In true prayer you turn within not without, where you contact both the immanent and transcendent power that is released in prayer.
5. You unfold in prayer power gradually, normally, as you are ready for it. There is no strain in prayer.
6. You always have all the prayer power you need to meet life victoriously. There are degrees and levels of prayer to meet your needs at the various levels of your life experiences. No

two people pray quite the same way and no one person prays the same way all the time.

7. Prayer is an art and science that requires practice, as does the development of any skill.

8. Prayer is the path to instant good. Prayer is the most practical way to solve all problems. *Pray first instead of last.* Prayer is the supreme combination of all that will produce riches in its tangible and real manifestation as financial independence and spiritual joy without limits.

2

What to Do When Your Prayers Have Not Been Answered

There are those who say, "Why pray? Prayer is a farce. My prayers have never been answered." Yet there are others who can attest to a long list of answered prayers. If God ever answers prayer, He always answers prayer, being the same God. Therefore, if there seems to be any failure of principle, the trouble is not with God, but with the one who prays.

There is also a belief among many people that when their prayers have not been answered, it is because God has said "no" to their prayer requests.

Prayer is no farce. And God never says "no."

God always says "yes"—but to the highest desires of your heart—not to the surface, limited ones. Most of us can recall times that we prayed limited, selfish prayers that did not get answered, and how grateful we were later.

Since God always says "yes"—but to the highest desires of your heart—there is often much you need to do to clear out false beliefs and negative emotions, in order to make way for your prayers to be answered.

When it seems that your prayers are not being answered, it is usually because there is something *within* you that is blocking the answer—some limited idea or negative emotion.

Prayer often has to work amazing results *in* you before it can work amazing results *through* you and *for* you. So often after we've prayed, we've been inclined to snap our fingers and expect instant results. Often if we did get an instant result in prayer it would not last because we would not have changed sufficiently to accept and retain the answer.

If you refuse to let prayer work in you, changing you deep within, then you stop prayer from working *for* you. *There must be an inworking before there can be an outworking*.

After praying, you must be ready to change and change and change. The change must be within your own thought and feeling nature, so that you will be big enough in consciousness to accept the answer for which you are praying—probably in a more expanded form than you had in mind.

Most people who complain that their prayers have not been answered fall into a certain mental and emotional pattern: They are people who are too rigid in their outlook on life. They need to give a little in their attitudes. They need to unbend mentally; they need to stretch emotionally. They are too set in their thinking. They are not willing to change the inner, so that God can change the outer phases of their lives.

They are like the woman who prayed earnestly for a healing of her eyes. Yet everytime she came to church she would say (almost triumphantly): "I notice that Mr. and Mrs. Smith haven't been attending church lately. What's wrong?" Or she would complain that the temperature was either too hot or too cold in church that morning. Always something was wrong. This lady unconsciously looked for what was wrong rather than what was right in life, and so she was not an open, receptive channel for her prayers for healing to be answered.

As with this woman, rigidity in our outlook on life and mental resistance to people and conditions often keep our prayers from being answered. We must be willing to change the inner so that God can change the outer phases of our lives.

HOW TO "GROW" INTO THE ANSWER TO PRAYER

So often we miss our answers to prayer because we insist upon an immediate result, rather than being willing to grow into it. We want every good thing at once—"instant good"—before we have unfolded to the point of receiving it, so we miss the answer. We are not yet ready to receive it.

It will encourage you to know that spiritual giants such as Abraham and Isaac had to wait from twenty to twenty-five years to get some of their prayers answered. Abraham waited twenty-five years for the birth of his son Isaac. During that time he realized that God's delays were not denials and that, as promised, God would fulfill in His own time and way. Meanwhile, Abraham had to cleanse his thinking of fear, doubt and bitterness and grow into answered prayer. The birth of Isaac was that answer.

Later Isaac had to learn this same spiritual lesson. After twenty years of married life, his wife Rebekah was still childless. Her barren condition caused her to be reproached by the daughters of Canaan, and her childlessness was also a trial to Isaac's faith. Finally Isaac prayed anew and Jacob was born. Still later, Jacob waited twenty years before receiving the blessing of the Lord, though he worked hard in the meantime to redeem himself from his mistakes. So Abraham, Isaac and Jacob learned the great spiritual lesson: that God does not hurry the fulfillment of His plan, but does answer the great desires of men's lives in His own time and way.[1]

Thus, when you pray, do not insist upon immediate results or rewards. *They will come as and when you are ready to receive them.* The Greek philosopher Epictetus said, "No great thing is created suddenly. If you tell me that you desire a fig, I answer you that there must be time. Let it first blossom, then bear fruit, then ripen."

The prayer you want answered is the prayer of the whole man: spirit, soul and body . . . the one that will satisfy your whole being. It may or may not be what you cry out for in a moment of pain or desire. The only thing you have to be concerned about when you pray is that you grow big enough in consciousness to receive and maintain the answer to your prayers when it comes.

Many people are not willing to do this so they stop the answers

---

[1] The success secrets of Abraham, Isaac and Jacob and their mental attitudes that led to answered prayer are shown in my book, *The Prosperity Secret of the Ages.*

to their prayers completely and then bitterly complain that God has let them down.

The mystics of old had a three-part formula for getting their prayers answered. Their three mystic steps to answered prayers were: (1) Purification (2) Illumination (3) Union.

How often we try to bypass that first step of purification and rush on to get illuminative guidance and then attempt to make union with results.

That famous 16th Century Spanish priest, St. John of the Cross, described the purification periods through which we must pass to answered prayer as "the dark night of the soul." In my book, *The Dynamic Laws of Healing*,[2] you find this cleansing experience described as "chemicalization, a healing process." The steps in chemicalization or soul-cleansing are therein explained.

OVERCOMING BLOCKS TO ANSWERED PRAYER

Purification, the first step in answered prayer, works through forgiveness. When your prayers have not been answered, there is someone or some experience of the past or present that needs to be forgiven by you. Forgiveness is purification. Forgiveness dissolves the mental and emotional blocks between you and answered prayer. (More about this in Chapter 4.)

The very pain you suffer, the very failure to demonstrate over some matter that touches your life deeply, may rest upon just this spirit of unforgiveness that you harbor toward the world in general or toward someone in particular. You must release it to get ready for answered prayer: "I RELEASE THIS TO A LOVING FATHER, WHO PERFECTLY HEALS IT NOW, AND I GET READY FOR ANSWERED PRAYER!"

The thoughts that most frequently work ill to you and stop your prayers from being answered are thoughts of criticism and condemnation. If you are criticizing or condemning anyone, you are keeping your own prayers from being answered. Where there

---

[2] Catherine Ponder, *The Dynamic Laws of Healing* (West Nyack, N.Y.: Parker Publishing Company, 1966).

should be an open channel in your thinking, there is a big grudge blocking the way to your good.

A Healing for Riches Through
Forgiveness

In my book, *The Dynamic Laws of Prosperity*,[3] is the story of a man who appeared one cold winter day for my counseling. He was in pain, out of work, lonely, unhappy, just "down and out" in every way. One of the most critical people I have ever met, he hated the politicians in Washington and blamed them for all his problems.

After realizing his spirit of unforgiveness could be the cause of his many problems, including finances, this sick man agreed to join me in humbly speaking words of forgiveness and to stop all his name-calling.

A few months later when he paid me another visit, this man had changed so much that I did not recognize him. Cleaned up and healed of the pain in his body, he had gotten a wonderful job and a fiancée, whom he brought along for me to meet. They were later married, and there was little he desired in his business life that he did not eventually get.

This man proved that getting results in prayer demands that anger must be overcome. It simply is not possible to get any results worth talking about, or even to exercise much prayer power in the way of healing, unless and until you have gotten rid of resentment and condemnation toward your brother man. Until you are prepared to rid yourself of such critical emotions, your prayers will go on and on being unanswered.

The Secret of Dissolving Negatives
Within You

To dissolve resentment declare often: "CHRIST IN ME NOW FREES ME FROM ALL RESENTMENT TOWARD PEOPLE, PLACES OR THINGS OF THE PAST OR PRESENT. CHRIST IN ME NOW FREES ME FROM ALL

---

[3] Catherine Ponder, *The Dynamic Laws of Prosperity* (Englewood Cliffs, N.J.: Prentice-Hall, Inc., 1962).

RESENTMENT FROM PEOPLE, PLACES OR THINGS OF THE PAST OR PRESENT. I MANIFEST MY TRUE PLACE WITH THE TRUE PEOPLE AND WITH THE TRUE SURROUNDINGS NOW."

The reason that forgiveness is the first step to answered prayer is because it cleanses your mind, body and affairs, and gets you ready to receive your good. A fine cleansing prayer to use daily for this purpose is: "CHRIST IN ME IS MY FORGIVING POWER."

For those whom you wish to forgive and by whom you wish to be forgiven, affirm: "CHRIST IN YOU IS YOUR FORGIVING POWER." For all involved, affirm: "CHRIST IN US IS OUR FORGIVING POWER. CHRIST IN THIS SITUATION IS ITS FORGIVING POWER. THE CHRIST IN THIS SITUATION PRODUCES THE PERFECT FORGIVENESS NOW."

Every marriage counselor, minister, prison official, psychiatrist, psychologist and worker in mental health problems has known persons whose lives were blighted and problem-filled because of unforgiveness. These problem-filled people held to grudges, were in bondage to hate, and had plans for revenge, all of which boomeranged upon *them*.

When you find yourself saying, "It serves him right," or "She got just what she deserved"—watch out! This is an attitude that can stop *your* prayers from being answered. *Holding to such a grudge is like holding to a hot coal. It will burn you again and again until you let it go.*

Fear, doubt, worry also close the door to answered prayer. *Your hurts stand in the way of answered prayer.* Do you dwell on wrongs and mistreatments and carefully preserve them in your memory? You must have the courage to loose them and let them go. Excuses, self-pity, blaming another for your problems, all stand in the way of answered prayer.

Prayers of forgiveness from and toward those who have abused you or who have persecuted you is the highest form of prayer, yet the hardest. But it is also the most rewarding and soul-cleansing! For this purpose affirm often, "I PASS FROM PREJUDICE, HATRED OR CONDEMNATION TO GENTLE, FORGIVING LOVE."

The love of God simply cannot enter a bitter, hardened, unforgiving heart, whereas prayers of forgiveness break down walls and barriers to your good, often instantly, and so are well worth the soul effort they demand of you. *Forgiveness is the secret formula for answered prayer!*

HOW TO CHANNEL YOURSELF FOR ANSWERED PRAYER

So often people who complain that their prayers have not been answered are those who are not doing their part by observing daily prayer periods. They want their prayers answered, yet they are not even attempting to make daily contact, through which they can be. This is as inconsistent as wanting their doctor to heal them when they haven't even made an appointment to see him!

There once was a lady whose condition of arthritis steadily worsened in spite of fine medical treatment. There were also inharmony and financial problems in her life.

One day, while browsing through her Bible for guidance, she noted that almost every passage she read talked about prayer. It was then that she realized she had not been taking time daily for prayer, meditation or spiritual study. She had not made spiritual contact nor become a channel for answered prayer.

From that day forward she made prayer and meditation a part of her daily schedule. As she did, things first became harmonious in her home life. Regarding financial matters, she soon received a letter informing her that certain insurance and salary benefits, which had previously been withheld, would now be paid her on a monthly basis.

As she continued having daily prayer periods, the pain diminished, new strength and vitality were generated. A whole new life gradually opened to her as she persisted in observing those daily prayer periods. Eventually she was completely free of this supposedly incurable disease. Prayer had healed her.

God always says "yes," but we have to make contact with Him before that answer can appear. Daily prayer opens the way. There are people who say you can pray anytime, anywhere, informally—that you do not have to go formally to God. In a sense they are right. But if you were trying to contact an important person, wouldn't you extend the courtesy of an appointment? The 13th Century German mystic, Meister Eckhardt said, "God is bound to act, to pour himself into thee, as soon as He shall find thee ready."

In the little pamphlet, *God Has the Solution*,[4] Emmet Fox explains:

> God can do anything. It is never too late. There is always an answer even when we cannot see it. When praying, ask yourself bluntly if you really expect an answer to your prayers. Do you really expect what you pray for? Could you accept it if it came?
>
> If you are not sure, then it's better to pray for faith, and release the problem to God. Pray for the divine solution and for the right arrangement of your affairs. Then leave the details to God. If you feel you have not received an answer to your prayers, then pray for understanding.

HOW TO DENY ALL THAT SAPS YOUR PRAYER VITALITY

Often a person's prayers are not answered because he scatters his forces so that he dissipates the spiritual power accumulated in prayer and there is no channel through which his prayers can be answered.

After you pray, learn to say "no" to unnecessary things, people and activities in your life. Conserve your time and energy more, so that your prayers can get answered. Do not pray and then dissipate that prayer power through endless activities with needless people.

One of the first things a praying person learns is to say "no" to activities and people who would fritter away his time and energy, thereby keeping his prayers from being answered.

There is a certain inner discipline that goes with getting one's prayers answered. Nobody places this inner discipline upon us but ourselves. I have seen many potentially fine people just never make the grade spiritually and never get their prayers answered because they had not learned to say "no" to the unnecessary people and events in their lives.

---

[4] Emmet Fox, *God Has the Solution* (Lee's Summit, Mo.: Unity School of Christianity).

As you expand and uplift your thinking, you change. The people and activities of your life should often change too. What was perfectly right at one period in your life is no longer right, because there is something bigger and better trying to open to you. You have outgrown the former good.

But if you do not give up the lesser first, the greater cannot come through. Then you complain that your prayers have not been answered. Yet no one stopped the answer but yourself. Learn to say "no" if you want your prayers answered.

As long as you scatter your forces, frittering away your time on unnecessary people and events, you will have to go on paying a high price for your folly, and that high price is unanswered prayer.

Dr. Emilie Cady has explained in her famous book, *Lessons in Truth*:[5]

> Every man must take time daily for quiet and meditation. In daily meditation lies the secret of power. No one can grow in either spiritual knowledge or power without it. You may be so busy with the doing, the outgoing of love to help others, that you find no time to go apart. Doing is secondary to being. When we are consciously the truth, it will radiate from us and accomplish the works without our running to and fro. If you have no time for this quiet meditation, make time, take time. You will find there are some things better left undone than that you should neglect regular meditation.
>
> You will find that some time is spent every day in idle conversation with people who just run in for a few moments to be entertained. If you can help such people, well. If not, gather yourself together and do not waste a moment idly dissipating yourself to gratify their idleness. You have no idea what you lose by it.

A previously unglamorous housewife, whose life suddenly took on better health, an inner radiance and beauty, increased job benefits for her husband, success for her only son, and even a sudden, vast financial inheritance from a totally unexpected

5 Emilie Cady, *Lessons in Truth* (Lee's Summit, Mo.: Unity School of Christianity, 1934).

source, was beseiged with requests for her success secret. It was simple: "I learned to say 'no' to the lesser. Through spending more time in prayer and spiritual study, I got ready for the greater good I desired. It came."

Until you learn to say "no" to the lesser, your greater prayers will never get answered.

ANSWERED PRAYER WILL NOT BE RUSHED

The shocking truth about prayer is that many people pray in the correct way, but then are in too much of a hurry for results. When results do not immediately appear, they lose heart and complain their prayers haven't been answered.

If you sowed seeds today, the harvest would not be available tomorrow, would it? Of course not. A certain amount of time, *an orderly unfoldment* of events, would first be expected.

This is true of prayer too. God is just never in a rush. He knows our wants before we ask him.

God does not violate the orderly arrangement of events. Instead, He withholds the next development until order is first established in the present situation.

In my book, *The Healing Secret of the Ages*,[6] is the story of a schoolteacher who had prayed and prayed for life's blessings. She was in ill health, dangerously overweight, out of harmony with her family, and unable to keep a job.

Finally a spiritual counselor visited her in her home and discovered the basic cause of her many ills: Her house, as well as her outlook on life, was in a state of total confusion. The counselor pointed out to this unhappy woman that God does not violate the orderly arrangement of affairs to answer our prayers. Instead, He withholds the next development until order is first established in the present situation.

Grateful to know the cause of her difficulties, this schoolteacher then got busy bringing order into her thinking and environment. As she daily affirmed, "DIVINE ORDER IS NOW ESTAB-

---

[6] Catherine Ponder, *The Healing Secret of the Ages* (West Nyack, N.Y.: Parker Publishing Company, Inc., 1967).

LISHED AND MAINTAINED BY THE POWER OF THE INDWELLING CHRIST," restoration of her health, family happiness, and professional success gradually took place.

This schoolteacher came to realize that you must live as normally as possible when you are trying to get your prayers answered. Do the next logical thing to bring order into your life. Then hold up your head and keep going. Do not give into the problem. Do not waste time worrying about "what people will say." Let them think or say what they will. Go your way in peace, affirming "divine order" every step of the way.

WHY ONE MUST CLEAN UP ONE'S LIFE FOR ANSWERED PRAYER

You must clean up your life if you truly want your prayers answered. The "skeletons in the closet" that you think no one knows about have got to go!

It is useless to pray for benefits, protection, financial supply, guidance and instruction when all the time you are doing those things which you know are not right in the sight of God or man.

An attractive businesswoman developed a mysterious disease in her feet and legs, which the finest of doctors, including specialists at the Mayo Clinic, had been unable to heal. They could find no organic reason for her health problems.

Meanwhile she had many of her friends praying for her healing—all to no avail. What her physicians and praying friends did not know was that she had been having an affair with a married man for years, and the subconscious guilt generated from it had affected her health and his.

She needed to have the courage to clean up her life. God was withholding the next development until order was first established in the present situation. Many people are like this attractive woman. They refuse to clean up and clean out their lives. They refuse to let go the lesser and trust God to give them their greater good. Meanwhile their prayers go unanswered and their problems mount.

In still another instance, a successful but lonely businesswoman longed to be happily married. She had long indulged in a life of compromise, going from one illicit love affair to another, reasoning that these transient experiences in love were better than none at all.

Finally realizing she was neutralizing any hope of answered prayer by her immoral actions, she vowed to clean up her life, which had been dissatisfying and frustrating at best.

As she deliberately closed the door on old relationships, former nicer friends came back into her life and they one day introduced her to a fine widower. She soon married him and he gave her a lovely home and the life of peace, contentment and emotional security she had longed for. But none of these desirable blessings had appeared until she courageously cleaned up her life.

This lady discovered like Joshua of old that sin had to be put away (Joshua 7:20) before her prayers could be answered. The Bible is filled with illustrations of the bitter experiences that come upon man when he persists in being disobedient to the divine will. Often a cleansing or purging has to take place, as in the case of Joshua's disobedient soldier, Achan, before Joshua's prayers for victory were answered.

Remember that there is no hurt or harm to yourself or to others in answered prayer. If your prayers are not being answered, it may be that their answer would harm someone involved. Clear your mind by asking honestly, "Is this desire for answered prayer obedient to the divine will? Will this prayer hurt anyone if answered? Is this desire in accord with God's will for everyone involved? Is it for the Lord's own purposes?" Dedicate your prayers to God's good will and to His high and holy purposes, and a lot more of your prayers will then be answered, though they may surprise you by being answered in a far higher and better way than you had anticipated or would have dared hope!

PERSISTENCE IN PRAYER ALWAYS BRINGS RESULTS

Many people do not get their prayers answered because they do not persist. Verily, it pays to be persistent! It is the "praying through" attitude of Jacob, his "holy boldness" of vowing, "I will not let thee go, except thou bless me" (Genesis 32:26).

Some years ago, a man in New York City visited a spiritual

counselor, asking for help with a supposedly incurable skin disease. The counselor assured this discouraged man that nothing was incurable with God. This man suffered great pain in his back; a part of his mouth and the lobe of one ear had been eaten away.

The counselor asked this suffering man to go home and spend three days in persistent prayer, believing he would be healed. During this time he was to take no medicine or food, but was to fast and pray. He was instructed to spend four hours a day meditating upon some healing affirmations given him. The balance of the time he was to study the healings of Jesus in the Four Gospels.

The affirmations he used four hours a day for three days were these:

"I NOW CONSECRATE MY MIND AND BODY TO GOD. I AM NOW WILLING AND READY TO GIVE UP FALSE IDEAS ABOUT MYSELF AND OTHERS. I KNOW THAT GOD HAS FORGIVEN ALL MY MISTAKES. I NOW SEE MYSELF AS GOD SEES ME, WITH HIS RADIANT LIGHT FILLING EVERY CELL OF MY BODY. I AM CLEAN, PURE, HEALTHY, FREE. I THANK GOD FOR HEALING POWER. I THANK GOD FOR FULFILLING THE DESIRES OF MY HEART. I THANK GOD THAT I AM WHOLE, FREE, WELL NOW AND FOREVER."

This man was persistent in prayer. Three days later when he returned to the counselor, he had been healed. The lobe of his ear and his mouth were free from the disease. The pain was gone. As with Jesus Who healed the epileptic, this man proved, "This kind can come out by nothing, save by prayer and fasting" (Mark 9:29).

HOW TO MEET ONE DAY AT A TIME PRAYERFULLY

If your prayers have remained unanswered, begin now asking God again, but in a different way. Ask God for the wisdom, courage, strength to live just one day at the time. Pray to be able to meet just the present day, the present experience, victoriously. Stop straining and reaching out to tomorrow's challenges.

Ask God unhesitatingly for that which you need for the next twenty-four hours. Stop straining about next week, month or year.

Day by day, ask for God's help to live that moment victoriously. As you do so, the miracle of answered prayer will unfold in your life as never before.

God always says "yes." The answer *will* come. The blessing will appear as you persist in prayer and quietly grow into the answer. Let your understanding of Eternity be in the Eternal Today.

PRAYER HAS MANY FRINGE BENEFITS FOR YOU

If your prayers seem a while in being answered, that is an indication there will probably be fringe benefits accompanying the answers to your prayers. When your prayers make long voyages, they come back laden with richer cargoes of blessings. It seems that when God keeps you waiting for an answer, He gives liberal interest for the interval you may have had to wait.

There once was a young man who became very ill. His mother was informed there was no hope of recovery from a medical standpoint. To complicate matters, he was also an alcoholic. But friends continued praying for his healing.

One day his doctor left town for a vacation and the case was taken over by another physician who believed in giving massive doses of vitamins to his patients. As the sick young man began absorbing these large doses of vitamins, not only was he healed of the physical condition that had been considered hopeless, but the desire to drink left him too. Healing of alcoholism proved to be the fringe benefit to his mother's prayers.

When your prayers seem not to be answered, that is the time to affirm "the divine idea," "the divine plan," "your true place" in life: "I AM A DIVINE IDEA IN THE MIND OF GOD, AND I AM NOW GUIDED INTO MY TRUE PLACE. I LET GO EVERYTHING AND EVERYBODY THAT IS NO LONGER A PART OF THE DIVINE PLAN OF MY LIFE. I NOW EXPAND QUICKLY INTO THE DIVINE PLAN OF MY LIFE, WHERE ALL CONDITIONS ARE PERMANENTLY PERFECT."

A businessman, nearing retirement age, had been without work for some months because his former employer had gone out of business. Prayers offered by himself, family and church friends seemed of no avail, until one prayer group began declaring for him: "JOHN BROWN IS A DIVINE IDEA IN THE MIND OF GOD AND IS NOW GUIDED INTO HIS TRUE PLACE. JOHN BROWN NOW LETS GO EVERYTHING AND EVERYBODY THAT IS NO LONGER A PART OF THE DIVINE PLAN OF HIS LIFE. JOHN BROWN NOW EXPANDS QUICKLY INTO THE DIVINE PLAN OF HIS LIFE, WHERE ALL CONDITIONS ARE PERMANENTLY PERFECT." He was then quickly offered a series of jobs in the executive category for which he had longed, one of which he immediately recognized and accepted as his "true place." It prove to be his best placement.

PROVED TECHNIQUES FOR ANSWERED PRAYER

When you pray, you must be willing for everyone involved to be just as much benefited from your prayers as you wish to be. You must be willing for your enemies as well as your friends to be blessed. You must be willing for everyone else involved—no matter who they are or what they have done to you—to receive an answer and a benefit, not just yourself. There is no hurt in answered prayer! Unselfishness is the hidden key to answered prayer.

Furthermore, *praying for others causes your own prayers to be answered!*

A teacher of judo had sprained her foot while teaching a class. Her doctor put her on crutches and informed her she would be unable to walk for at least two months.

Having a full schedule of civic and church activities, as well as heavy family responsibilities, this young matron did not feel she could accept this well-meant diagnosis. On Tuesday night, after having sprained her foot the day before, she attended on crutches a prayer group whose members prayed for her healing. On Thursday night when she could not sleep, she remained up most of the night praying—not for her own healing—but individually for each name on her long prayer list. The following Sunday—less than a week after her accident—she attended church, minus the crutches and bearing no sign of a limp. The only irregularity was that she wore flat-heeled shoes rather than the higher-heeled pumps usually worn. She felt that her complete healing came the night she had spent praying for others.

When you have prayed for a long time for certain prayers to be answered and they seem not to have been, that is the time to decree "divine completion": "THIS IS A TIME OF DIVINE COMPLETION. IT IS DONE. IT IS FINISHED. IT NOW MANIFESTS, IN THE NAME OF A LOVING GOD."

Then, whether your prayers seem to be answered or not, just continue to "seal" the answer by declaring often, "THANK YOU GOD FOR ANSWERED PRAYER."

Thereafter, *let go and trust*. Dare to observe "a Sabbath" or a resting period from trying to manifest results. As you do, you will discover that the Lord never said "no" to your prayers.

And the ultimate answer to your prayers will amaze you!

SUMMARY OF CHAPTER 2

When your prayers have not been answered, it is because:

1. There is something within you that is blocking the answer, some limited idea or negative emotion.
2. Prayer often has to work amazing results in you before it can work amazing results through you and for you. There must be an inworking before there can be an outworking.
3. You may have gotten too rigid in your outlook on life. You may need to unbend mentally and stretch emotionally. You may have gotten too set in your thinking. You must be willing to change the inner so that God can change the outer phases of your life.
4. The prayer you want answered is the prayer of the whole man: spirit, soul and body. This answer will satisfy your whole being. Such an answer may or may not be what you cry out for in a moment of pain or intense desire.
5. Getting results in prayer demands that anger must be overcome. Your hurts stand in the way of answered prayer. The love of God simply cannot enter a bitter, hardened, unforgiving heart. Forgiveness is the secret formula to answered prayer.

6. There is a certain inner discipline that goes with answered prayer. Until you learn to say "no" to unnecessary people and events in your life, your prayers will never get answered.

7. God is never in a rush, nor does He violate the orderly arrangement of events. Often a loving Father withholds the next development until order is first established in the present situation. Getting your life in divine order is one of the first steps to answered prayer.

8. You must clean up your life if you want your prayers answered.

9. Many people do not get their prayers answered because they do not persist. When results do not immediately appear, they lose heart and complain that their prayers have not been answered. When your prayers have not been answered, a season of persistent prayer and fasting can bring the answer.

10. If your prayers have not been answered, begin praying in a different way. Ask God for the wisdom, courage, strength to live just one day at the time.

11. When you pray, be as willing for everyone involved to be benefited as much as you wish to be. Then let go and trust. Praying for others gets your own prayers answered.

12. Remind yourself that God never says "no." He always says "yes"—but to the highest and best answer for you—not a limited one, which may be what you have had in mind.

3

The Constructive Prayer
of Relaxation

People who complain that it is hard to pray are people who do not know about the prayer of relaxation.

When you practice the prayer of relaxation you learn how to "pray easy." Many folks think that the prayer that gets results is just the opposite—the prayer that "prays hard." As in everything else—"easy does it."

Perhaps you have heard the story about the Catholic girl who fell in love with the Protestant boy and wanted to marry him. Since they had different religious backgrounds, the girl and her mother agreed to pray about the situation. The first week after they prayed, the young man passed by their church. This was encouraging. The second week after they had prayed, he not only passed by it, but this time he looked in. The third week he went in and sat down. The fourth week, as their hopes of answered prayer were mounting, he stated he had talked to their priest; and the fifth week he announced he had decided to join their church. But alas, their sixth week of prayer for this young man brought a surprise. The girl lamented, "Mama, we prayed 'too hard.' Now he's going to be a priest!"

The prayer of relaxation helps you do just the opposite—"pray easy." The prayer of relaxation helps you become open and receptive to your good. This happens because your objective in prayer is not to fight against conditions but rather to commune with God in anticipation of that good you would like to experience in your life. The prayer of relaxation has definite effects upon the body, too. Tests show that up to 75 percent of the pain which exists when a person is tense and jittery vanishes when he relaxes.

A tense businessman was concerned about a desperate business problem. When he wrote to a prayer counselor in our organization, she advised him to give his problem "the light touch," explaining that to give it the light touch would be to give it the "touch of life." They suggested he do this by practicing prayers of relaxation. As he learned to "pray easy," the turmoil in this man's life subsided. Solutions came.

When it seems your prayers have not been answered, if you review how you prayed, you may discover that you just never relaxed; you never released the problem or condition that bothered you to God in prayer. You tried to pray in a tense way and you only held onto, rather than releasing and getting release from, the problem. You may have fastened yourself too well to the problem.

Dr. Emmet Fox once explained in his booklet, *The Mental Equivalent,*[1]

> The great enemy of prayer is a sense of tension. . . .
> Tension in prayer is probably the greatest cause of failure.
> . . . The mind always works inefficiently when you are tense.

Perhaps you are apt to take yourself, other people and life in general too seriously. The mystics spoke of "attachment in detachment." *In prayer it is good to detach yourself from people, places and things for a while.* Otherwise you become too concerned, too tense. When that happens, your attention and inner forces flow outward and dissipate. You can become tense, rigid, losing your balance. That tension can become a habit. But when you deliberately practice detachment and relax your grasp, your inner forces are then reconnected with your source. You function at a higher rate of vibration and the blessings of the universe then flow to you instead of from you.

A minister who is famous for helping people develop their prayer powers once explained:

---

[1] Emmet Fox, *The Mental Equivalent* (Lee's Summit, Mo.: Unity School of Christianity).

"I have had many cases of people who had strong, powerful minds, and who had reached a place in their spiritual unfoldment where it seemed impossible for them to get their prayers answered. An examination into the consciousness and habits of such persons revealed that their mental and spiritual work was done under strain. They were invariably anxious or tense, rarely relaxing, with the result that they generated inharmonious energy and constructed such an inharmonious wall around themselves invisibly that they were enclosed in it as in a shell. This prevented them from demonstrating the very things they desired and which they were working, even straining, to realize mentally and spiritually. Just as soon as this wall of inharmony and strained thinking could be dissipated and dissolved, the things they desired came to them. These people were taught how to relate affirmations of relaxation and peace to deep breathing. This practice always brought desirable results."

TO RELAX IS TO LOOSEN, RELEASE YOURSELF FROM A SITUATION

The word "relax" means "to loosen" and "to release." When you practice the prayer of relaxation, you learn how to "loosen" and "release" your problems, so that they can be resolved.

You also learn how to loosen your mind and body, to let the activity of the Holy Spirit—the whole spirit of God's good—work in, through, on, and 'round about you. When you are relaxed you gain power because you become an open, receptive channel for the power of the universe to flow in and through.

Perhaps you are thinking, "But that *is* the problem. I cannot relax. I cannot turn loose."

You have not turned loose because you have not known how. We hear much these days about the desire for relaxation. People pay hundreds, even thousands of dollars for tranquilizing drugs, psychiatric treatments, and for exotic vacations in faraway places, all in an effort to relax.

Yet one of the simplest methods of relaxation is one that costs nothing but a little time and practice. It is one that people generally know nothing about and would underestimate at first glance as "too simple to work"—the prayer of relaxation. However, this method proves all-powerful for health and release from nervous strain, as well as a delightful way of getting one's prayers answered, when practiced for even a little while.

And so I repeat: You have not turned loose because you have not known how. There is a way! As you practice the prayer of relaxation herein outlined, you will find yourself turning loose more and more. Relaxation *will* come, first in mind, then in body. You will be filled with a power greater than your own, so that tense striving will cease. Problems will be resolved. "Easy does it" will become your theme song for successful praying and successful living.

The prayer of relaxation should be the beginner's method of prayer, as well as the first step in all methods of prayer.

HOW TO TUNE IN TO A UNIVERSAL COSMIC CURRENT

The prayer of relaxation is truly the easy method of prayer, because in the prayer of relaxation you just do "what comes naturally," by turning within and relaxing both mind and body. When this happens, you then tune in on the magnetic or cosmic current of the universe which pulsates through your whole being, as well as through the whole universe, constantly. However, until you become still, quiet, relaxed, you are not aware of this pulsating, magnetic, power-filled current and its tremendous vibratory energy which longs to fill you and your world with its good.

There is no limit to what you can accomplish through relaxing and becoming attuned to this magnetic current within and around you. The Buddha taught that, through using this current, a man could become so peaceful that nothing could ever hurt him again. Confucius taught that by using this God-force, man would no longer say unkind words to, or perform unkind deeds upon, his neighbor. Job spoke of this magnetic current as a "spirit in man" (Job 32:8). Jesus described it as "the kingdom of God within you" (Luke 17:21). Paul thought of it as "Christ in you, the hope of glory" (Colossians 1:27).

Modern scientists describe it variously as electrical energy, an innate intelligence, and as an atomic vibration of light that fills every cell of man's being. Occultists have long described it as "the white light of spirit" in man, and traditional churchmen refer to it as the Holy Spirit or Holy Ghost.

I first became aware of this inner magnetic current when I attended a spiritual retreat for the first time about twenty years ago. There in an atmosphere of peaceful, prayerful relaxation, this universal current came alive in my body. Its activation within me almost frightened me out of my wits. It seemed especially strong in my hands and I recall carrying my right arm around in a peculiar upright position as though it were in a sling for days, until an enlightened soul explained what was happening to me. Since that time, as related in my book, *The Healing Secret of the Ages*, this universal current has served as a healing power flowing through me to my readers in the words of Truth found in the pages of my books.

Regardless of the name you give it, this magnetic current may be contacted and released through relaxation. Through the practice of deep breathing and deliberate relaxation of the mind and body, you tune in to this magnetic current which flows through, within and around you. Through regular practice, you can attune yourself to the magnetic forces of the universe, which will renew, inspire and uplift you in mind, body and affairs.

Through practicing the prayer of relaxation, you will find yourself tuning in more and more to an inner stillness you have never known before. In that inner stillness is all the power, energy, and guidance you will ever need or desire. In that inner stillness you will receive spiritual manna from heaven in whatever earthly form best suits your needs. Once you have "tasted" that heavenly inner stillness and partaken of its manna, you will never again be satisfied without it. You will find yourself returning again and again in prayer to partake of that heavenly communion, to taste its sweetness and peace, and then to experience its earthly benefits as increased health, wealth and happiness in your outer world. Like St. Francis of Assisi you may even be tempted to retire to a cave to pray often, so as to be overcome by "the heavenly sweetness" of prayer.

PRAY IN THE BODY

The importance of including the body in prayer cannot be overemphasized. You must pray *in* the body, rather than straining to reach outside of it in prayer. The body is the third part of the trinity of spirit, soul and body. The body *is* the sacred temple of the living God and should be included in your prayer development.

Only as man is able to pray *in* the body, causing it to relax and become an instrument of the universal life current, can his prayers have power and be answered. *Any method of prayer that bypasses the body also bypasses the way to answered prayer.*

Not only in the formal act of prayer, but also as you go about your day, say to your body often, "RELAX, LET GO, LET GOD." However, do not let the informal acts of prayer take the place of formal ones. Sometimes people say, "Oh, I do not have to take time formally to pray. Since God is omnipotent, I can pray silently as I work and play." Such misguided souls cheat themselves of one of the greatest experiences in life: The act of formal prayer.

Your first duty in prayer is to bless your body and help it to relax. Sometimes the mind gets so anxious about what it wishes to do that it tends to neglect the body. The mind is often inclined to reach out so much, especially when one is praying, that the body is neglected and suffers. *Pain and suffering can be a means of drawing the attention of the mind back into the body.* Often the pain begins to subside and even to disappear when one turns his thoughts inward into every part of the body, telling it to relax, loose, let go.

The body is like a child. It needs constant praise and appreciation. When you try to push and force the body to do your will, this produces tension and pain. But the act of praise and blessing causes it to relax and cooperate.

Your body needs your attention and your love, and it awaits your mental instructions. Give your thoughts of love and appreciation to your wonderful body temple. It is precious to you. Your body is an instrument of the mind, which enables you to live on this earth plane. You need to let the spirit of God take hold of your mind and set it doing its perfect work in the body.

Stop crucifying and start resurrecting the body as an instrument of your divinity. For this purpose, declare often: "I AM CALM, SERENE, RELAXED."

As you relax the body more and more, gaining control of it, you are then able to become less conscious of it in prayer, and to go deeper in consciousness into the more advanced prayer levels of meditation, the silence and realization. *The prayer of relaxation leads into every other method and type of prayer, and must always come first.* Over and over in developing your prayer powers, return to the prayer of relaxation. It is both the beginner's and the advanced prayer's method of prayer.

FIRST STEP IN PRAYER OF RELAXATION

When you sit down, kneel down, or lie down to pray, your first conscious act of prayer should be to speak to your body, as though it were a little child, telling it to relax. Your body is filled with intelligence and its cells will actually hear your decrees for relaxation and will respond. You will be amazed how the body will take you seriously and follow your instructions. Say, "YOU NOW RELAX AND LET GO. YOU NOW RELAX AND LET GO ALL TENSION, STRESS, AND STRAIN. YOU ARE NOW REAXED IN MIND AND BODY."

Then declare in a more personal way, "I NOW RELAX AND LET GO. I NOW RELAX AND LET GO ALL TENSION, STRESS AND STRAIN. I AM NOW RELAXING IN MIND AND BODY. I RELAX AND LET GO."

Get your thoughts right down into your body by turning your thoughts inward, within the body, as you gently instruct the body to relax. You may need to say to it a number of times, "RELAX, LET GO, LET GOD." If you do not feel relaxed after telling the mind and body to let go, perhaps it is because you have not let go enough. Relax all you can. Then relax some more. Keep on relaxing more and more. From the top of your head to the tip of your toes, go through your body telling it to relax. When anxious thoughts try to gain your attention tell them to "RELAX, LET GO, LET GOD." Let go and then let go some more.

HOW TO RELAX YOUR EMOTIONS

After telling the body to relax as a first step in the prayer of relaxation, then quiet your thoughts and emotions by declaring to them, "BE STILL. BE STILL AND KNOW THAT I AM GOD."

Many busy people have attested to the fact that these words of the Psalmist make a fine prayer for producing a relaxed mind and body, or a relaxed atmosphere in which to work. Say often to your mind, body and affairs: "BE STILL AND KNOW THAT I AM GOD. BE STILL AND KNOW THAT I AM GOD AT WORK IN THIS SITUATION. BE STILL AND KNOW THAT I AM SUPREME GOOD AT WORK IN THIS SITUATION."

A businessman once told me that he found this method to be a remedy for sleeplessness. After retiring at night, if his mind still seemed wide awake, attempting to go over and over business problems, he would say to it, "BE STILL AND KNOW THAT I AM GOD. BE STILL AND KNOW THAT I AM GOD AT WORK IN THIS SITUATION." Invariably this method worked. He relaxed into restful sleep and awakened in a peaceful, confident state of mind.

In the prayer of relaxation, think of surrendering your entire world to a loving Father—spirit, soul, body, relationships, financial affairs, spiritual understanding. Say to yourself, "I RELAX IN MIND AND BODY. I FEEL THE PEACE OF GOD. I REST IN HIS LOVING PRESENCE."

Then as taught in the Delsartean philosophy, just "decompose," mentally as well as physically, by dropping from the mind all thought of having much to do, of being crowded or pushed. Dwell upon the words of the prophet, "Not by might nor by power but by my spirit, saith the Lord" (Zech. 4:6).

A Professional Woman Healed
Through Relaxation

A professional woman had become tense and nervous over various family matters. Her mind was filled with agitation and her body with fatigue, as well as with vague but definite pain. A heavy schedule faced her in her work, so that she did not feel free to take the time for an exhaustive medical examination. She realized, also, that the tense state of her mind had undoubtedly caused the physical symptoms and if she could clear the tension from her mind and body, the pain would doubtless subside.

She began to practice daily the prayer of relaxation. In her prayer time she would breathe deeply and say, "I RELAX, LET GO, LET GOD." She would place her hands on the area of the body that was in pain, declaring these words of relaxation.

Often she would decree: "I AM FREE FROM TENSION, STRESS AND STRAIN. I SURRENDER MYSELF ENTIRELY TO GOD. I AM AT PEACE IN MIND AND IN BODY. FROM THE TOP OF MY HEAD TO THE SOLES OF MY FEET, I FEEL RELAXED. I AM CALM, SERENE, RELAXED. I FEEL GOD'S PEACE FILLING MY MIND AND BODY. I REST IN GOD'S GOODNESS."

When tension would try to overtake her during her busy days, she would say, "RELAX, RELAX." As she dwelled much upon prayers of relaxation, her whole world responded. Her body seemed less fatigued, the pain diminished considerably within only a few days, and then gradually faded away completely. Her business life became more relaxed and harmonious, as did her entire outlook on life. Harmony, order, peace became more and more evident as she continued to dwell on prayers of relaxation.

How often problems of health, human relations and finances work out quickly and quietly for those who practice the prayer of relaxation, as they declare to those problems: "I RELAX. I RELEASE YOU. I LOOSE YOU. I LET YOU GO. I LET GOD HEAL YOU IN HIS OWN WAY. I FREE YOU TO THE PERFECT SOLUTION." *Sometimes it is a surprise and a jolt to your ego to find that your problem remained with you because of your fierce, tense, possessive hold on it. The prayer of relaxation produces freedom wherever it is needed, and then the divine solution can come!*

SECOND STEP IN THE PRAYER OF RELAXATION

As you loosen the mind and body by telling them to relax, you then want to make prayer contact with your own indwelling God-nature. Job explained how to do this: "There is a spirit in man, and the breath of the Almighty giveth them understanding" (Job 32:8).

Breath is very important to prayer. The word "breath" and the word "spirit" have the same root meaning in all languages. It is through the breath that you make contact with the spirit. *The God within (immanent) and the God without (transcendent) are united by breathing!*

The ancient Greeks believed that there was a creative or ruling spirit within man, which they called the "breath." Socrates was the chief advocate of this theory. The Greeks looked upon man as a "breath being" and any illness of man was diagnosed as a disturbance of his spirit in his breath.

The ancient people advised people to breathe outward, to entirely empty their lungs of breath, and then draw in the breath with some affirmation of good. When they breathed outward again, they had only a healing breath going through their bodies and affairs. *The ancients believed that your breath is vitally connected with your happiness! They felt that all despondency and depression could be overcome by breathing in and out words of praise.*

When you speak words of relaxation to your mind and body and then deliberately breathe deeply, you unite your spirit, soul and body. You unite your conscious mind (located in the front forehead), your superconscious mind (located in the crown of the head), and your subconscious mind (located in the chest and abdominal region).[2]

When you relax and take a deep breath, this unites all three phases of your mind power, bringing them together at the top of

---

[2] Catherine Ponder, *The Healing Secret of the Ages* (West Nyack, N.Y.: Parker Publishing Company, Inc., 1967).

the lungs, where the conscious and subconscious mind activities meet in prayer. As you bring these mind activities under your thought control in the area of the breath, you then have real power for prayer and meditation, for it is in that area of the body that you literally "feel" the activity of spirit as it works to dissolve problems lodged in the subconscious mind, thereafter producing peace. (More about this prayer method in Chapter 8 on meditation.)

You actually pray through your breath. You can tell when your prayers have been effective, because of the peaceful feeling that will permeate the lungs-breath area. That good feeling then works throughout the subconscious area, clearing up negative emotions, producing peace in the entire chest-heart area. It is then that you know your prayers have been answered on the inner plane and that the outer results will manifest in due season. (See Chapter 10 on realization.)

After a good prayer period, you find you can breathe more freely. The burdens seem lifted from the subconscious breath-area in the body. Your feeling nature is uplifted, renewed, peaceful, filled with new power.

As you practice the prayer of relaxation, you will find that instead of breathing from the top of your lungs, you will breathe more deeply. As you continue to practice relaxing the body in prayer, you will find yourself breathing from as deep in the body as the abdominal area.

You will discover that deep breathing relaxes your body and gives you mental and spiritual powers previously unknown. Deep breathing in prayer seems to awaken your intuition, telepathy, deeper prayer powers, such as meditation and the silence. Your extra-sensory perception powers will come alive too, without any effort on your part. You will know things about the past, present and future which no human voice ever reveals to you.

Thus deep breathing helps you to relax so that your good can come on through into visibility. Deep breathing adds to your health, improves your looks, opens your mind and affairs to success.

As you develop your prayer powers, not only will you find yourself breathing more deeply without realizing it. You will also crave fresh air, which will quickly revitalize you within and without.

When your prayers have not been answered, and you are trying to realize greater good, do a lot of deep breathing. Then relax, and release your desires, saying, "I RELEASE THIS TO THE FATHER. I LET GO AND TRUST."

HOLY BREATH—WHAT IT MEANS

Job spoke of the "breath of the Almighty." Sometimes it is good to declare: "THE BREATH OF THE ALMIGHTY NOW GIVES ME UNDERSTANDING ABOUT THIS." Or "THE BREATH OF THE ALMIGHTY GIVES ME NEW LIFE."

This "holy breath" is to the intellect what air is to fuel, as it lifts the weight of human problems off the soul, warming it with the fires of divine love, the warmth of which permeates man's whole being, healing it with peace.

God created man with this "holy breath" according to Genesis 2: "And the Lord God breathed into his nostrils the breath of life; and man became a living soul."

Elijah apparently had developed this "holy breath" for healing because when he placed his mouth upon the body of the dead child, life was restored (II Kings 4:34).

Jesus attempted to awaken fully the spiritual consciousness of his disciples when he "breathed on them and said unto them, 'Receive ye the Holy Spirit'" (John 20:22).

Paul revived Eutychus after he had been killed by falling from a balcony, apparently by exercising "holy breath healing" (Acts 20:10).

The mystics of old felt that this "holy breath" was the pure breath of the Almighty; that it was filled with universal life energy which could heal incurable diseases or incurable situations; and that it longed to pour itself forth through receptive man. However, experiencing the "holy breath" isn't something you do mechanically or mentally. It simply happens to you and through you as soon as your prayer development allows it entrance. You will become aware of it in times of quiet, prayerful, relaxed meditative periods.

Prayer, generally, might be described as a sort of spiritual breathing which will cause the soul of man to live again, just as physical breathing, mechanically induced, has caused the body to live again.

THIRD STEP IN THE PRAYER OF RELAXATION

Remember that when you pray, you turn your attention within by speaking words of relaxation to your mind and body, and by breathing deeply. Your good is within your indwelling God-nature, and you are trying to release it through the prayer of relaxation. You are then ready to take the last step in the prayer of relaxation: You are ready to speak the word of "peace" to your mind and body.

As you keep relaxing and breathing deeply, you can gain a sense of peace by saying to any noisy, racing thoughts, or any upset emotions, "PEACE, BE STILL." *You can control the body as well as the mind by speaking words of "peace" to it.* Say often whether it seems to be so or not, "I FEEL THE PEACE OF GOD. I REST IN HIS PEACE."

It is good to dwell upon the phrase from that old hymn, "PEACE, SWEET PEACE." *The mystics have long known that the consciousness of peace in prayer is the forerunner of victory, of healing, and of answered prayer.* The peaceful state of mind is the powerful state of mind. It is the healing state of mind. In the word "peace" is every element of good.

In the consciousness of peace is released all the blessings of life which man seeks: health, abundant supply, a full and replete life, talents, strength and happiness. Peace includes every good thing that is possible to the human being.

If you can get into and remain in a peaceful state of mind, you become a receptive channel for every other rich blessing in life. This is true because peace releases a strong vibratory force, which is teeming with life and recharges one quickly. Establishing peace interiorly has been known to heal diseases.

In my book *The Healing Secret of the Ages* is the story of the businessman who had smoked for years to the detriment of his health, but had been unable to terminate the habit until he attended a religious lecture on "peace." On his way home, he reached for a cigar and suddenly realized that the realization of peace received at that lecture had dissolved all desire within him to smoke. The habit had simply fallen away. There was not a minute's nervous distress or emotional reaction—only a great sense of freedom and gratitude. This man never smoked again.

St. Francis of Sales, in his devotional writings of the 16th Century, gave this advice:

> Strive everywhere and in all things to be at peace. *If trouble comes from within or without, receive it peacefully— without excitement.* If we must needs fly from evil, let us do it calmly, without agitation, or we may stumble and fall in our haste.
>
> Let us do good peacefully, or our hurry will lead us into sundry faults. Even repentance is a work that should be carried out peacefully.

LAST POINTS ON PRAYER OF RELAXATION

So you have the three easy steps to be practiced in the prayer of relaxation:

First, speaking words of relaxation to mind and body; second, breathing deeply; third, dwelling upon words of peace for your whole being. It is a simple and delightful practice.

Last points include these: Do not practice the prayer of relaxation for long periods of time when you first begin to pray daily in this manner. Instead make your prayer periods short (and sweet). Practice makes perfect in prayer, as in anything else.

Do not try to perfect your prayer powers at the very first sitting. Do not try to force the unfoldment of any of these methods of prayer. If you do not relax and become as peaceful as you would like at the first prayer attempt, do not become concerned. Prayer is an art and a science and must be practiced as any art or science in order to be perfected. You should daily practice developing your prayer powers just as you would practice music or the development of any other talent.

The main point is to go back to the prayer of relaxation day after day for just a little while. You will become fascinated with its quiet power in your life; you will begin immediately to feel better and you will gradually note the development of a more tranquil, happier state of mind, as well as vast improvement in your health and in your relationships with others.

Many beginners become discouraged in prayer because they try to pray for long periods when they are not yet mentally trained or emotionally prepared to do so. Keep your prayer periods short, so that your mind does not wander and so that you do not become "heady" in your prayer efforts. This would only cause tension—the very thing you started praying in the first place to overcome!

Remind yourself often: "I DO NOT PRAY TENSELY, ANXIOUSLY, OR HEAVILY ABOUT ANY SITUATION. INSTEAD, I PRAY ABOUT ALL THINGS WITH A LIGHT AND EASY TOUCH."

"Easy does it" where your prayer practice is concerned. Give it the light touch, the relaxed thought. Prayer is meant to be a delightful, satisfying, uplifting experience. When you give the practice of prayer the light touch by practicing short periods of prayer and relaxation daily, you quickly come to enjoy it and look forward to the quick lift it will give you. The more you enjoy your daily prayer periods, the more prayer power you will seem to have and the more easily the blessings you long for will begin to flow to you.

It is then that you will know what Tennyson meant when he promised, "More things are wrought by prayer than this world dreams of." Relaxation will make you strong if prayerfully cultivated by you—and riches always gravitate to the strong in spirit.

SUMMARY OF CHAPTER 3

1. When it seems your prayers have not been answered, you review how you prayed; you may discover that you never relaxed. You never released the problem or condition in prayer. You tried to pray in a tense way and only held onto, rather than releasing and getting released from, the problem.

2. The prayer of relaxation should be the beginner's method of prayer, as well as the first step in all methods of prayer. The

prayer of relaxation leads into every other method and type of prayer and must always come first.

3. The word "relax" means "to loosen," "to release." In prayer it is necessary to detach yourself from people, places and things for a while.

4. There is no limit to what you can accomplish through relaxing and becoming attuned to the magnetic current within and around you, which is divine.

5. Relaxation is an ancient form of prayer which helps you to recognize the body as a temple of the living God and to turn within and pray *in* the body.

6. Any method of prayer that bypasses the body also bypasses the way to answered prayer.

7. The first step in the prayer of relaxation is to get your thoughts right down into your body by turning your thoughts inward within the body as you gently instruct the intelligence within the body saying, "RELAX, LET GO."

8. The second step in the prayer of relaxation is to breathe deeply. When you speak words of relaxation to your mind and body and then deliberately breathe deeply, you unite your spirit, soul and body. The God within (immanent) and the God without (transcendent) are united by breathing. You pray through your breath.

9. When your prayers have not been answered and you are trying to realize greater good, do a lot of deep breathing.

10. The third step in the prayer of relaxation is to speak the word of "PEACE" to your mind and body. You gain control of the body as well as the mind by affirming peace. Peace in prayer brings realization and healing. The peaceful state of mind is the powerful state of mind because every element of good is contained in that word "peace." In a peaceful state of mind you become receptive to all the blessings of life.

11. When you first begin to practice the prayer of relaxation, make your daily prayer periods short. This keeps you from getting "heady" and tense. Give your prayer periods the light touch, the relaxed mood, and you will grow into the practice of renewing, uplifting, soul satisfying prayer.

4

The Prayer of Cleansing
to Receive Riches

In recent times we have heard much about the power of positive thinking. Truly, it is a great philosophy that has helped millions to better their lives. But if your prayers have not been answered, almost in spite of your positive thinking, it may be because you haven't used prayers of cleansing first to unblock hostile emotions and buried resentments which must be cleared out before positive thinking can be permanently effective. Remember even the Bible said new wine was not to be placed in old bottles (your old attitudes).

If people around the world knew about the prayer of cleansing and used it faithfully, they could revolutionize their lives for all good in a matter of hours!

The ancient mystics felt that the development of prayer powers always began with purification, which eventually led to illumination and finally to union. The initiates of Dionysus, the mystery cult of the Greeks, felt so strongly about it that they observed "rites of purification."

How often most of us have tried to skip that first phase of prayer—purification—as we attempted to race on into illumination and union; and how often we have complained bitterly that illumination and union continually evaded us.

The Bible is filled with cleansing symbology used by the Hebrews of old. Their acts of sacrifice, renunciation, repentance —even their "wailing wall"—were all symbols of inner cleansing, release of negative emotions, and purification of their thoughts and emotions.

Life is a constant purification process. However, purification is nothing to be feared! If you try to bypass that purifying process, you stop your good because you have not cleansed your mind and emotions to receive it. Furthermore, the prayer of cleansing is master of purification. The prayer of cleansing gets you ready to receive your good. To bypass the prayer of cleansing is to bypass your good.

Famous prayer authority Friedrich von Hugel once said that it is your own fault if you do not get purified in this life! Dante described the gradual cleansing of the soul in his *Purgatorio*. The pray-ers down through the centuries have described it as "the purgative way."

Thomas Aquinas spoke of the seven deadly sins of the mind and heart of man which must be cleansed in this "purgative way." Perhaps he knew about the ancient belief that there were seven layers of the mind that needed constant cleansing. Modern metaphysicians speak instead of the "seven senses" that must be cleansed as man takes up the spiritual life: his five human senses, and his two superhuman senses of intuition and telepathy.

Bible symbology might have been referring to cleansing the seven layers of the mind, or of cleansing the seven senses of man, in the story of the leper, Naaman, who was healed after following Elisha's instruction to wash in the Jordan River seven times (II Kings 5). After making grave mistakes David cried, "Purify me. . . . Create in me a clean heart, O God; and renew a right spirit within me." His "cry" became the famous "Psalm of Cleansing" known as the 51st Psalm. Jesus might have been describing man's experiences on "the purgative way" when he spoke of the necessity of cleansing the inside of the cup first so that the outside of the cup might become cleansed also (Matt. 23:26).

Most people turn to prayer at a time when their lives seem filled with evil. Though they do not realize it, they are in the mystic process of purification. They are on "the purgative way."

Though it seems uncomfortable, this "purgative way" is a healthy process of soul-cleansing in which negative thoughts, feelings, memories rise out of man's subconscious mind to the surface of his thoughts, feelings, body and relationships, and seem to present him with problems of evil.

Through meeting these experiences of evil, man learns lessons that are necessary for his growth and understanding. Although he seems in the midst of an evil experience, when he learns that it is a purifying process and dares to invoke the prayer of cleansing, he can then turn that experience of evil into one of good.

And so I repeat: *Purification is nothing to be feared. It is a healing process, and the prayer of cleansing is master of purification! It is a joyous process!* And it always can create more riches for you.

THE "LESSON" OF EVIL

Evil is not a "problem" but a "lesson." It is an experience in purification. *An understanding of this purification process through which the soul passes is a first requirement for one on the pathway of prayer.*

It is not enough to pray to God to remove evil appearances from your life. You must find out *why* they are there, and *what* lesson you are to learn from them. Cease fighting and resisting evil. Pray for the humility and patience to learn the lessons evil is trying to teach you.

All evil is corrective. It becomes a teacher to those who are willing to learn. Those evil experiences did not begin somewhere outside yourself, but within your own secret thoughts and feelings. There within you they can be erased as you invoke the prayer of cleansing. Then, as you learn the lesson those evil experiences have to teach you, they will fade away.

Concerning evil experiences you probably wail, "But I did not know any better." Of course you didn't. There is no evil in the universe which is not the result of ignorance, and which would not, if you were ready and willing to learn its lesson, lead you to higher wisdom and then vanish. When men remain in an evil experience which does not pass away, it is because they are not willing to learn the lesson that it came to teach them.

Since evil is the direct outcome of ignorance, when the lessons of evil are fully learned, ignorance passes away as wisdom takes its place. But as a disobedient child refuses to learn its lessons at school, so it is possible to refuse to learn the lessons that evil tries to teach, and thus remain in bondage to it, fighting, resisting, resenting, multiplying its presence in one's life.

To do so only causes one to suffer continually recurring punishments in the form of disease, disappointment and lack. He who would shake himself free of evil must be willing and ready to undergo a disciplinary cleansing process, through which he gains new wisdom and strength that lead him to abiding happiness. However, this disciplinary, cleansing process is not hard or difficult, but has to do with invoking simple prayers of cleansing as described in this chapter. His "lesson" in evil having taught him what he needs to know then dissolves, having served its purpose. Thus nothing is evil that brings forth good.

HOW TO INVOKE THE POWER OF THE PRAYER OF CLEANSING

The first thing you wish to do in the midst of a "lesson" in evil is to cleanse your mind of any fear you have about it. *If you want your prayers answered you must often turn from evil appearances and cleanse your mind of any fear about them by saying "no" to them.*

This you do through the prayer of denial, in which you deny that the problem has any power over you as you simply say "no" to it. (See more detailed explanation of the philosophy of evil in my book, *The Dynamic Laws of Healing.*)

This gives you a sense of detachment or "holy indifference" to it. As you continue saying "no" to a troublesome situation, you first cast out fear about that situation. With the release from fear, then comes release from the problem which you no longer are clutching mentally or emotionally, and so it is free to adjust itself. You also feel a new freedom as the "no" power cuts away negative beliefs which were the cause of your problems in the first place. Through saying "no" to those situations that have harassed you,

you not only clear up emotional blocks but you also open the way for divine intelligence to circulate freely and produce a solution.

A businessman who was healed of arthritis through using prayers of denial by saying "no" to the appearance of disease later explained:

"From the day I began to say 'no' to the pain, declaring, 'NO, I WILL NOT ACCEPT THIS CONDITION AS PERMANENT. WITH GOD'S HELP I AM GOING TO BE HEALED'—from that day forward, I never allowed my attention to dwell on anything else. When the old doubts and fears tried to creep in, I quickly shut the door on them with a 'no, no, no.' The arthritic pains disappeared and I never knew exactly when they left me. They tried to return often, but I constantly dwelled upon God's love and God's healing power, saying 'no' to the pain. Since that experience I have enjoyed over twenty-five years of splendid health, because I refused to accept anything else."

A man in the real estate business was told that he had an incurable disease. While awaiting further clinical tests, he began to cleanse his mind of fear by using "no" prayers: "NO, I DO NOT ACCEPT THIS DIAGNOSIS. THERE IS NO ABSENCE OF LIFE, SUBSTANCE, OR INTELLIGENCE IN ME. I PRAISE MY BODY AS THE PERFECT CREATION OF DIVINE LIFE, SUBSTANCE AND INTELLIGENCE. I AM THE PERFECT CHILD OF GOD AND I MANIFEST HIS PERFECTION NOW!"

As he continued to invoke the "no" power of prayer, various situations arose that delayed further immediate clinical tests. Several weeks later, when the tests were finally made, the X-rays were clear. The incurable appearance had faded away. That was more than five years ago. This man continues in fine health.

All improved conditions in the world, with every step of progress from the beginning of time to the present, have resulted because someone said "no" to limiting appearances along the way and then worked to improve conditions. *If you want your prayers answered, you must often turn from evil appearances and cleanse your mind of any fear about them by saying "no" to them.*

A district sales manager was assigned a new territory. She said to her superior, "No, I do not accept this limited territory as all I am to have. I do not accept this area as my final assignment." A

few days later she received word from the home office in another
state informing her that her new territory was being enlarged!

Evil conditions of mind, body or affairs are built up by someone feeling bad about them. This bad feeling not only builds up
but sustains the unhappy condition. When the bad feeling is
pulled out from under the negative appearance, that evil has
nothing to sustain it and has to fade away.

This is true because evil conditions have no life, substance or
intelligence of themselves. They are created by the fears, resentments and other negative beliefs of man. Saying "no" to those evil
conditions and then refusing to be fearful, impressed, or even to
give them further attention is the greatest way you can begin to
dissolve them into their native nothingness.

When you say to any apparent limitation of mind, body or
affairs, "NO, I DO NOT ACCEPT THIS APPEARANCE. MY LIFE (HEALTH,
WEALTH, HAPPINESS) CANNOT BE LIMITED!" *you are dissolving fear.*
You are saying "no" to negative appearances. You are *not accepting them,* or giving them power, and so they have to fade away.
The omnipresent good, which has been in your midst all the time,
is then free to manifest as a happy result.

*Thus, saying "no" to evil appearances can help you dissolve
your hardest trials!* A simple praying "no, no, no" to apparent
limitation, or quietly saying "no, no, no" to yourself when others
about you speak of evil, is a marvelous way to invoke the prayer
of cleansing.

A Young Executive's Experience
with Cleansing Prayer

A young executive had just been transferred abroad by his
company. His family was to join him there, just as soon as housing was available. However, the area to which he had been transferred was very crowded and housing facilities were scarce.

After several months without his family, this young executive
became very homesick and threatened to give up his fine job and
return home to the United States unless his family was able to
join him shortly.

His wife realized this job was the opportunity of a lifetime and that he would doubtless regret his impatience later if he gave up and came home at this point. However, several other executives' wives for the same company were also awaiting overseas housing.

They kept saying, "It is just an impossible situation. Things are so crowded that we will never get housing." This young wife learned of the "no" power of prayer and she began to say to herself, "No, I do not accept that for us." Then to prove her faith, she began packing and making ready for their journey abroad. She and her children received their overseas shots. As she kept getting unfavorable reports about crowded housing conditions, she kept saying "no" to them.

Suddenly her husband wrote, "This week there will be a meeting about housing. There is only one house now available in this area and there is a long list of people trying to get it, including several of my superiors. Our chances for getting this house seem dim. If we don't get this house, it may be months before another is available. Please pray for the right outcome of this situation. I will telephone or cable you as soon as the meeting is over."

The night of the meeting, her husband did not call or cable and she assumed they had not gotten the house. However, one of the other executives' wives, who had been saying so many negative things about the situation, *did* receive a call from her husband saying they had not gotten the house. (In fact, they never did get housing and as this wife decreed, her husband finally was sent back to the United States to work at a much lower rate of pay).

Two nights later a telephone call came to the first executive's wife, who had been mentally denying the crowded housing conditions. Her husband said, "I don't understand it. Of all the people trying to get this one house, including some of my superiors who supposedly have seniority and influence, I was assigned the house! I will be flying home in just three days, and you and the children will be flying back here with me within a week."

The "no" power of prayer can dissolve apparently impossible blocks to your good because it cleanses your mind of fear and negative beliefs that block your good. You can stop evil "dead in its tracks" with the "no" power of prayer, because you cleanse your mind of the belief in evil, which is actually the cause of all your problems. As this is done, then there is nothing to stop your good!

THE CROSS A SYMBOL OF HEALING

The cross has long been considered a symbol of healing. There are many stories about the transforming power of the cross. The Emperor Constantine's conversion to Christianity three hundred years after Christ is attributed to his vision of the cross in the sky. In this vision of the cross he saw the words, "In this conquer," on the eve of a battle. As he dwelled upon that vision of the cross and its message, he won the battle.

We win our battles in life the same way: By keeping our vision on the cross, as we cross out any fear about those battling appearances. We too then conquer.

There is a legend about Emperor Constantine's mother visiting Palestine in the year 326 A.D. On this visit she was guided to the site of Jesus' crucifixion by an aged Jew, who had inherited knowledge of the site of the cross.

The mother of Emperor Constantine, on this visit, had the ground dug to a considerable depth, trying to find the cross of Jesus. Legend states that three crosses were found. The cross of Jesus was identified when the miraculous cure of a sick woman occurred, after she stretched out upon the cross of Jesus. This was supposed to have occurred 362 years after Jesus' crucifixion. There is another legend that one of the nails from Jesus' cross, which was found by Constantine's mother, was cast into the sea during a storm and subdued it.

The symbology of these stories is significant: We, too, subdue the storms of life through crossing out our beliefs in their power to hurt or harm us. We subdue and cross out the storms of life when we say to them, "THIS TOO SHALL PASS. THIS HAS NO POWER. MY LIFE CANNOT BE LIMITED. MY GOOD CANNOT BE LIMITED." Or "I NOW CROSS OUT ALL LIMITATION FROM MY LIFE IN THE NAME OF JESUS CHRIST."

Through saying "no" to limitation in your life, your cross can become a crown.

The early Christians constantly used the sign of the cross. That was one of the secrets of their spiritual power for performing miracles. Historians say that on each journey, at each coming in and going out, at the putting on of shoes, at the bath, at meals, at the kindling of fire, at the sitting down, and at whatever occupation they were engaged, they marked their brow with the sign of the cross.

St. Francis of Assisi once healed a paralyzed man by making the sign of the cross over him from head to feet. That there is still literal healing power in the cross has been proved in modern times. One mother healed her son of acute indigestion and later of whooping cough by making the sign of the cross over him and declaring, "By this sign we conquer." Another woman came through a period of severe depression and ill health after she began to use the sign of the cross and affirmed often, "By this sign I conquer."

A Canadian was puzzled by apparently psychic visitations in her home which resulted in mystifying noises and queer happenings the moment the lights were out at night. In the morning she would find furniture overturned and articles missing or misplaced. Friends advised moving, but this lady loved her home and did not wish to leave for such strange reasons.

Finally a spiritual counselor advised her to use the "no" power of prayer, denying the mysterious noises any power. It was also suggested that the troubled one spiritually raise the cross of Christ in every room. This advice was taken literally as the troubled one cut out paper crosses, placing many of them in each room. The noises quickly disappeared and never returned.

COMPLETE RELEASE: THE SECOND PRAYER OF CLEANSING

The prayer of cleansing takes several forms. Following the "no" power of denial, there is the prayer of release that "lets go and lets God."

In order to become cleansed and freed from many of life's problems, it is necessary to practice renunciation or release, especially in the human relations department. This proves a pleasant process, since it frees you from people whose burdens you should not be bearing anyway!

Most human relations problems would melt away if the people involved would pray prayers of release, instead of trying to make people over in their own image, forcing those people to *their* will and *their* way.

The prayer of cleansing includes cleansing one's thoughts and world of possessiveness. You must cleanse yourself of possessively clinging to other people in your life, telling them what to do in the name of "love," if you want your own prayers to be answered. Through possessive emotional ties, you direct the substance of your thoughts and feelings into someone else's life, which you should be using in your own; thus you deplete yourself so that you are not a fit channel for answered prayer.

After hearing a recent lecture on the prayer of release, almost everyone attending had interesting experiences in answered prayer:

A businesswoman mentally released her troublesome daughter, declaring for her: "I FULLY AND FREELY RELEASE YOU. I LOOSE YOU AND LET YOU GO. I LET GO AND LET GOD HAVE HIS WAY IN YOUR LIFE." The daughter soon married and went abroad to live.

An overly protective mother released her married daughter in the same manner, then moved out of her daughter's home to a distant city and went back to work, though she was beyond the usual retirement age. The daughter and son-in-law were then able to adopt children, which they had tried to do many times previously without success. As both mother and daughter continued praying the prayer of release, the daughter and her husband inherited money with which they bought a larger home, another car, and happily prepared for a comfortable life with their adopted children.

One couple's troublesome son settled down emotionally, went back to college and finally happily married, after his parents mentally released him. As two concerned mothers spoke words of release for their teen-age daughters, these daughters enrolled in colleges away from home and became honor students. *Peace was restored in all these households through the spoken word of release.*

Strong possessiveness sets up a block in your consciousness, so that you are not open to the guidance and illumination of answered prayer. The prayer of release frees you from trying to outline, dominate, or force another's good. Not only does the prayer of release free your mind and your world to become a channel for answered prayer, but it also frees those you love to follow the guidance of their own indwelling Lord, and to unfold the divine plan of their lives in their own God-appointed ways.

For everything and everybody that concerns you, instead of clutching them to you, trying to force them into your will and your way, let them go to their good by declaring: "I NOW PLACE YOU LOVINGLY IN THE HANDS OF THE FATHER. THAT WHICH IS FOR YOUR HIGHEST GOOD NOW COMES TO YOU IN YOUR OWN TIME AND IN YOUR OWN WAY."

Thereafter, when that person or situation tries to get your attention, keep releasing him or it by affirming, "I HAVE RELEASED YOU LOVINGLY INTO THE HANDS OF THE FATHER, AND I HAVE FAITH THAT THAT WHICH IS FOR YOUR HIGHEST GOOD MANIFESTS."

A troubled mother, who had tried everything from psychiatric to ministerial counseling as a means of straightening out her delinquent daughter, found that nothing worked until she emotionally released her. Thereafter, when she thought of the daughter she would say, "I HAVE PLACED MY DAUGHTER IN GOD'S HANDS. WHAT BETTER HANDS CAN SHE BE IN? NOT MY WILL BUT GOD'S WILL IS BEING DONE IN HER LIFE." Shortly the daughter began to mature and later married and became a fine wife and mother.

A father had a visit with his son for the last time before his son was returning to Vietnam for further duty with the Marine Corps. This father cleansed his mind of fear about his son's destiny and released any sense of possessiveness about him by praying, "I RELEASE YOU TO THE FATHER." Many months later his handsome son returned safely from war.

In praying the prayer of release for your loved ones, remember that nothing relinquished is ever lost. Everything finds its true balance, its equilibrium, when freed to do so. Give each soul in your life freedom to swing into his own accepted place in the scheme of life; give him freedom to do so in his own time and way, whether his methods please you or not. As you fully let go, each one will find his true place. As you give all people absolute freedom in your thoughts about them, your act of release will cause them to do whatever is best for them at their present level of understanding. They must learn life's lessons for themselves. You cannot grow or overcome for another. Through the act of releasing them to their own indwelling Lord, you not only free them to their good, but you also free yourself to become an open, receptive, peaceful channel for answered prayer.

Emerson might have been describing the sheer necessity of releasing our loved ones when he wrote: "If you put a chain around the neck of a slave, the other end fastens itself around your own."

PRAYER OF RELEASE BRINGS MARRIAGE

When you let go of strain, of pushing and shoving, of self-assertion and the determination to have things go your own way regardless; when you cease fighting, struggling, swinging mentally, reaching, grasping for your good; when you stop striving and relax, release, let go, leaving everything to the perfect outworking of the Power Within after having done all you know to do to make things right; when you give up your human efforts and accept what comes, you find that what comes is fulfillment of the very desires of which you had let go!

A businesswoman, for many years widowed, had tried every physical and mental trick she knew to remarry. But in her zealousness to marry, she had subconsciously repelled every man who crossed her path. Finally she began to speak prayers of release saying, "FATHER, I FULLY AND FREELY RELEASE MY DESIRE TO MARRY. I LOOSE AND LET GO. I LET GO AND LET THY PERFECT WILL BE DONE IN MY LIFE. I WOULD LOVE TO HAVE A HAPPY HOME, BUT I RELEASE THE MATTER TO YOU. I AM YOUR DAUGHTER AND YOU LOVE

ME. YOU KNOW WHAT IS BEST, SO DO WITH MY LIFE WHATEVER YOU WISH." With that, she gave a sigh of relief and released the matter completely.

Within a matter of weeks she was introduced by friends to a fine widower, whom she happily married within a matter of months. When later asked by astonished friends the secret of her sudden success she explained: "It's simple. Nothing worked out until I practiced the prayer of release. I had to let go completely and trust God to make my life right. That was the key to results."

THE PRAYER OF RELEASE INCLUDES CONFESSION

Along with speaking words of release for and to those people in your world; along with speaking words that you are released, another healthy form of release is the act of confessing to a priest, minister or trusted friend. The Bible spoke of this act as "repentance."

An unhappily married man had had a series of affairs with "other women" and in the mounting frustration finally was hospitalized. Neither his health nor his state of mind improved until he confessed his severe unhappiness to a minister, who had the wisdom to release him from his mistakes by saying to him: "Do not condemn yourself for your unhappy marriage, for the affairs you entered into with other women, or for your present illness. You did the best you knew at your level of understanding. Release it all, let it go and let God show you the way out of your dilemma." They then prayed together prayers of release for everyone involved in the marital mix-ups of past and present, and asked for forgiveness of the sins of all involved. With that act of prayer, the unhappy man cried tears of relief, and his healing began.

Later he and his wife were reconciled, their marriage became happier than ever before, and he went on to business success such as he had never known. But only after confession in which a wise spiritual counselor did not condemn his sins but prayed with him for release from them.

It is an established fact that people who go regularly to a

church confessional rarely end up on a psychiatrist's couch or in a mental hospital, so potent is confession as a form of relief and release from life's problems.

If no priest, minister or trusted friend is available to hear your confession (and many ministers have neither the training nor the spiritual or emotional understanding for it, so be careful to whom you confess), then go directly to God with your confession. Talk directly to Him as a loving Father who cares. You may wish to do this on your knees in the formal act of prayer.

The wife of a brilliant corporation lawyer became an alcoholic and no amount of treatment or therapy seemed to help. After three years of searching for healing in countless ways, one night this troubled woman realized that not once in those three years had she prayed directly to God, asking His help. Getting down on her knees in formal prayer, she confessed: "Oh God, what can I do? Help me to conquer this habit. I have tried but nothing has helped. I am laying this burden at Your feet, Father. Only You can save me. Only You know what is best."

Suddenly she felt God's presence enfolding her as an indescribable warmth and love. A feeling of peace then came and the desire for drink was gone by the time she arose from her knees. She never needed it again. Simple confession direct to God in prayer had done for her quickly what no amount of expensive treatment or therapy had been able to do for her in three years of searching. She proved what statistics show: That far more people are still healed through prayer and spiritual methods than through all other methods of healing combined! You do not always hear about these spiritual healings because people wisely keep quiet about them, knowing that what is sacred should often remain secret.

Another simple, satisfying method for confessing your sins directly to God is to write them out honestly and fully, leaving out nothing. Then, placing your hands on your written confession, pray asking God's help and forgiveness. Finally, give thanks for cleansing of those mistakes: "THE FORGIVING LOVE OF JESUS CHRIST HAS NOW SET ME FREE FROM MISTAKES OF THE PAST, AND FROM RESULTS OF MISTAKES OF THE PAST. I FACE THE FUTURE WISE, FREE AND UNAFRAID." A real soul cleansing will take place and you will be freed of the previous guilt and condemnation that had kept you emotionally bound to past sins. Your last act should be to destroy your confession and rejoice in your freedom.

Through his famous book of *Confessions,* St. Augustine revealed himself as the last of the great metaphysicians of the Patristic period, and also the first of all modern psychologists. In his *Confessions,* St. Augustine gave consolation to the frustrated and neurotic that no psychologist since has ever been able to top. He proved that true peace of soul is found not so much on the psychological couch as on the bended knee, and that help comes as soon as man realizes he cannot lift himself by his own bootstraps, and then confesses his need to God. It is little wonder that his book, *The Confessions of St. Augustine,* has been a best seller since 400 A.D.—or for fifteen hundred years!

GETTING RELEASE FROM OTHERS

Sometimes the problem is to get others to release you emotionally from their possessiveness and domination. This can come secretly as you speak words of release that cause them subconsciously to free you. Simply declare "JOHN BROWN, YOU NOW FULLY AND FREELY RELEASE ME. YOU LOOSE ME AND LET ME GO. YOU LET GO AND LET GOD." If there is a need for freedom both ways, you might declare: "CHRIST IN US IS OUR RELEASING POWER." For situations that need freedom from a number of personalities declare: "CHRIST IN THIS SITUATION IS ITS RELEASING POWER." As you daily declare prayers of release, the freedom will come, sometimes suddenly, sometimes more slowly; often severe unpleasantness cuts clean the release. But that severe unpleasantness is like the pain connected with physical healing. It is necessary and thus a blessing in disguise.

COMPLETE FORGIVENESS: THE THIRD PRAYER OF CLEANSING

Forgiveness is the third type of prayers of cleansing.
One of the major causes of unanswered prayer is unforgiveness.
Jesus repeatedly emphasized that you cannot pray aright if you

are bound to grudges, prejudices, bitterness, and an unforgiving attitude toward God, man, yourself, or the world in general. (And *all* of us are holding unforgiving thoughts in one or more of these areas of life.)

If you want to develop your prayer powers and get your prayers answered, you must pray the prayer of forgiveness often. *Forgiveness can dissolve whatever has stood between you and your good as it cleanses your mind, body and relationships, opening the way for your dreams to come true.*

You can solve more problems through prayers of forgiveness than in any other way: health, financial and human relations problems all quickly respond to forgiveness. When there is a problem of any kind there is a need for forgiveness. One person speaking prayers of forgiveness for a situation can dissolve the emotional blocks and clear up the problem, regardless of what others are saying or doing. That is the potency of forgiveness, which simply means "to give up."

When I have problems on any level of life—health, financial or human relations—I give myself a "universal forgiveness treatment." I simply speak the word of universal forgiveness for the situation declaring that everything and everybody connected subconsciously joins me in forgiving whatever needs to be forgiven, thus dissolving the invisible cause of the problem: "CHRIST IN THIS SITUATION IS ITS FORGIVING POWER. THE CHRIST IN ME FORGIVES THE CHRIST IN YOU. THE CHRIST IN YOU FORGIVES THE CHRIST IN ME. WE ARE ALL FORGIVEN AND GOVERNED BY THE CHRIST WITHIN AND THE PERFECT RESULTS NOW MANIFEST." Invariably they do!

HOW FORGIVENESS HEALS, PROSPERS, HARMONIZES

A fine couple was faced with problems of every kind. They both suddenly found themselves without jobs. Their debts mounted and their creditors harassed them. Furthermore, the wife had a painful lump in one breast, and her husband's former wife was causing them legal and financial difficulties.

Learning that all problems can be resolved through forgiveness, this couple decided to prove it. While the husband continued looking for work, the wife remained at home daily declaring prayers of forgiveness, writing out statements of forgiveness to both friends and foes alike: "I FULLY AND FREELY FORGIVE YOU. I LOOSE YOU AND LET YOU GO. I LET GO AND LET GOD. THE FORGIVING LOVE OF JESUS CHRIST HAS SET US FREE FROM ALL MISTAKES OF THE PAST OR PRESENT."

These acts of forgiveness first brought great peace of mind. After a week of daily practice of forgiveness in this way, this previously sick woman realized that the painful lump in her breast was gone. (It is estimated that 70 percent of all disease is caused by suppressed emotion. Forgiveness releases that suppressed emotion.)

Meanwhile, her husband had been promised several jobs but none had materialized. After her healing, she went out to look for work too. On the street one day she saw a former business associate. Meeting him brought to memory a period several years previously when she had been in business with a man who bankrupted her. Facing their mutual friend on the street she said, "Do you ever see my former business partner?"

"Yes," he replied.

"Will you please deliver a message to him for me? Will you please tell him that I have forgiven him for bankrupting me. It was a blessing in disguise. I did not need that job with all the responsibility, worry and problems it presented."

Relieved, the mutual friend went on his way. Whether he ever delivered her message of forgiveness, she never knew. But the next day, she obtained the best job of her life! Speaking words of forgiveness had turned the tide.

On still another day, she saw a man across the street who had promised a good job to her husband but had not come through with it. Her first reaction was silently to resent and criticize him. Her second reaction was: "He has come to my attention to be forgiven." Mentally, she said to him, "I forgive you for not giving my husband that job you promised him. I release the matter completely."

The next day that man telephoned her husband, again offering him the job that had been previously promised! He took it on a part-time basis while seeking a better paying job. As the prayers of forgiveness were continued, suddenly he was offered not one or two but six fine jobs! He took the best of the lot and is now enjoying the greatest success of his life.

As for the former wife who had caused this couple so much trouble, their prayers of forgiveness for her began to bring peace. Often they had prayed: "YOU FULLY AND FREELY FORGIVE US. YOU LOOSE US AND LET US GO. YOU LET GO AND LET GOD. CHRIST IN YOU IS YOUR FORGIVING POWER. THE FORGIVING LOVE OF JESUS CHRIST HAS SET US ALL FREE FROM MISTAKES OF THE PAST OR PRESENT. WE ALL GO FREE TO BE HAPPY."

Finally harmony was established to such a point that this couple was able to give the former wife my book, *The Dynamic Laws of Healing*, even suggesting the chapter on forgiveness in it to her. She later confessed to them that she was "living with that book."

Thus health, good jobs, and harmony were re-established for this couple through the prayer of forgiveness.

If you will sit for half an hour every day and forgive yourself, the people of the past and present in your world, and also forgive your wrong ideas about God (knowing that instead of being a hostile faraway Entity, He is a loving Father who is near and dear), you will soon be describing forgiveness as "the miracle prayer." Declare often, "I AM FORGIVEN AND GOVERNED BY GOD'S LOVE ALONE. GOD LOVES ME, GOD IS GUIDING ME, GOD IS SHOWING ME THE WAY."

VACUUM: THE FOURTH PRAYER OF CLEANSING

Along with the "no" prayer, the prayer of release, and the prayer of forgiveness, there is also a last type of cleansing prayer: the vacuum prayer.

In effect, the other three prayers of cleansing are for the purpose of forming a vacuum in one's mind and emotions, cleansing them of negative emotions which have blocked one's prayer powers. After invoking the cleansing prayer through saying "no" to fearful appearances, after releasing one's loved ones and forgiving one's enemies, it is then time to cleanse one's world through forming a vacuum in outer ways too.

There is psychological value in cleansing one's world by forming a vacuum in outer as well as inner ways: the subconscious mind becomes more quickly convinced that you mean business about all the praying you have done when you follow through by taking some outer action as well.

Through saying "no" to fearful appearances, thereby cleansing yourself of fear, through emotionally releasing your loved ones, and by forgiving the unloving people in your life—you have already begun forming an inner vacuum. It is good to complete the cycle by forming a vacuum in an outer way too.

Recently I lectured to a group of insurance executives who got very excited about this vacuum law and rushed home afterward to form a vacuum. A number of them later reported to me the satisfying results that followed.

The vacuum prayer of cleansing is this: Nature abhors a vacuum. If you want your prayers answered, form a vacuum to receive that answer! Get rid of what you do not want to make room for what you do want.

A doctor of chiropractic recently told me how his little daughter learned of this vacuum method and immediately used it with gratifying consequences: She wanted some new clothes, so she secretly formed a vacuum by giving away some she had in the faith that the vacant places in her closet would cause new substance to rush in and fill it with new clothes. That very afternoon her mother came in with some new dresses explaining: "I didn't expect to buy these for you now, but they were on sale." When her daughter did not seem surprised the mother asked why. "I formed a vacuum only this morning to receive them," was her quiet reply.

A businessman had been praying for some time for the healing of a relative who was suffering from a chronic heart condition. In studying my book, *The Dynamic Laws of Prosperity*, this businessman realized his relative needed to invoke the vacuum law as a phase of cleansing, so he gave her a copy of my book and asked her to study the law of vacuum.

In the book she read: "You can form a physical vacuum for new peace, health and plenty by releasing, giving away, selling or otherwise getting rid of what you no longer want or need. Do not retain items of clothing, furniture, letters, files, books, or any other personal possessions that you no longer need or use. Get them out of the way to make room for what you do want. As long as you retain them, they take up space in your world that is needed for your new good. Declare to yourself as you go through your personal effects: 'I FULLY AND FREELY RELEASE. I LOOSE AND LET GO. I JOYOUSLY MAKE WAY FOR NEW GOOD, WHICH NOW APPEARS QUICKLY IN SATISFYING, APPROPRIATE FORM.'"

This ailing relative immediately went up into the attic (forgetting that because of her heart condition she was not supposed to climb stairs). Among the clutter she found there was some antique furniture that she had previously offered as a gift to a charitable institution.

Since there had been no response to the offer, she now contacted an antique dealer, who arrived, inspected the antiques, purchased them, and immediately gave her a check for a substantial sum of money. As she continued to dwell on the various inner and outer ways she could release, loose, let go, and get out of her old negative state of mind, it occurred to her that she needed to forgive a daughter with whom she was out of harmony. As she daily spoke words of forgiveness for the daughter who lived away from home, this daughter subconsciously responded by paying an unexpected visit. Furthermore, she offered as a gift to her mother and father round-trip tickets to Europe. This, with the money acquired from the sale of antiques, made the trip possible.

As this previously sick woman continued speaking prayers of forgiveness and release, and then followed through by forming a vacuum in outer ways, she realized that her former heart condition had faded away. That a complete healing had occurred became obvious on her trip to Europe, from which she suffered no ill effects, and she enjoyed Europe immensely.

Pray the prayer of vacuum by declaring: "I NOW GET RID OF WHAT I DO NOT WANT IN MY LIFE TO MAKE WAY FOR WHAT I DO

WANT. DIVINE INTELLIGENCE NOW SHOWS ME IN WHAT AREAS OF MY LIFE TO FORM A VACUUM. I NOW LET GO THE LESSER TO MAKE ROOM FOR THE GREATER GOOD TO RUSH INTO MY LIFE. I LET GO AND TRUST."

Another marvelous prayer of vacuum for freedom from possessions and possessiveness is this: "CHRIST IN ME NOW FREES ME FROM EVERY ATTACHMENT TO PEOPLE, PLACES OR THINGS OF THE PAST OR PRESENT. CHRIST IN ME NOW FREES ME FROM EVERY ATTACHMENT FROM PEOPLE, PLACES OR THINGS OF THE PAST OR PRESENT. I MANIFEST MY TRUE PLACE WITH THE TRUE PEOPLE AND WITH THE TRUE POSSESSIONS NOW."

The mystics of old formed a vacuum by taking vows of poverty, not so much because they wished to be poor but because they wished to be free. Their vows included freedom from negative emotions and freedom from being possessed by things. When you form a vacuum and get rid of outer possessions as well as inner negative emotions through the prayers of cleansing described in this chapter, you too free yourself from the chains of possessiveness and possessions that are inclined to bind so many, and keep them from developing their prayer powers and the deeper, more satisfying qualities that truly make life worth living.

Freedom is one of the first requirements for answered prayer. The prayer of vacuum and the other types of cleansing described herein give you that inner and outer freedom. Take it!

HOW FASTING IS A FORM OF CLEANSING PRAYER

The act of fasting is another method of invoking a vacuum in mind and body, thus cleansing them of both mental and physical poisons. Indeed, fasting can be an act of cleansing prayer. Mohammed said, "Prayer leads halfway to God, fasting brings one to the doors of heaven."

I was first introduced to the power of fasting by a doctor who pointed out that the body can easily go without food for thirty days, taking only water; that instead of starving the body, fasting rejuvenates it and cleanses it; that the fast is not an ordeal, but a rest of mind and body; that after the first twenty-four hours of fasting all desire for food gradually leaves one until the body has been cleansed and is ready to again receive food, at which time hunger will return normally.

This doctor suggested plenty of fresh air and sunshine while fasting, though it is not necessary to abstain from one's regular activities. He felt that prayer and spiritual study should be a "steady diet" during the fasting period.

This doctor often used fasting as a method for overcoming personal problems. I know of one instance in which he went on a fast because of some troublesome personality conflicts that had arisen in his private life. After he quietly went on a diet of prayer and fasting, the troublesome personalities suddenly left town, moving out of the state!

Fasting existed in prehistoric cultures, and was an accompaniment of prayer common to the people of both the Old and New Testaments alike. As Gibbon's famous book, *The Decline and Fall of the Roman Empire*, pointed out, the healing success of the early Christians even into the end of the Second Century was extraordinary. They were able literally to raise the dead, who often lived for many years afterward. Their secret seemed to lie in their practice of prayer and "great fasting."

Jesus pointed out the power of fasting as a means of overcoming severe problems, as in the case of healing the epileptic boy: "This kind cometh out by nothing save prayer and fasting" (Mark 9:29). Jesus' definite advice on fasting was: "But thou, when thou fastest, anoint thy head, and wash thy face; that thou be not seen of men to fast, but of thy Father who is in secret; and thy Father, who seeth in secret, shall recompense thee" (Matthew 6:17).

Famed minister Kathryn Kuhlman of Pittsburgh, whose prayers have healed so many, has often advised those seeking healing to fast as well as pray. The remarkable results of prayer and fasting are related in the Kuhlman book, *I Believe in Miracles.*[1]

Hippocrates, the father of medicine, suggested fasts up to seven days. Fasting in modern times has returned as a method prescribed by some doctors for losing weight. Dr. Herbert M.

---

[1] Kathryn Kuhlman, *I Believe in Miracles* (Englewood Cliffs, N.J.: Prentice-Hall, Inc., 1962).

Shelton, who has conducted over thirty thousand fasts, has found, as the title of his book points out, that *Fasting Can Save Your Life*. It is also a fine method for loosing and releasing one's problems and letting them go to solution. Those who do not wish to abstain from both food and liquids and go on a severe fast of distilled water only often find it helpful to go on a fast consisting of liquids such as vegetable juices.

This seems to cleanse the mind and body and raise the one fasting to a higher level of consciousness where his prayer powers are heightened and illumination comes more quickly. *Fasting is especially powerful for overcoming severe problems, because fasting intensifies your prayer consciousness.*

A friend of mine recently had a puzzling problem which she did not know how to resolve and decided to go on a fast, consuming only liquids, until the problem was solved. The prayers she used with her fast were these: "JESUS CHRIST IS IN ABSOLUTE CONTROL OF THIS SITUATION, AND JESUS CHRIST IS PRODUCING PERFECT RESULTS IN THIS MATTER NOW." Amazingly, a man she had never seen called her "out of the blue," informing her just how to resolve her problem.

It was as though the act of prayer and fasting had set up a high-powered vibration that went forth into the ethers and worked through a total stranger, who then went to the trouble to seek her out and supply the answer to her prayer. Thus, within a week from the time she secretly went on the fast and began using special prayers to clarify the problem, it was solved by an individual she is yet to meet!

And so I repeat: Fasting is especially powerful for overcoming severe problems, because fasting intensifies your prayer consciousness.

There is a saying: "First the fast. Then the feast."

Surely the dramatic accomplishments of Paul and the apostles, both in their healing ministry and in their strenuous missionary travels for establishing the early Christian church all over the ancient world, seemed to be accompanied by strenuous fasting. However, the severities of the ancient fasts, particularly as they were practiced in the 3rd and 4th Centuries, were abandoned by later Christians, since they in some instances caused bodily damage to the fasters. In many religious groups down through the centuries, fasting has remained as a spiritual practice strongly suggested as an accompaniment of prayer in time of stress, strain or spiritual overcoming, however.

CLEANSING: A CONSTANT AND SELF-RENEWING PROCESS

The prayer of cleansing includes (1) the "no" power of prayer, often known as denial; (2) prayers of release from possessiveness, particularly in one's human relationships; (3) prayers of forgiveness for one's self, one's fellow man, one's experiences of unhappiness of past or present, and even of one's false ideas about God; and (4) the vacuum prayer, which includes both inner and outer methods of letting go that which is no longer of value in one's life, to make way for the good one is praying for. Purification and cleansing of one's thoughts and life is a constant process. You will never get through invoking these various prayers of cleansing. But you will pleasantly discover that each time you use them anew, they unblock the good in your life, and open fresh new ways to answered prayer for additional riches in your life.

SUMMARY OF CHAPTER 4

1. The development of your prayer powers *always* begins with purification of your thought and feeling nature. This dissolves mental and emotional blocks and makes you an open, receptive channel to answered prayer.
2. Purification is nothing to be feared but is a healing process. The prayer of cleansing is master of purification. To bypass the prayer of cleansing is to bypass your good.
3. Evil is not a problem but a lesson in purification. An understanding of this purification process through which the soul passes is a first requirement for one on the pathway of prayer. All evil is corrective and becomes a teacher to those who are willing to learn.

4. The prayer of cleansing includes the "no" prayer of cleansing. If you want your prayers answered, you must often turn from evil appearances and cleanse your mind of any fear about them by saying "no" to them.

5. The word "no" has power to erase. The "no" prayer has power to dissolve unhappy appearances of mind, body, affairs, relationships. There is a cleansing, freeing, redeeming power in the word "no."

6. The prayer of cleansing is symbolized in the cross, which is the oldest known spiritual symbol. The prayer of cleansing and purification is also symbolized through the Biblical acts of sacrifice, renunciation, repentance, even by the "wailing wall" in Jerusalem.

7. The second prayer of cleansing is release or letting go and letting God. This includes release of willful attitudes and possessive relationships. Willfulness and possessiveness have often blocked answers to prayer.

8. The act of confession and speaking words of release are both powerful methods of letting go and letting God.

9. Forgiveness is the third prayer of cleansing. Where there is a problem there is always a need for forgiveness. One person speaking prayers of forgiveness can dissolve the emotional blocks in a situation, regardless of what others involved are doing or saying. This is the potency of forgiveness, which simply means "to give up."

10. The fourth prayer of cleansing is the vacuum prayer, in which you get rid of what you do not want, in both inner and outer ways, to make way for what you do want. This action convinces your subconscious mind that you expect your prayers to be answered.

11. Freedom is one of the requirements of answered prayer and forming a powerful vacuum gives you that freedom.

12. The act of fasting is a form of the cleansing prayer and is powerful for overcoming severe problems, because fasting intensifies your prayer consciousness.

5

The Prayer of
Complete Protection

One of the most powerful, yet least known, forms of prayer is the prayer of protection. Through the prayer of protection, you can mentally say "no" to negative experiences and even stop them completely for yourself or others. Though the act of prayer itself protects, definite prayers of protection are even more powerful.

Through prayers of protection, you can dissolve unhappy experiences in which you have gotten involved. You can also help dissolve the negative experiences of others.

The 91st Psalm is one of the most powerful prayers of protection in the Bible. The Psalmist knew how important it was to pray prayers of protection as he guarded his helpless sheep against wild animals, inclement weather and a thousand and one ills. Thus he filled his psalms with protective prayers.

F. L. Rawson, who was a noted engineer and one of England's great scientists, got interested in spiritual healing and became a fine metaphysician soon after the turn of the century. He was a firm believer in prayers of protection for those in war.

He relates the story of a British regiment under the command of a Colonel Whittlesey, which served in World War I for more than four years without losing a man. When asked how his regiment was able to serve four years in the thick of battle without a single casualty, Colonel Whittlesey said it was because the officers and men in that regiment memorized and repeated regularly the 91st Psalm, which they called their "Psalm of Protection."

A man once lived through a shipwreck that took the lives of

many. When asked how he survived when death came to all those around him, this wise man replied he had prayed over and over the 91st Psalm.

As a spiritual being, made a little lower than the angels (8th Psalm), you can gain dominion of your world, and completely cast out or dissolve negative experiences from your life! The word "protect" means to shield from injury, danger or loss. The prayer of protection helps you do just that, as it shields you against loss, injury, danger, unhappiness and all the unnecessary experiences of life.

A very successful businesswoman has often stated that one of her success secrets is that she sends forth prayers of protection before her into her business world each day. At a time when almost everyone in her company was being fired by the new owner and was suffering the loss of thousands of dollars in income, this woman retained her job and went on to work in peace and harmony with her new boss as she daily used this protective prayer: "I CLOTHE MYSELF SAFELY ROUND WITH INFINITE LOVE AND WISDOM."

If you are already in the midst of unhappy experiences, prayers of protection can get you out of them! Immediately after the great fire in San Francisco in 1906, a businessman rose one hour earlier than usual each morning through those first chaotic months, in order to meditate upon divine protection, wisdom and peace. The results were astonishing to his friends and business acquaintances. Many of them asked him how he was able to re-establish his office in an orderly working manner when people all around him were still so unsettled.

As he daily affirmed divine protection, wisdom and peace, he was able to locate workers easily, systematize his work, and harmonize his records. All this was done without experiencing the weariness, confusion, exhaustion and depression that other people thought a necessary part of those hectic days.

In these challenging times, when one hears so much about war, crime, disease, poverty and a thousand inharmonies of mind and body, you should constantly use prayers of protection so that "it will not come nigh thee." *If some of these inharmonies are al-*

ready in your life, prayers of protection can help you meet them victoriously.

HOW TO BE PROTECTED FROM ROBBERY

A little girl was disappointed when she realized that one of her playmates had taken a doll and cradle from her room. At first she got angry and blamed various friends, planning to complain to her teacher at school about the theft.

But her mother reminded her of the power of speaking a prayer of protection and together they declared, "LOVE ENVIETH NOT," and stated that no one wanted her doll and cradle or anything else that was hers by divine right. That very night the doll and cradle were returned to their usual place in her room.

A woman once saved her house from being robbed, at a time when burglaries were being committed on all sides, as she declared these same words, "LOVE ENVIETH NOT."

There once was a woman in San Francisco who was suddenly approached by two masked men as she descended from a streetcar one dark night. They said to her, "We are short of cash and we want the money in your handbag."

She replied with an affirmation of protection: "GOD IS MY PROTECTION. THERE IS NOTHING IN THE SEEN OR THE UNSEEN THAT CAN HARM ME OR MAKE ME FEARFUL. I AM OVERSHADOWED BY DIVINE LOVE."

One masked man said to the other one, "Take her pocketbook. We've got to have it." As the other man snatched it the robbed woman kindly said, "I hope it will do you some good." Then she added, "We are all God's children. We are all brothers and sisters in the one human family. If one has a need, the other should be glad to divide with him. I hope that money will be a blessing to you."

The two robbers looked at each other helplessly, shook their heads, and returned the pocketbook to the victim, whereupon she bade them, "Good night, boys." As she went on her way, she realized they had never even opened her bag!

At a time when nearly every house in the neighborhood was

being robbed, a housewife spent time in nightly meditation, mentally building a wall of protection around her home and that of her next-door neighbor's. She would picture the wall of protection as a brilliant white light about a foot thick, and she would affirm: "WE ARE SURROUNDED BY THE PURE WHITE LIGHT OF THE CHRIST, INTO WHICH NOTHING NEGATIVE CAN PENETRATE AND OUT OF WHICH ONLY GOOD CAN COME." Her property and that of her next-door neighbor were never touched.

Paul might have been pointing out this protective method to the Romans when he advised: "Let us therefore cast off the works of darkness, and let us put on the armor of light" (Romans 13:12).

PRAYERS OF PROTECTION FOR HEALTH

Prayers of protection work in all departments of life, for health, wealth and happiness. A businessman was very worried about his wife, who fretted over everything. She got very upset at night if he did not arrive home on the dot. They were heavily in debt because of his wife's illness, and this man worked at a distasteful job as a bill collector in an effort to make ends meet. It was very unpleasant work, and life seemed just a series of unhappy experiences for this couple.

One day when his wife was in town shopping, she noticed a sign that read "Silence hour. Come in. You are welcome." The word "silence" interested her, because she was trying to get free from fear and gain peace of mind. Hopefully she attended this noon prayer meeting. The speaker on the platform, with his eyes closed, kept affirming over and over these words of protection: "THERE IS AN INFINITE POWER WITHIN US THAT PROTECTS US FROM ALL HARM."

For an hour, over and over, this speaker declared these words and the audience joined him. Following the use of this prayer, there would be long periods of silence in which the people meditated upon these words of protection.

At the end of this quiet hour, the formerly nervous, high-strung woman felt like a completely reborn person. She realized that most of her fears were groundless; she determined to go home, clean house, prepare a good meal for her husband, and just relax and enjoy life. She vowed to stop worrying about so many little things.

When her husband arrived home for dinner after a trying day of bill-collecting, he could hardly believe the change he saw in his wife. Instead of being distraught that he was late, she was calmly sitting by the fire sewing, while the evening meal remained warm in the oven.

When he asked what had brought about this change, she related the day's events and the great impact that the prayer of protection had made upon her: "THERE IS AN INFINITE POWER WITHIN US THAT PROTECTS US FROM ALL HARM." Amazed, he told her that that very afternoon, one of his customers who had not been able to pay his bill for some time, had told him that he too, had attended that same noon prayer meeting and was using that prayer of protection in faith that he would soon be able to pay up. This couple found as they continued using this protective prayer that it opened the way to a whole new life of peace, health and plenty.

HOW YOUR PROTECTIVE PRAYERS REACH OTHERS

You also have the ability constantly to do protective mental and *spiritual work for others, as well as for yourself. In fact, some of the greatest prayers you can ever pray for other people are prayers of protection.*

A worried widow was concerned about her headstrong teenage son who insisted upon racing his new car. He had met with several accidents in driving and his mother feared for his life, but had been unable to persuade him to stop racing. At a weekly prayer group, the members joined her in using the well-known Unity Prayer of Protection for him: "THE LIGHT OF GOD SURROUNDS YOU. THE LOVE OF GOD ENFOLDS YOU. THE POWER OF GOD PROTECTS YOU. THE PRESENCE OF GOD WATCHES OVER YOU. WHEREVER YOU ARE, GOD IS, AND ALL IS WELL."

The mother then said no more about the forthcoming races but trusted to divine protection and the results were interesting:

When her son's car was tested at the "time trials," it was found defective and he was not allowed to race it. Continued prayers of protection helped this energetic teenager begin to mature and develop other interests.

A young businessman was driving across the country to Southern California on a business trip. His mother read in the morning paper of a flood and she immediately spoke words that her son was divinely protected. Later she heard from him saying some local business had interfered with his leaving home when originally planned. By being detained, he had avoided the flooded areas, whereas if he had left when originally planned, he would have been in the midst of the flooded district.

One of the humorous stories that Florence Shinn relates in her book, *The Power of the Spoken Word*,[1] is that of a lady who had seven children. Instead of worrying about them all the time, she casually spoke words of protection for them, and they all grew up safe and sound.

One day a neighbor had rushed in and said, "You had better call your children. They are all climbing up and down trees. They are going to kill themselves." This mother calmly replied, "Oh, they are only playing tree tag. Don't look at them and nothing will happen." She refused to worry about them, and nothing did happen.

If worried mothers of teenage daughters and sons, and worried wives of philandering husbands would fret less and surround their loved ones more with prayers of protection, there would be fewer unwanted pregnancies, less illegitimacy and adulterous behavior in their family circles. Through prayers of protection by even one member of the family, true family happiness can be restored for its members. *Replace nagging and name-calling with prayers of protection. The results will astound you!*

People in public life should be surrounded by prayers of protection so that they will not become the subconscious victims of the jealousies and criticisms of others. As pointed out in my book, *The Healing Secret of the Ages*, ill health and even death can

---

[1] Florence Shinn, *The Power of the Spoken Word* (London, England: L. N. Fowler & Company, Ltd., 1959).

result for a person from someone else's "ill" thoughts about him, if
he is not protecting himself mentally. Cold, critical, envious,
jealous thoughts directed toward the sufferer can cause everything from overweight to cancer and emotional disturbances.

Pray protectively for yourself: "I AM SURROUNDED BY THE PURE
WHITE LIGHT OF THE CHRIST. I AM FREE FROM THE NEGATIVE
THOUGHTS OF OTHERS." Declare for other people: "YOU ARE SUR-
ROUNDED BY THE PURE WHITE LIGHT OF THE CHRIST. I PRONOUNCE
YOU FREE FROM THE NEGATIVE THOUGHTS OF OTHERS.

It is a good practice to begin the day with prayers of protection, both for yourself and others. Upon rising in the morning,
entrust the day to God's keeping. Place yourself and your loved
ones in His loving care. This attitude will give calmness and
strength. If there is any special challenge or troublesome situation that has to be met that day, declare for it, "I RELEASE YOU TO
DIVINE PROTECTION. GOD IS IN CHARGE AND ONLY GOOD SHALL COME
FROM THIS EXPERIENCE. EVERYONE INVOLVED SHALL BE DIVINELY
SATISFIED AND BLESSED.

Remind yourself that God is truly taking care of that which
you have given into His charge. This will give you the assurance,
conviction and realization that you, your life, and all whom you
hold dear are safe and secure in God's loving presence, and you
will go forth into your day relaxed and happy.

If you have been harboring thoughts of fear for yourself or for
your loved ones or if you have feared storms, accidents, disease,
epidemics, war, then prayers of protection will help you release
such negative fears. As you go forth to meet your day, you will
find yourself denying fear as you continue affirming God's protective presence in each experience. Slippery roads, speeding
cars, and all the seeming hazards of modern living will cause you
no uneasiness. As you meet each experience you will find yourself
releasing it to divine protection. Through this prayerful, protective outlook on life, you will find yourself guided and blessed
with wisdom and good judgment day by day, and you will be
brought safely through every experience. *Daily use of prayers of
protection can truly be the secret to successful living in this challenging age!*

HOW CROPS AND WEATHER CONDITIONS ARE PROTECTED THROUGH PRAYER

There once was a farmer who believed that a "praying man" comes under divine protection in his fields. This man's father had been a successful farmer in England. In the process of raising potatoes, his father had united with a number of neighbors in leasing a long strip of land, which was divided so that every farmer had two rows of potato hills. The men bought seed together and plowed and planted at the same time. However, this man's father was a strong believer in the presence and power of divine protection in the affairs of man. So while planting his seed, he made it a habit to invoke the blessing of the Almighty upon them, for he believed that all his prosperity came through remembering God in his financial affairs.

When the time came to gather the potatoes, the farmers found that a potato disease called "dry rot" had attacked every tuber, causing almost a total loss to each farmer—except this one man. When he turned over the soil in his two long rows of hills, he found that not one potato had been touched. This made a very deep impression upon all the country round, especially since this farmer ascribed his protection to the goodness of God in answering his direct and believing prayer for the perfect yield of his crop.

A protective prayer that has been used by many to produce good crops is this: "DIVINE ORDER IS ESTABLISHED IN THE ATMOSPHERIC CONDITIONS PRODUCING THE KIND OF WEATHER NEEDED FOR THE EARTH TO BRING FORTH ITS BOUNTIFUL HARVEST."

There once was a woman in Southern California whose home was in the midst of a large orange grove, which was then in full bearing and promised a fine crop and income that year.

This woman had a neighbor who also owned orange groves and was expecting a good crop, but this neighbor did not believe in the power of divine protection. She scoffed the idea as "simple and silly."

One night a report was carried through the town that they

were likely to have a black frost before morning and that every person had better "smudge" his orange groves. This "smudging" consisted of building fires in the groves, and letting the smoke keep the air warm, so that the cold air could not get to the oranges.

The husbands of both these women were away on business, and there was no one on hand to do the job of smudging. So the woman who did not believe in divine protection spent that night walking the floor wringing her hands. But the woman who believed in divine protection was quiet and calm, and spoke these words of protection: "GOD CAN PROTECT MY GROVE. THE PRESENCE OF GOD IS THERE, AND EVEN NOW FOLDS IT ROUND AND KEEPS IT FROM EVERY HARMFUL THING." She remembered the 91st Psalm and affirmed it over and over. Suddenly she got the impression that her grove was covered over with a great invisible canvas of protection. With this realization came a sense of peace, so she retired for the night and slept peacefully.

That night the black frost came, and every orange grove that had not been smudged was lost—except this woman's. The grove of her unbelieving neighbor was a total loss. Yet this woman who had spoken words of protection for her grove found not one orange damaged! Through prayers of protection her grove had been saved, and an income of thousands of dollars salvaged. Needless to say, her previously scoffing friend never again criticized her belief in divine protection.

A powerful prayer of protection regarding weather conditions for good crops, safe travel, etc., is this: "DIVINE ORDER NOW BLESSES THE EARTH WITH PERFECT WEATHER AND THE PROPER AMOUNT OF MOISTURE. ORDER, HARMONY, AND SAFE CONDITIONS ARE ESTAB-LISHED AND MAINTAINED."

HOW PROTECTION PRAYERS PUT OUT FIRE

There once was a fierce fire raging out of control in the northern part of the province of Ontario, Canada. The flames had been spreading rapidly for three days, destroying hundreds of homes in their wake, when a homeowner decided to telephone a spiritual counselor in Toronto for prayers of protection.

Within fifteen minutes from the time the spiritual counselor and members of her prayer ministry started speaking words of protection, that fire of three days was completely wiped out as the wind stopped and the whole area was flooded with rain. What was their method that so quickly put out a three-day fire?

The spiritual counselor had spoken directly to the wind: "IN THE NAME OF JESUS CHRIST, I SAY TO YOU: PEACE, BE STILL."

Then to the flames of the fire she had said: "YOU HAVE NO POWER IN YOU TO HURT OR DESTROY ANY GOOD THING. IN THE NAME OF JESUS CHRIST YOU ARE NOW FINISHED. YOU ARE WIPED OUT."

In conclusion she had said, "THE WET BLANKET OF JESUS CHRIST NOW LOWERS AND SPREADS OVER THE WHOLE LAND AND THE FIRE IS OUT. FATHER, I THANK YOU THAT IT IS NOW DONE."

As for the spiritual validity of praying about crops, weather, and atmospheric conditions, the prophet Zechariah advised: "Ask ye of Jehovah rain in the time of the latter rain . . . and He will give them showers of rain, to every one grass in the field" (Zech. 10:1).

PRAYER PROTECTION IN WAR

There is an interesting World War I story that came out of France about the power of protective prayers: A young lieutenant and his eighteen men were cut off from both communications and supplies. The enemy was closing in on them and there seemed no way of escape. This young officer suddenly remembered a letter from his sister, which he had not had time to read. Upon impulse he opened it. She wrote that her prayers were surrounding him and his men with divine protection, and that she had a number of other people praying for their safekeeping.

The lieutenant and his soldiers were haggard and scared, as well as hungry and tired. In his sister's letter she quoted from the Psalms:

I will say of the Lord, He is my refuge and my fortress. My God in whom I trust. . . . His truth is a shield and buckler. Thou shalt not be afraid for the terror by night, nor for the arrow that flieth by day. Or the pestilence that walketh in the darkness, nor for the destruction that wasteth at noonday. A thousand shall fall at thy side and ten thousand at thy right hand, but it shall not come nigh thee (Psalm 91:2, 4–7).

The young officer read these words, then folded the letter, placing it inside his shirt. No longer fearful, he said to his men, "Keep your chin up. Nothing is going to harm us, because we're being prayed for. If you guys have a prayer in you, I suggest you pitch in and help."

One soldier replied, "The Lord be with us." The others chorused "Amen" solemnly. They had barely finished when the big guns of the enemy tore loose and for five hours there was terrific gunfire. These soldiers were completely helpless. Annihilation seemed inevitable, to all human appearances. In spite of this, none of these soldiers was hit, nor was their quarters in an old house disturbed in any way. It was as though a circle had been drawn around the house and barn that they occupied, though the rest of the village was wiped out.

The young lieutenant later concluded: "Nobody ever again has had to convince me of the power of prayers of protection. It's too potent and dynamic a method to take lightly. It works."

YOUR ANGEL PRAYER PROTECTORS

The ancients believed that the Angel of God's Presence is a miracle-working presence that is available to every man; that there are angel-protectors all around us who are only too glad to guide and protect us, when called upon to do so. They felt that every person has an angel or higher self. (Read about the healing method of writing to a person's angel in my book, *The Dynamic Laws of Healing*.)

When challenges arise, say to yourself, "I HAVE NOTHING TO FEAR. MY GUARDIAN ANGEL GOES BEFORE ME, MAKING RIGHT MY WAY." Decree this often for others, too. A businesswoman was concerned about having to make an out-of-town buying trip, since she would have to drive two hundred miles in rain and fog accompanied by her sick husband, whom she could not leave at home alone. A friend said, "You have nothing to fear, because I prayed that your guardian angel will be with you."

Upon returning from the buying trip, this businesswoman reported, "I did seem to be accompanied by an angel. As I drove out of town, the sky cleared of fog, the rain stopped, and the sun shone through. There was no more bad weather on the entire trip. The drive lifted my husband's spirits and he suffered no ill effects from it. Financially, this proved to be the most profitable buying trip I have made in a long time."

Two missionaries were passing through a dangerous jungle region where two robbers were waiting to attack them. But as the missionaries prayerfully approached, the robbers saw a "third person," much larger than life-size, traveling with them and apparently hovering over them protectively. The presence of this third party, or Angel of Protection, both puzzled and frightened the robbers, so that the missionaries were saved from harm.

ANGELS OF PROSPERITY AND HEALING

The Hebrews of old felt that Raphae was the angel of healing. At times you may wish to decree: "ANGEL OF HEALING, COME FORTH HERE AND NOW." Or you may wish to call on the Angel of Prosperity, or the Angel of Love, Harmony and Marriage in the same way.

Before traveling or going forth into any challenging situation, it is well to affirm: "THE ANGEL CALM GOES BEFORE ME, PROTECTING ME FROM ANY NEGATIVE EXPERIENCES" or "THE ANGEL OF GOD'S PRESENCE GOES BEFORE ME AND PREPARES MY WAY." The prophet Malachi might have been speaking of his angel-protector when he said, "Behold, I send my messenger, and he shall prepare the way before me" (Mal. 3:1).

Once when I was going on a six weeks' lecture trip, I decided to test the angel idea by affirming that the Angel of Prosperity went before me making prosperous and successful my way. When lecturing for business, professional or convention groups, a professional lecture fee is in order, whereas the offerings received when lecturing in churches are often so small they do not pay one's expenses—and this was to be a lecture trip for churches.

However, on this trip, after sending the Prosperity Angel before me, something happened that had never happened before: Along the way people kept privately saying, "I have read your books and have been helped by them. I want to show my appreciation by sharing a special tithe offering with you." The result was that I came home carrying a number of tithe checks as special gifts to me individually, which helped defray costs I had so often had to meet personally. That experience convinced me that there is an Angel of Prosperity—an Angel of Riches without limitations!

As for the Angel of Healing, a story came out of England many years ago, appearing in the *London Daily Mirror* and *The Central News Agency*, about a woman who had been ill for five years and was dying from advanced tuberculosis. Doctors had long despaired of saving her, and relatives had gathered round as she stopped breathing and appeared to be gone. Eight minutes later, she suddenly took a deep breath and roused as she said conversationally, "Yes, I am listening. Who is it?" At that moment she saw an angel bending over her who said, "Your sufferings are over. Get up and walk."

When she asked for her robe so that she could walk, it caused a great commotion among her relatives, because she had not walked for months. She then walked into another room and asked for food, though she had not had a solid meal for six months.

As she quickly regained her health, medical tests revealed there was not a trace of the disease left in her body, after five years of intense suffering. Thereafter, she ate well, slept well, and was quite calm and peaceful. Nothing seemed to tire or excite her. The angel had told her that her life was being spared so that she might help to heal others, so she spent a great deal of time in intercessory prayer for the sick in her village, asking the Angel of Healing to make them whole. Many healings occurred and her life took on new meaning and new satisfaction.

The Psalmist seemed to know about the protective power of angels summoned by prayer when he promised: "There shall no

evil befall thee. Neither shall any plague come nigh thy tent. For
he will give his angels charge over thee, to keep thee in all thy
ways" (91st Psalm).

SUMMARY OF CHAPTER 5

1. One of the most powerful, yet least known forms of prayer, is
   the prayer of protection. Through prayers of protection, you
   can dissolve unhappy experiences in which you have gotten
   involved and you can also help dissolve negative experiences
   of others.
2. If you are in the midst of unhappy experiences, prayers of
   protection can get you out of them, and prayers of protection
   can keep you from such unhappy experiences in the future.
3. Some of the greatest prayers you can ever pray for others are
   prayers of protection.
4. Replace nagging and name-calling in your family circle with
   prayers of protection. The results will astound you.
5. Prayers of protection are especially powerful in dissolving ill
   health, warding off accidents, protecting crops and the weather,
   even putting out fires. Prayers of protection have often saved
   lives in war.
6. The office of the angels is to guard, guide and direct you. Affirm
   often that the angel of healing, protection, prosperity goes
   before you making healthy, safe or prosperous your way.
7. The Psalmist prayed often prayers of protection to ward off
   wild beasts, inclement weather, and other ills. The 91st Psalm
   is a powerful prayer of protection. Use it often.

6

The Powerful
Prayer of Decree

A businessman quipped, "Of course, I believe in the power of prayer. I pray—every morning—for the stock market to go up!"

Whether he realized it or not, that man was invoking the prayer of decree, though in a rather casual way.

Prayers of decree have been described as "handles of power" and I agree. When you know how to pray affirmatively, without fear, through prayers of decree, you know how to take hold of "handles of power" which can guide you victoriously through life's experiences.

Many of the blessings of life are not obtained simply because you have not asked for them affirmatively. Affirmation, or the prayer of decree, releases power into the subconscious mind, where it is freed to go to work and produce positive results. Prayers of decree, especially the type described in chapter 7, reach the deepest level of the mind, which is the superconscious, and often release miracle power that is dormant there.

Knowing about the simplicity and power of affirmative prayer gives you a sense of spiritual and emotional security that nothing else does because, once you know how to use prayers of decree, you will never again feel alone or defenseless. You will be armed with spiritual ammunition with which to meet life's challenges and come out "the winner."

Though I had been reared in a religious family, I never really knew how to pray until I learned about the prayer of decree.

Suddenly it was as though I had discovered the greatest treasure on earth, because at last I had something to hold to, to steer me through life's good times and bad. For twenty years now, I have been using affirmative prayers for myself and others. I have found that you can literally "blast your way" out of limitation, if you will but speak the word of truth and decree your good regardless of appearances. Prayers of decree can be your "spiritual dynamite" to remove troublesome barriers to your good in all areas of life.

Recently after I had served as guest minister at the Unity Temple on the Country Club Plaza in Kansas City, Missouri, the main comment about my lectures was, "Why, she's nothing but a bundle of affirmations!"

However, if the belief you have previously given to evil were consistently turned to the belief in good for even one hour, it would be sufficient to revolutionize your life! You can begin to revolutionize your life through prayers of affirmative decree, which help you to dwell upon the good in life and call it into expression. Your words can dissolve obstacles and remove barriers. Affirmation seems to be the form of prayer that sets in motion the whole power of God.

The word "affirm" means to "make firm" and prayers of affirmation help you to make firm the good in life. The prayer of affirmation is so simple that it takes away the feeling of mystery and complexity generally associated with prayer. Its simplicity dissolves the usual psychological blocks about prayer being difficult.

The prayer of affirmation has been described as "scientific prayer," or "spiritual treatment," in modern times. The Bible is filled with affirmative prayers which were known then as "decrees." Job described the simplicity and power of affirmation when he promised: "Thou shalt decree a thing and it shall be established unto thee and light shall shine upon thy ways" (Job 22:28). Jesus used the power of decree often to heal and prosper his followers. The Lord's Prayer, in some translations such as the Fenton, is a series of affirmations. The Psalmist loved affirmative prayers and filled his psalms with them. A good example is the beloved 23rd Psalm. The creation story of Genesis emphasized the creative power of decree over and over with the phrase: "God said 'Let there be . . .' and there was."

Owing to the vibratory power of words, whatever you decree— that you release within yourself and your world. The word "utter" and the word "outer" have the same root meaning. What you "utter" literally becomes an "outer" part of your world!

HOW AFFIRMATIONS PRODUCED A BOOK

Study shows that nearly all Bible prayers were spoken in a loud voice. Historians assume this was true because they were usually prayed before a large assembly. However, Biblical prayers were also spoken in a loud voice because the ancients knew about the dynamics of sound: That every spoken word has tremendous power; and that by certain arrangements of words, such as in an affirmative decree, a tremendous vibratory force could be set up in the invisible which profoundly affected substance and produced the specific results decreed.

The power of the spoken word was used for healing long before Bible times. Chanting of affirmative decrees was used in the healing temples of Atlantis, Egypt, Persia, India and Greece to bring again into harmony the vibratory forces in man. In the East, Mantra Yoga, or salvation through affirmation, has long been practiced.

My first book, *The Dynamic Laws of Prosperity*, got into print as a result of affirmations. During the recession of 1958, by request I taught a class on the spiritual and mental laws of prosperity. The people in my ministry were helped so much by it that they asked me to put the material from that class into a book. Having never written a book, I felt I had neither the time nor talent for such a project and plainly said so.

However, one fine businessman in that prosperity class felt so strongly that I should write such a book that he offered to meet with me for an hour every morning in the prayer room at the church to pray affirmatively about it. At the time we started making affirmations, I had neither a book, a title, a publisher, or any experience for such a task, so it seemed a fantastic prayer project.

Nevertheless, as we began daily to use decrees, the whole format for the book unfolded to me in prayer, even to the chapter headings. As we next prayed for a name for the book, a stock-broker in that prosperity class suggested the appropriate title, *The Dynamic Laws of Prosperity*. Then we needed a publisher. Under the circumstances, it seemed preposterous that I could just "break into print" successfully as an unknown writer. But as we prayed affirmatively, decreeing the God-appointed publisher, an amazing thing happened: A man in the public relations business who had been helped by the class instruction walked into my office one day and said, "Your prosperity class has helped me and my business so much that I want to do something for you. What can I do?"

When I explained my writing project he exclaimed, "I have a friend in New York who is a well-known literary agent. Ordinarily she does not take on unknown writers, but I will ask her about representing you." The result was that I soon had a fine agent and publishers.

Thus the book, its title and publisher all came after the power of decree was employed. Then, as we affirmed that I would have the time to write the book amid a heavy schedule of church work, somehow the book got written in the middle of the night and at odd moments.

Affirmative prayer did a very thorough job of providing me with all that was needed to launch my books into print! The only "contact" or "influence" I had as an unknown writer was the "contact" or "influence" of affirmative prayer!

The prayer of decree is the only contact or influence you need to get your prayers answered too.

PRAYER BEGINS WITH WORDS

Perhaps you are asking, "But why does just speaking forth words have spiritual power? Isn't prayer more than just words?" Yes, prayer is more than words, but *prayer begins and ends with words.* As the great religions of the world have always known, the word is God in action. "In the beginning was the Word . . . and the Word was God . . . and without him (the word) was not anything made," explained the mystical John (John 1: 1,3).

The word is dynamic because it creates. Speech is the very breath of God because it creates. Nothing is more alive with power, nothing has more creative power than affirmative words. This is true because words of truth have life, intelligence and substance within them, which are released through decree.

The reason the prayer of affirmation has been used by all civilizations and cultures from the beginning of time until the present is because the great minds down through the ages have known that the word has creative power. Words of truth are sharp as a two-edged sword (Hebrews 4:12) and quickly cut through negation and dissolve it, thereby releasing the omnipresent good.

The Hindu scriptures pointed this out "If a man speaks or acts with an evil thought, pain follows him. If a man speaks or acts with a pure, affirmative thought, happiness follows him." The Egyptian creation story emphasized the power of affirmative words for creating, just as does our own Genesis story of creation: "It was the Egyptian god who made the world, speaking it into existence. That which flows from his mouth happens, and that which he speaks comes into being." The Greeks said the word is filled with cosmic power. In India, the spoken word of affirmation is considered the greatest power in the world. The Chinese have long believed that words are so powerful that no piece of paper containing written words should ever be destroyed, even when it is no longer of value.

RESULTS OF PRAYERFUL AFFIRMATION

One of the Popes of the early Christian Church decided, when he was just a little boy working out in the fields, that he would become Pope of Rome. As he affirmed it, he released the most dynamic, creative power in existence which then shaped circumstances and events that caused this farm boy to become Pope, as he had said he would.

A little Greek boy, the son of a fruit dealer, affirmed as a child that he would make his life worth something, and he rose from the son of that fruit dealer to the friend of Socrates.

One of the early Roman poets had been a baker's son. Then he lifted his thoughts so high in affirming the good that he became a great poet and playwright, and the Roman people showed him the same reverence they paid their emperors. There was also a Greek slave who was sickly and badly deformed but, through affirmation, was lifted from the bondage of slavery to a cruel master and became the honored companion of lords and princes.

The Scottish philosopher, Thomas Carlyle, said that if you will proclaim your freedom from bondage, that bondage will vanish, and you can lay hold of some new good each moment. He promised that through the affirmation you will notice you are becoming free from sickness. As you continue affirming the good, you will see how much better you get along with people who previously seemed difficult. As you persist in affirmation, you will notice that your disposition improves. You will soon be more prosperous. Many things that previously hurt you will change in your favor. *Affirmative prayer is among the simplest, yet most powerful ways offered to mankind to change and improve life!* This is why people in all ages have known and used the prayer of decree.

WHY VERBAL PRAYER IS ALWAYS A NECESSITY

Many people become frustrated in prayer because they try to pray silently, through meditation and the silence, when they have not first relaxed, dissolved their fears through prayers of cleansing, and then spoken affirmative decrees. If you do not learn how to pray the prayer of relaxation, the prayer of cleansing, the prayer of affirmation first, you cannot possibly skip these and learn how to pray the deeper, more spiritual types of prayer such as meditation, silence and realization.

Sincere seekers on the pathway of prayer sometimes become discouraged because they try to master the deeper phases of prayer when they have not yet learned the first basic types of prayer, which include the spoken word of decree. They are trying to get their master's degree in prayer when they have not even learned the kindergarten phases of prayer!

Do not underestimate the prayer of relaxation, the prayer of cleansing, and the prayer of decree. These verbal phases of prayer must come first in your prayer development. Verbal prayers (such as prayers of cleansing and decree) break up all kinds of negative thought patterns in your conscious and subconscious mind. It is these old, negative thought patterns of inharmony, unforgiveness, resentment, fear, jealousy, envy, condemnation, that have kept your good from you, and that have kept you from being able to pray in a deeper way.

Spoken words clear away these old negative thought patterns that have crowded your mind and emotions. When these are cleared away, and your mind and emotions have been cleansed, then you can pray in deeper ways through meditation, the silence, realization.

But there are layers and layers of thought in your mind and emotions that have got to be cleansed first, before you can pray more deeply. The ancients believed that man had seven thicknesses or layers of the mind that constantly needed to be cleansed of negative thought in order for his prayers to be answered.

Verbal words, verbal prayers, which often seem more mental than spiritual, are the one thing that can clear these layers and layers of negative thought out of man's mental and emotional strata. It is only after such a mental and emotional cleansing that man's prayers get answered.

VERBAL PRAYER HAS PSYCHOLOGICAL VALUE

Psychology, as well as religion, agrees that you should use a lot of verbal prayer. Psychology insists that the spoken word has more suggestive power, is more likely to reach and improve the deeper psychic levels of the mind, than mere inarticulate thought. Psychology insists that verbal prayer is very powerful for cleansing and improving the mind and emotions, because psychology has found that *your centers of speech are closely connected with your mental life. Thus, when you speak forth good words, you improve your mental life.*

The early Christians, as well as the Christian mystics of the Middle Ages who were such experts in prayer, insisted that some vocal prayer should enter into the daily life of even the most contemplative, silent souls. They said that the use of higher degrees of prayer did not and should not ever mean giving up or totally abandoning the lower phases of prayer such as verbal prayer.

The early Christian mystics pointed out again and again in their writings, from their own profound prayer experiences, that health in your spiritual life, like that in your mental life, depends to a great extent on variety in your prayer life.

Therefore, you should never be afraid of variety in prayer. You should never feel that you are losing ground spiritually if you again find yourself using verbal prayers after having learned how to practice meditation and the silence.

St. Teresa, St. John of the Cross, and others insisted that for your own spiritual balance you must constantly go back to affirmative prayer. There are "prayer neurotics" who insist they have "outgrown" verbal prayer; they feel that prayer of decree is too "simple" for them. Invariably such warped individuals become confused, upset, unbalanced as they try to be "advanced," practicing only meditation and the silence. Often they end up having psychic obsessions and other psychological problems, because they did not balance their prayer life.

Through variety in prayer, you open your soul to fresh new areas of spiritual development. The great Christian specialists in prayer always began with vocal prayer, the most direct and powerful instrument of suggestion, which tuned up the psychic levels of the soul. They then proceeded to meditation, the silence and the deeper levels of prayer. Verbal prayer is all powerful in the beginning of your prayer development, and later on, too! You never outgrow the verbal prayer of decree.

There is one theory that for every fifteen minutes of spiritual study, there should be five minutes of affirmation to balance it.

Study helps you know *about* the truth. Affirmation helps you to
release it.

VERBAL PRAYER BRINGS QUICK FINANCIAL HELP

*Anyone can pray, anyone can get results, who dares to pray the
prayer of decree! This is true because prayer power is centralized
at the root of the tongue.* "Death and life are in the power of the
tongue," explained Solomon in the Proverbs (Proverbs 18:21).

Because prayer power is centralized at the root of the tongue,
the ancients believed that the word must be tried and tasted
before it became powerful, that it is not enough just to say an
affirmation, but that you should "eat" your decrees. Take a bite—
a few words—then chew, assimilate, think about them. Swallow,
digest, meditate upon them. The word then becomes flesh and
dwells among you as results (John 1:14).

To speak forth words of life, health, prosperity, success, happiness and peace over and over releases an atomic vibration. Those
words then move in the ethers to form the conditions described
right out of the omnipresent intelligence of the universe! Affirmation is a simple, easy method of prayer. It is a handle of power
which anyone can take hold of and then produce satisfying
results.

A shopkeeper in England suddenly found herself in dire financial circumstances. She owed a considerable amount of money on
her business property. The mortgagor of this property had passed
away and his heirs wanted to settle the estate. They notified her
that she must pay off her indebtedness or be sold out. She wished
to retain her property, but did not have the money to meet their
demands.

Realizing that prayers of affirmation "make firm" one's good,
she began affirming: "ALL FINANCIAL DOORS ARE NOW OPEN TO ME.
ALL FINANCIAL CHANNELS ARE NOW FREE TO ME. DIVINE SUBSTANCE
NOW APPROPRIATELY MANIFESTS FOR ME."

As she continued in affirmative prayer "at the eleventh hour" a
stranger walked into her shop. While he browsed through the
merchandise, they chatted. Their conversation revealed that he

was a bank manager. Although her own bank had refused her a loan, this bank manager offered the services of his bank to cover her financial needs. Thus the right financial door opened, but only after she decreed it—verbally and definitely.

Speak forth your prayers of decree verbally into the ethers at regular, daily intervals. As you do, your spoken affirmative words move on the substance of the universe, set up an atomic vibration, form your good into definite results and manifest it visibly for you. *You literally release atomic energy through spoken decrees of good.*

Phillips Brooks once said, "Prayer is not the beseeching of a reluctant God, but the opening of ourselves to God's willingness." Affirmative prayer helps you to do just that: Open your mind and heart to God's willingness to shower you with infinite blessings!

Emerson described God as a "vast affirmation," and he described prayer as "God in man pronouncing His works good." A powerful prayer technique is to affirm for *every* experience in life—positive or negative—"I PRONOUNCE THIS GOOD."

MOST POWERFUL TYPES OF AFFIRMATION

Though all my books are filled with prayers of decree (See *The Dynamic Laws of Prosperity* for specific prosperity decrees; and see *The Dynamic Laws of Healing* for specific healing decrees), over the years I have observed that there are certain types of affirmative prayers that seem the most powerful for getting results.

First: The Prayer of Talking Directly to God

You may be amazed how quickly your prayers will be answered when you treat God as a loving Father and speak directly to Him. For instance, talk to God about the good things you want in life. Robert Collier has described this simple process in his book, *Riches Within Your Reach:*[1]

---

[1] Robert Collier, *Riches Within Your Reach* (Tarrytown, N.Y.: Robert Collier Publications, Inc., 1947).

Start with what you have, and suggest to Him each day that you are getting stronger, healthier, richer, happier. Talk to Him as a rich and loving Father, describing the improvements you would like to see in your affairs, the finer body you have in your mind's eye, the more important work you should be doing, the lovelier home, the richer rewards. Talk them over for ten minutes each day when you are alone with Him. You will be amazed at how readily He will help you to carry out your suggestions. Don't worry about how He is to bring about the conditions you desire. Just talk to Him confidently, serenely, happily—and then leave the rest to Him.

The person who faithfully prays in this way is certain to succeed, because he is attuning himself to the most successful force in the universe. This method of prayer is a simple way of fulfilling the promise of Jesus: "All things whatsoever ye shall ask in prayer, believing, ye shall receive" (Matthew 2:22 ASV).

Many people have not employed the power of prayer because they have the erroneous idea that it is wrong to pray for *things*. Jesus did not mean that praying for things was the only form of prayer, or even the highest form of prayer, when He made this promise. But He knew that if you first pray for things, you will learn the power of prayer as a means of communing with God and His goodness.

It is right and just that you should pray for things if you need them. You are living in a rich God-created universe that desires to fulfill all your needs. Among Biblical figures who prayed for definite things and got them were Abraham, Asa, Daniel, David, Elijah, Ezekiel, Habakkuk, Hannah, Jehoshaphat, Jeremiah, Jonah, Joshua, Moses, Nehemiah, Samson, and Solomon. On a number of occasions Jesus prayed for things and they manifested.

When you are in doubt about whether you should pray for a certain thing or not, ask yourself three questions:

First, is it spiritually legal? Would getting it hurt anyone else? Would getting it be good for all concerned? There is a saying, "The good of one is the good of all."

Second, do you really want what you are asking for—to the extent that you are willing to accept the responsibility that having it will bring? New good always brings new responsibilities and challenges.

Third, are you willing, if necessary, to give up something you now have to make way for the good you want which would replace it? Emerson was right when he said that for everything you gain, you lose something.

You never go wrong, when praying for things, to pray for "divine results."

Second: The Prayer of Asking

At times man is inclined to decide personally what he wants, then formulate an affirmation to get it, and through use of that decree, try to force God to give him his desires. Struggle and strife often result. Delay, disappointment, barriers and obstacles may stop the answer.

However, the "prayer of asking" simply asks God for what you want, knowing you do not have to try to force Him to give it to you, because it was God in you wanting it for you that gave you the desire in the first place! You cannot ask for anything that has not already been given you on the invisible plane. The simple prayer of asking wipes out time and space between you and the receiving. Often just saying, "This or something better, Father. Let thine unlimited good appear," is all that is needed to get results—either the result you had in mind or a far better one.

Remind yourself often that if it were not God's good will for you to experience fulfillment of the deep desires of your heart, you would not desire them in the first place. Selfish, human, limited, surface desires do not last. They soon pass away, whereas the deep desires of the soul quietly persist, seeking fulfillment.

The word "desire" means "from the Father." If God did not want you to be happy and successful, you could not possibly achieve happiness and success no matter what you did, no matter how hard you tried. Regardless of how much you might strain and press toward success, you would fail if God did not want you to succeed!

A housewife once related how just by asking God for what she wanted, her needs were met in an incredible way:

One summer day I had to drive from Graham to Tyler, Texas, and I had only $15 in cash, which was enough for the trip since I planned to return the same day. I started at 4 A.M. in order to be there at 9 A.M. My husband had been in Tyler for several days and planned to return home with me, but he too was out of funds. We had a fairly new car with which we had had no trouble, but on the return trip from Tyler back to Graham before we had eaten lunch, the car stopped running. We gave a man $1 to get it started. He then pushed us to a station, worked on it some more, and after finally getting it running, charged us $2.50 more. At this point, we were left with only $9 (having used a portion on the earlier trip that morning) to buy gas to drive two hundred and twenty miles home.

After we drove about ten miles the car stopped again. This time we were near a garage, so the mechanic there got it started. By then it was 6 P.M. and we were only thirty miles from where we had started four hours previously. We were tired and hungry, but felt we should drive a while and stop for coffee, since we did not have enough money to spare for a meal.

About 5 miles from the garage, the car stopped again in a desolate area. Since we had done all we knew to do, we pushed the car off the road and decided to spend the night there. My husband walked up the road looking for water for us before we retired for the night.

I had been praying all day but things looked hopeless. Worse still, my son was ill in Graham and I was concerned about him. The sky turned black, became stormy and it looked like rain. During the long wait, I kept wondering why my prayers had not been answered that day. Then suddenly I remembered having read an incredible story about two ladies who had a flat tire and no spare. *So they closed their eyes and asked God for a tire and kept affirming that God had a tire for their car.* All of a sudden they heard a lot of noise and opened their eyes to see a tire rolling down the street, until it hit their car. It was the right size and they used it! Its origin remained a mystery. They were never able to discover just where it came from.

I decided if God could do that for them, He could fix our car. *So I was busy praying, asking God to repair our car and get us home safely,* when a lady and her husband stopped their car and asked, "Lady, can we help you?" Before I could answer, her husband raised the hood and with the use of a flashlight in the dark, looked at the engine. She said to me, "Don't worry, honey, my husband is a good mechanic and he will know what to do." By the time my own husband returned with some water, this man had our car running again. He and his wife invited us home with them, where he had parts and equipment to make further repairs.

On the way to their house, my husband and I wondered how we would pay for the parts, but I told my husband how I had been asking for help when they arrived and that we should just go in faith, knowing somehow our prayer was being answered. Upon arriving at their home, the wife fixed sandwiches and coffee and asked me to telephone my son in Graham. The phone call revealed that other relatives had come in and were caring for him, so everything was fine.

After our car had been repaired that night, we had a good night's rest and a nice visit the next day with these people. They explained there was no charge for the car's parts and repairs because they made it a habit to help people in trouble. It seems they always prayed and asked God to guide them to those who needed help, and this mechanic had repaired many a car for a stranded traveler. Often this mechanic had prayed, "Now, God You know everything. Should I help these people?" He felt this was one way he could tithe his time and talent. No wonder that couple was so happy and prosperous. *This experience proved to me the power of asking God directly for what you need and want. When I finally got around to that, my prayer was immediately answered!*

Third: The Prayer of Asking for Direct Guidance

If you don't know what to ask for directly, pray for guidance. Say, "Father, what is the truth about this? Make the truth about this situation so plain and clear that I cannot mistake it." The people of the Bible called it "asking for a sign." They often asked God to give them a sign of answered prayer. You can too!

More than a decade ago, while driving from Missouri to my home state of North Carolina, I had stopped at a little rustic restaurant in the mountains of Tennessee. As I sat there tired and travel-worn, awaiting my meal, I kept wondering whether I should accept the offer of a job in Birmingham, Alabama.

For some time I quietly pondered all aspects of the situation. There was a time element involved that made it necessary for me to make a quick decision. There were grave financial considerations involved that would affect both myself and my small son. Logically it didn't seem the thing to do, but intuitively I felt strongly that it could be a great step in the right direction.

Finally the thought came, "You do not have to try to figure this out or reason it through on the human level. Just ask for direct guidance, ask for a sign, and then release the matter. You will be shown what to do." And so I quietly thought, "Father, what is the truth about this job? Am I to take it or not? Make your guidance so clear that I cannot mistake it." As I then relaxed and again became aware of my immediate surroundings, I suddenly realized that background music was playing in the distance and the tune being played was, "Stars Fell on Alabama." That song led me into the ministry and to my first church—in Alabama.

About a year ago, my prayer group and I were praying about my son's future. There was some question about whether he should go to college or into the armed forces. As we sat quietly on two separate Tuesday nights affirming for him, "YOU ARE A DIVINE IDEA IN THE MIND OF GOD, AND YOU ARE NOW GUIDED INTO YOUR TRUE PLACE," suddenly Air Force planes roared overhead so low that the sound of their engines drowned out our prayer. When it happened the second time consecutively, I realized this was "the sign" of answered prayer. Within a matter of weeks, my son had enlisted in the Air Force.

Many times a day I pray aloud, "Father, help me," or "Father, what is the truth about this?" or "Father, let there be light," or "Father, what do you want me to do about this?" or "Father, what is the answer, what is Your guidance, what is your good in this situation?" or "Father, if you love me, show me!" How often these direct prayers for guidance produce quick results.

You should make it a practice to ask God about anything that concerns you—from finding a parking place on a crowded street to obtaining an appointment with a busy person whom you suddenly need to see. The 17th Century French mystic Brother Lawrence called this prayer method "practicing the presence of God." It certainly makes for a delightful, easier way of life.

When Solomon asked for wisdom to discern between the true and the false, he was asking for guidance, and that guidance brought him all the blessings of life, plus. Paul pointed out the power of simply asking for guidance and wisdom to meet life victoriously when he promised, "If any of you lacks wisdom, let him ask of God . . . and it shall be given him" (James 1:5).

In her book, *The Healing Gifts of the Spirit*,[2] Agnes Sanford emphasizes the importance of praying for guidance or wisdom. She relates how she was once unable to be a channel of healing to someone, because she did not first ask for the wisdom to know what to do. The decree for guidance or wisdom will always lead you to answered prayer, if you but follow that guidance when it comes. George Fox, founder of the Quakers, wrote in his *Journal* about becoming blind when he did not follow definite guidance that came to him. Later, when he realized his mistake and made the effort to carry through on that guidance, his sight returned.

Fourth: The Decree of Divine Intelligence

Along with asking for guidance and wisdom from a universal Father, it is sometimes wise to call on the "divine intelligence" within you. Psychologist William James has written that, along with a conscious mind and subconscious mind, man also has a deeper level of the mind in which resides infinite intelligence that longs to work for and through man. By recognizing it, giving it

---

[2] Agnes Sanford, *The Healing Gifts of the Spirit* (Philadelphia, Pa.: J. B. Lippincott Co., 1966).

your attention, and decreeing it, you release this superwisdom within. Decrees of "divine intelligence" tap it.

If you will invite this divine intelligence to solve any problem that concerns you, it will. "THERE IS AN ANSWER. DIVINE INTELLIGENCE NOW SHOWS ME THE PERFECT ANSWER TO THIS PROBLEM. I RELAX, LET GO, AND LET IT."

A schoolteacher decreed that divine intelligence was showing her what to write in a contest, so that she might win a trip to Europe. The ideas came in a rush and she quickly submitted her entry, which won her the trip. Later she could not remember what she had written—only that it came quickly after she asked. Infinite intelligence is just teeming with right answers and solutions and awaits your attention. Your act of asking opens the channel for receiving that intelligence, as it did for this schoolteacher.

When things in your life seem to be going wrong, affirm that "divine intelligence" is showing you the way. When business or other conditions appear to have reached a deadlock, affirm that divine intelligence is producing a solution. When you seem up against a stone wall and there is apparently no way out, affirm that divine intelligence is producing perfect results. For health, financial or human relations problems affirm, "I RELEASE YOU TO THE PERFECT OUTWORKING OF DIVINE INTELLIGENCE NOW." Set aside a little time every day and meditate upon divine intelligence at work in every phase of your life. This is the way to bring vast improvement quickly!

Fifth: The Decree of Divine Love

After the more contemplative phases of decree, such as asking for guidance and then being flexible to receive it, you now come to actual affirmation or decree, which positive method of assertion Walt Whitman described when he said, "I no longer ask for good fortune; I *am* good fortune."

One of the most powerful prayers of decree is that one which decrees divine love. To affirm "divine love" releases the all-powerful "love vibration" which then moves among people and events producing harmonious results.

Why are decrees of divine love so powerful? Certain words used persistently release mind power to mold and transform conditions in the mind, body and affairs of man. The words "divine love" dissolve hate, resistance, opposition, anger, and other mental and physical frictions that cause pain in mind, body and relationships. *Through decrees on "divine love," you can free yourself from all kinds of problems!*

I have often heard a housewife say, "Divine love always has and always will work any miracle that needs working!" And "work it" she has. For every problem—physical, emotional, financial, and in family relationships—she uses decrees of divine love. The result is that she is putting a son through college on "divine love." She obtains part-time jobs when she needs extra money by affirming divine love. Recently she came into a sizable inheritance after affirming divine love. And she has healed a number of physical ailments, her own and others', after affirming divine love. Some of her favorite decrees are these: "DIVINE LOVE IS DOING ITS PERFECT WORK IN THIS SITUATION NOW FOR THE GOOD OF ALL CONCERNED." "DIVINE LOVE GOES BEFORE ME AND PREPARES THE WAY." "I CALL ON DIVINE LOVE TO WORK ANY MIRACLE THAT NEEDS WORKING IN THIS EXPERIENCE."

A businessman had become bored with his job, having gone to the top in it, and wanted a change into something better, but did not know which way to turn to find it since he was "at the top" professionally. Remembering the power of love to work any miracle that needs working, he began affirming, "I INVITE THE POWERFUL, LOVING ACTION OF GOD INTO MY LIFE NOW. I INVITE THE POWERFUL, LOVING ACTION OF GOD TO PROVIDE ME WITH MY OWN TRUE PLACE IN LIFE NOW."

Shortly, the president of the board of trustees of a large, successful corporation "got the idea" to fly across country and invite this man to head up the corporation, whose previous director had retired. The change of scene, pace and work proved to be the perfect answer to this previously bored executive's prayer. Love *had* worked its miracle!

A widower with six children was assured by all his relatives and friends that he would never find a woman who would love him enough to marry him *and* his six "live wires." It seemed for several years that they were right, until he remembered to call on divine love. The affirmation he used was, "THE IRRESISTIBLE LOVE OF JESUS CHRIST NOW DRAWS MY OWN TRUE WIFE TO ME." Soon thereafter he met a beautiful lonely widow, who was only too glad to have a new family to care for. They were married and it proved a happy union.

Sixth: The Decree That God's Will Is Being Done

Contrary to what most people think, to declare that God's will is being done in a situation is the highest form of prayer and always brings the perfect, happy, satisfying answer for all involved. This is true because God is a God of love, so His will for His children is always the highest and best. A heavenly Father would hardly want less for His children than would an earthly father.

Among the most powerful prayers of decree you can ever pray—ones which often bring almost instantaneously happy surprises are: "NOT MY WILL BUT THINE BE DONE, FATHER." "I WILLINGLY DO THE GOOD WILL OF GOD IN THIS SITUATION." "GOD WORKS IN ME TO WILL AND TO DO WHATSOEVER HE WISHES DONE AND GOD'S GOOD WILL CANNOT FAIL!" "GOD WORKS IN THIS SITUATION TO WILL AND TO DO WHATSOEVER HE WISHES DONE AND GOD CANNOT FAIL!" "I CALL ON GOD'S WILL TO DO ITS PERFECT WORK IN THIS SITUATION NOW FOR THE GOOD OF ALL CONCERNED."

Jesus said, "My Father worketh . . . and I work" (John 5:17). When you affirm "God's will" you unconsciously cast the burden of the problem on the Highest Power of the universe, which is then free to resolve it in the highest and best way. Miracles happen when people dare to affirm God's will in their lives.

Several years ago I visited in Hollywood with television and movie actress Mala Powers, whose mother is a minister friend of mine. Beautiful Miss Powers related how in 1951, after returning from a USO Christmas show in Korea, she came down with flu in Hawaii. There she was given an antibiotic to which her system proved allergic. After she returned to California, it was discovered that this drug had destroyed the bone marrow and her system stopped making new blood cells. It also dissolved the blood cells that fight off disease. Her condition developed into complete anemia which, at that time, medical science could not cure. Most people with this malady died from hemmorhaging.

Finally, in a Los Angeles hospital with her mother, Silent Unity and her minister, Dr. Ernest Wilson, all praying with her, she realized the death sentence was hanging over her, so she prayed, "Father, if You want me to live, tell me what to do. If You want me to die, tell me what You want me to do before I go. Not my will, but Thine be done." With that prayer came an instant inner feeling that she would live, but that she had to contribute to her own recovery in terms of cheerfulness and inner peace, and by patiently believing she would be healed whether it seemed so or not.

In the weeks and months of slow recovery that followed, she often used an affirmation that Dr. Wilson had given her: "WITH-OUT HASTE, WITHOUT DELAY, IN PERFECT WAYS AND UNDER DIVINE GRACE, MY HEALING MANIFESTS." Though she was in and out of bed for nine months, the day came when her doctors assured her she would get well. Though she continued medication and treatment for some time, and tired easily for a couple of years after going back into movie-making, today she leads a normal life. The turning point from death to life came after she had prayed, "NOT MY WILL BUT THINE BE DONE." God's will is always supreme good for His beloved children. When you invoke His will, you also invoke His miracle goodness for you!

Seventh: Decrees of the Divine Plan

There is a divine plan for your life. The divine plan is the sublime plan and includes health, wealth, happiness and perfect self-expression. As you affirm "the divine plan," you begin to draw to yourself the ideas, opportunities, events and people that are meant to be a part of your divine plan.

I know a man who was suffering the agony of an unhappy

marriage and of divorce problems, indebtedness, confusion, and a limited income; but who went from that to a brand-new job filled with self-expression at double his previous income, a brand-new wife, a happy marriage, peace of mind, increased health, and a whole new lease on life, after he began affirming the divine plan at an apparently hopeless period in his life. This tranformation came within just six short months! Some of the prayers he used were these:

"I NOW RELEASE EVERYTHING AND EVERYBODY THAT IS NO LONGER A PART OF THE DIVINE PLAN OF MY LIFE. EVERYTHING AND EVERYBODY THAT IS NOT A PART OF THE DIVINE PLAN OF MY LIFE NOW RELEASES ME. I NOW LET GO AND LET GOD UNFOLD THE DIVINE PLAN OF MY LIFE. I AM NOW ATTUNED TO THE DIVINE PLAN OF MY LIFE. I NOW COOPERATE WITH THE DIVINE PLAN OF MY LIFE. CHRIST IN ME NOW MANIFESTS THE DIVINE PLAN OF MY LIFE IN LOVE AND IN PEACE. I NOW RECOGNIZE, ACCEPT AND FOLLOW THE DIVINE PLAN OF MY LIFE AS IT IS REVEALED TO ME STEP BY STEP. I REJOICE IN THE DIVINE PLAN WHICH IS THE SUBLIME PLAN, AND INCLUDES HEALTH, WEALTH, HAPPINESS AND PERFECT SELF-EXPRESSION FOR ME NOW."

Eighth: The Decree of Divine Order

Order is heaven's first law, and by affirming "divine order" you somehow release a heavenly form of order to manifest in your mind, body and affairs. *Answered prayer inevitably manifests when things get into divine order.*

One of the most powerful and popular affirmations which thousands have used to produce health, increased prosperity and personal happiness is: "DIVINE ORDER IS NOW ESTABLISHED IN MY MIND, BODY AND AFFAIRS BY THE POWER OF THE INDWELLING CHRIST. DIVINE ORDER IS NOW ESTABLISHED AND MAINTAINED." I have found that by placing this affirmation near my telephone, only necessary calls come through. My telephone becomes courteously silent.

Recently a housewife wrote of needing to leave her home to shop but the gas company had notified her the gas would be turned off that day for certain repairs to be made in that neighborhood. She was required to be at home when the gas man arrived and departed. Instead of fuming about the timing in the situation, she sat down quietly in her living room and affirmed "divine order" for the situation. At that moment the gas worker arrived and promptly completed his task and reconnected the gas service. Thus, no time and energy were wasted in needless fretting.

Another housewife often gets through a long waiting line at the check-out counter at the Air Force commissary where she shops by affirming "divine order," while housewives all around her gripe and complain about the long wait in their lines. In another instance, this housewife literally stopped a freight train with the affirmation of "divine order" when she was late to an appointment and needed to get around the shifting train cars quickly.

In situations where time elements are involved, it is also good to affirm "divine timing," or "perfect timing."

Ninth: The Decree of Blessing

The people of the Bible felt that the act of blessing carried great power to accomplish good. To bless means "to make holy or whole by spoken words," "to ask divine favor for some situation or person," "to wish a person or situation well," "to make happy or prosperous," "to gladden, glorify, praise." When you bless a troublesome person, financial situation, or bodily ailment, you are praising the good in it. You are invoking divine favor, which is then released to produce happy results for you.

Bless a thing and it will bless you. Curse it and it will curse you. To bless means to bring forth good in a situation or personality, whether there seems any good to be brought forth or not! How often you have condemned, criticized, or cursed a situation and only brought forth more problems and unhappy experiences from it, whereas if you had dared to take the opposite view and had blessed the situation, something good would have come from it.

A doctor's wife recently wrote me the sad story of her life:

How she had worked hard to help her husband through medical school; then more hard work to help get him established in his practice. Finally overwork and anxiety brought on her own bad health, after which her husband began having an affair with one of his patients.

Later he had a series of serious health problems and finally had to give up his practice, after which his wife went back to work, though she was not well physically. But she closed her letter by saying, "In spite of all our problems and a lifetime filled with hurt, disappointment and pain, I have begun using the practice of blessing, instead of cursing, our situation. As I have begun blessing my husband, these experiences, and our life together for the good that is in it, new blessings have begun to appear. The prayer of blessing is starting to work! For the first time in years, I have hope of a better life unfolding for us."

Tenth: The Prayer of Faith

One of the most powerful forms of affirmative prayer is the decree of faith. Jesus promised, "All things, whatsoever ye shall ask in prayer, believing, ye shall receive" (Matthew 21:22). "According to your faith be it done unto you" (Matthew 9:29).

The psychologist William James emphasized the power of faith to make things right: "Our belief at the beginning of a doubtful undertaking is the *one thing* that assures the successful outcome of our venture." Dr. Smiley Blanton, the noted psychiatrist, found that in dealing with people and helping them resolve their problems, *everything hinged on their faith.* Those people who did not have faith in anything—God, themselves, their business, family, the world—never got very far until they changed their beliefs and began to declare they did have faith.

If you have had a life of disappointment, how do you begin to believe in the goodness of God, man, the world? By decreeing it anyway! *Faith can be developed as the result of many affirmations.* (See the chapter on faith in my book, *The Healing Secret of the Ages.*) Charles Fillmore has scientifically explained the potency of faith to produce practical results in your life: "Just as the electric current precipitates certain metals in an acid solution, so faith stirs into action the electrons of man's brain and, acting concurrently with the spiritual ethers, these electrons hasten nature and produce quickly what ordinarily requires months of seedtime and harvest."

Thus, instead of complaining that you do not have enough faith to improve your life, begin decreeing that you do have faith; this act will hasten the power of faith in people and events and will produce quickly for you what ordinarily would require months or years!

A little old lady who ran a boarding house had always had trouble trying to collect the rent from her boarders. Then she learned of the amazing power of decrees of faith and began to affirm: "I HAVE FAITH IN GOD. I HAVE FAITH IN PEOPLE. I HAVE FAITH IN THINGS." Quickly her boarders responded by paying their rent on time or even ahead of time, as good things began to happen to them. Not only did their attitudes and financial situations improve, but the word of faith seemed to affect the cook, maid, janitor and everyone else connected with this boarding house. All were prospered and blessed as the landlady continued privately decreeing her faith in God, man, things. She proved that by affirming for another what you desire for yourself, both of you are blessed!

You can invoke the miracle prayer of faith by affirming often: "I DARE TO BELIEVE THAT ALL THINGS HAVE WORKED TOGETHER FOR GOOD IN MY LIFE. I DARE TO BELIEVE THAT ALL THINGS ARE NOW WORKING TOGETHER FOR GOOD IN MY LIFE. I DARE TO BELIEVE THAT ALL THINGS SHALL WORK TOGETHER FOR GOOD IN MY LIFE (or in this situation or person).

Eleventh: The Prayer of Divine Restoration

One of the least-known prayers of decree, yet one of the most important for getting your prayers answered, is the decree of divine restoration. If you could trace back in memory the cause of the unhappy experiences in your life, you would doubtless discover that most of those experiences in ill health, financial difficulties, and human relations problems were related to a belief in "loss." The thought of "loss" lodged in the conscious and subconscious phases of the mind causes many—perhaps most—of life's difficulties. The word "loss" literally means "destruction" and the thought of loss held in the mind is a destructive one.

However, a belief in present and future fulfillment blots out previous beliefs in loss as promised by the prophet Joel: "I will restore to you the years the locust hath eaten" (Joel 2:25). You can establish such a belief in present and future fulfillment by affirming "divine restoration." The word "restore" means "to make beautiful again." As you affirm "divine restoration" of your good, so much can be added to the present that it seems even to fill the emptiness of the past. In the process, whatever has been taken from you is then divinely restored. Always there is a balancing, restoring power for good at work in every person and in every experience of apparent loss. Instead of trying to force your good, affirm that it is now divinely restored in God's own time and way and it will still appear. Affirm often: "I CALL ON THE POWER OF DIVINE RESTORATION. MY GOOD OF PAST AND PRESENT IS DIVINELY RESTORED TO ME NOW. THIS IS A TIME OF DIVINE FULFILLMENT. I GIVE THANKS FOR DIVINE RESTORATION IN MIND, BODY, FINANCIAL AFFAIRS AND IN ALL MY RELATIONSHIPS NOW." (For more on this subject see my book, *The Prosperity Secret of the Ages*, Chapter 5.)

WRITE OUT YOUR DECREES

Along with speaking forth your prayers of decree into the ethers every day for at least five minutes or preferably fifteen minutes a day, another dynamic method for getting your prayers answered, is *to write* out your decrees. I have a prayer notebook in which I daily write out affirmations about all that concerns me or that I wish to accomplish that day. It is amazing in checking back later to see how often my prayers are answered, after I write out my affirmations.

By writing down your decrees and reading them over at intervals, both aloud and silently, you help fasten your mind on what you want. As one woman recently wrote me, "When I begin to feel depression coming on, I write down affirmations until I feel a sense of peace. This seems to be the turning point from negative feelings into a time of hope and renewed faith that good will come."

Another prayerful person who has gotten fine results from affirmations writes out her decrees in the form of a letter to God, saying "Dear God, grant this or endow that." An age-old prayer method is to write out affirmations of healing, prosperity, happiness and then to wear it secretly on some part of your body, or to carry it with you in your personal effects until it has manifested the answer you seek. Also, quietly putting your affirmative decrees in your Bible is a literal method of releasing them to their perfect outworking in your life.

Use often the various types of decree herein described: (1) talking directly to God; (2) the decree of asking; (3) the decree of guidance; (4) the decree of divine intelligence; (5) the decree of divine love; (6) the decree that God's will is being done; (7) the decree of the divine plan; (8) the decree of divine order; (9) the decree of blessing; (10) the decree of faith, and (11) the decree of divine restoration.

Now proceed quickly to Chapter 7 and learn of the prayer of decree that can produce miracles for you.

SUMMARY OF CHAPTER 6

1. You can begin to revolutionize your life through prayers of affirmative decree, which help you to dwell upon the good and call it into expression.
2. The word "utter" and the word "outer" have the same root meaning. What you "utter" becomes "outer" in your world of experiences.
3. Prayer begins and ends with words. The word is dynamic. It creates. You literally release atomic vibrations through spoken decrees of good.

4. Verbal words and prayers, which often seem more mental than spiritual, are the one thing that can clear those layers of negative thoughts out of man's mind and emotions. It is only after such a mental and emotional cleansing that prayers are answered.

5. Your centers of speech are closely connected with your mental life. When you speak forth good words, you improve your mental life.

6. Certain types of affirmative decrees seem the most powerful for getting results. They include:
    (1) the prayer of talking directly to God;
    (2) the prayer of asking;
    (3) the prayer of asking for direct guidance;
    (4) the decree of divine intelligence;
    (5) the decree of divine love;
    (6) the decree that God's will is being done;
    (7) the decree of the divine plan;
    (8) the decree of divine order;
    (9) the decree of blessing;
    (10) the prayer of faith;
    (11) the prayer of divine restoration.

7. Along with speaking forth your prayers of decree, write them out in your prayer book and read them over at intervals. This helps to fasten your mind on the good you want rather than on the problem.

7

The Prayer for Miracles

Miracles can happen to you when you learn how to use the miracle decrees for releasing them as given in this chapter! This is true because all things are possible to the Christ consciousness.

In the foregoing chapters, you have learned about the prayer of relaxation, the prayer of cleansing, and various forms of the prayer of decree. In most instances, these forms of prayer will work through the conscious and subconscious phases of your mind, clearing the way for answered prayer.

But at times none of the foregoing prayer methods will seem sufficient to meet your need, perhaps because you are ready to go more deeply into your prayer consciousness and tap another level of prayer power; or perhaps it may be because the situation about which you pray simply needs a miracle! It needs a release of power and energy more dynamic than the usual prayer methods seem to activate. You may be in desperate need of prayers that can crash through the negative thought stratum that has bound you, raising you to higher levels of consciousness quickly, where you automatically are in tune with divine energy that floods you with power. Nothing less will suffice.

There *is* such a prayer of decree to help you do this! It is the miracle decree—the prayer that releases the Christ consciousness. The ancient people who in their aloneness with nature knew the great secrets of the universe felt there was such a miracle consciousness, which when discovered and tapped, could perform miracles in an instant. I believe it!

In fact, I know there *is* such a miracle consciousness which you can tap and release. The first time I discovered it, I did so almost by chance and did not realize at the time what I had tapped. After I had prayed for guidance about an impossible situation over which I had struggled for some time, helplessly trying to extricate myself, the answer came in the mail from a stranger who seemed to have tuned in on my cry for help through the ethers, and responded by sending me an affirmation that literally released miracle power, as I faithfully decreed it. Had I not gotten that prayer when I did and used it to break out of a negative thought stratum in which I seemed helplessly bound by the limited thinking of others, I could not have remained on this earth plane much longer. The prayer of decree that literally saved my life was: "THE MIRACLE-WORKING POWER OF JESUS CHRIST IS RE-LEASED IN THIS SITUATION NOW FOR THE GOOD OF ALL CONCERNED."

At still another low level in my life when I was again bound by the negations of others from which I seemed helpless to free myself, I kept praying for the right thoughts and decrees that would loose me. The prayer that came that time through inner realizations, and which I then wrote down and decreed over and over in a loud voice as I walked the floor, was: "OF MYSELF I CANNOT DO IT, BUT JESUS CHRIST CAN AND IS PERFORMING MIRACLES IN MY MIND, BODY AND AFFAIRS HERE AND NOW!" I literally heard the ethers crack as I said that miracle decree and I could feel my whole consciousness lifted out of an inharmonious thought stratum that had previously almost smothered me. My outer life quickly changed and I found myself hundreds of miles away among new people in new congenial circumstances amid fulfilling work. I had had my miracle!

Sometimes in prayer we try to improve or change the people or situations for which we pray, and we become quite frustrated when they do not seem to respond to our prayers. God gave spiritual man the power of choice to improve or not improve as he wishes. In using the miracle prayer, instead of trying to change and improve others, you cast the burden of your prayers on that higher power of the Christ consciousness. *If the people and situations for whom you pray do not wish to respond to your prayers, their lack of cooperation does not stop your prayers from being answered!* The Christ consciousness simply helps you overcome or, literally, "come up over" those troublesome people and situations and be freed from them as you rise into higher levels of understanding, which invariably lift you into higher levels of living as well.

PSYCHOLOGISTS KNOW ABOUT MIRACLE CONSCIOUSNESS

Two noted psychologists were the Swiss doctor Carl Jung and the father of American psychology, William James. Both of these great men felt that man has not only a conscious mind with which he daily thinks, and a subconscious mind which contains his memory and emotions, but that man also has a deeper third level of the mind—a superconscious level—in which resides an infinite intelligence that longs to work for and through both the conscious and subconscious phases of the mind to produce fantastic good in man's life quickly.

What these psychologists referred to as superconsciousness, divine intelligence, or divine mind in man, is referred to by practical Christians as "the Christ mind" or "the Christ consciousness." The reason practical Christians refer to this deeper superconscious level of the mind as the Christ mind or Christ consciousness is because Jesus Christ seemed to know about and to have developed this miracle level of the mind, as is reflected in his life, ministry and teachings.

He knew that all men had the same Christ mind within them too, which, when activated, could produce apparent miracles for them in an instant. He promised His followers (and His promise applies to His modern-day followers as well): "He that believeth on me, the works that I do shall he do also; and greater works than these shall he do; because I go unto the Father" (John 14:12).

Jesus Christ broke through the negative thought stratum into which the race had fallen. By breaking through this mental negation, He opened the way for all who become attuned to His power to do likewise. Through the consciousness Jesus generated through His life, crucifixion, and resurrection, He aimed to arouse this superconscious miracle power in man and reconnect mankind with it, to get man back into an Eden state of mind where all things are possible, when man was given dominion over the earth and himself.

That Jesus did re-establish this miracle consciousness which man can tune in on is evident in the miracle power that the early Christians had. They knew how to tune in on the Christ consciousness Jesus had activated, and for several centuries they were able to do the works Jesus had done. This miracle consciousness was finally suppressed by human personality that took over the church and ruled it for many centuries. Even so, there are many isolated instances of great souls down through the centuries who became aware of and quietly developed and used the miracle consciousness that Jesus had aroused.

Then in 1894, Dr. Richard M. Bucke, an English doctor, predicted that this spiritual consciousness, which he called "cosmic consciousness," and which he described in his book by that title,[1] would soon become a common thing again. When Dr. Bucke spoke to the British Medical Association in Montreal in 1894, he told those physicians that this divine phase of man's being called "superconsciousness" was even then becoming "increasingly common" and that it would eventually become "general." Dr. Bucke predicted that not only was the spiritual consciousness of man becoming increasingly common and would eventually become general, but that the development of the cosmic, or spiritual, phase of the mind would soon lift the whole of human life to a higher plane.

Dr. Bucke was a medical doctor who had had a spiritual awakening and dared to tell the world about it, and he even dared to predict the spiritual evolution of mankind. He stated that the human race is in the process of developing a new kind of consciousness, far in advance of the human self, and that this new kind of consciousness would eventually lift the race above and beyond all the fears and ignorance and brutalities that beset it.

[1] Richard Maurice Bucke, *Cosmic Consciousness* (New York: E. P. Dutton & Co., Inc., 1901).

Certainly in this century, Dr. Bucke's prediction has been coming true as more and more people have quietly taken up a spiritual quest and have privately begun developing their prayer consciousness and their innate spiritual powers.

ANCIENTS KNEW HOW TO ACTIVATE SPIRITUAL CONSCIOUSNESS

People of all ages have searched for the superconsciousness within them and a method by which to activate it. Long before the time of Jesus, the ancient people had various secret names they intoned for activating this superconsciousness—this third deeper level of the mind—that is filled with miracle power in man. They felt that if you would hold to that secret word, motto or text in time of trial, it would rearrange your affairs, bringing you through to victory.

The priests of the Old Testament aroused this superconscious level of divine power in man by affirming and meditating, over and over, upon the words "I AM" or "I AM THAT I AM." Moses had learned this secret text from the Egyptians who had written it upon the walls of every Egyptian Temple.

The Hebrews of the Old Testament released the superconscious power within them by meditating upon the name "JE-HOVAH," which they considered so powerful that they did not speak it. They meditated upon variations of this name for producing specific results: "JEHOVAH-JIREH" for prosperity; "JEHO-VAH-RAPHA" for healing; "JEHOVAH-SHALOM" for peace of mind; "JEHOVAH-NISSI" for protection; "JEHOVAH-TSIDKENU" for claiming God's goodness; and "JEHOVAH-RA-AH" for guidance and love.

The word "Jehovah" is the Old Testament Hebrew word which corresponds to the New Testament Greek word "Christ." *By taking the word "Jehovah," meditating upon it, affirming it, you can feel its quickening power through and through. The word "Jehovah" (Christ) is charged with spiritual power far above and beyond any other word in the human language.*

The people of Asia have long intoned "AUM or "OM" as the name for God and the release of His goodness. An Eastern mystic releases the superconscious power within him by drawing in his breath and decreeing aloud the word "AUM" or "OM" twelve times. He then holds his breath and repeats the name twenty-four times, until he finally feels the God power which he has released within and around him. The Brahmins attained to great power and wisdom by meditating much on the word "OM."

HOW TO ACTIVATE YOUR MIRACLE CONSCIOUSNESS

Scientists tell us there are no miracles—only the working of higher laws not commonly understood. Actually there seems to be one set of natural laws for the physical world and another set for the invisible world of mind and spirit. The laws of mind and spirit are so much stronger that they can be used to neutralize, accentuate, or even reverse the laws of the physical world, when necessary. Jesus knew the higher laws of mind and spirit and used them to perform apparent miracles. By developing the Christ consciousness you also have access to that same miracle power!

The Christ consciousness is the miracle state of mind that contains within it the power to resurrect a miracle where previously there had seemed only crucifying problems. The Christ consciousness or superconsciousness within you is filled with peace, power, plenty. To bring it alive within you is to bring alive your spiritual nature, your divinity, the divine level of the mind, through which all things are possible. If people the world over knew about this indwelling Christ consciousness and would bother to develop it, mankind's problems could all be solved effortlessly, through the peaceful, powerful, efficient Christ mind within mankind.

When you invoke the Christ consciousness, you step up your prayer power. You speed up results!

How do you develop your miracle Christ consciousness, the divine intelligence, the divine mind within you? By first realizing that you have this third superconscious level of the mind within. You then develop it by recognizing this Christ consciousness, meditating upon it, affirmatively decreeing its presence and power at work in and through you. Decrees about "the Christ mind," "the Christ within," "Jesus Christ," and "Christ Jesus" help you do this. Writing and picturing it also helps. The following simple techniques will help you develop and invoke the Christ consciousness and release its miracle power in your life!

THE CHRIST MIND

You can develop the third level of the mind, the superconsciousness, by dwelling upon the Christ mind within you. Psychologists tell us that we develop whatever we concentrate our attention upon. If you turn your attention upon your innate divinity, the Christ mind within you, you will begin to arouse it, in the same way as did Paul and the apostles.

Paul knew about the Christ mind which had spoken to him out of the ethers as he trod the road to Damascus, and which converted him from a tireless persecutor of the Christians to a tireless advocate of Christianity. Paul developed the Christ mind to such an extent that he became known as the "versatile genius" of the early Christian church, teaching, preaching, traveling, writing and organizing churches throughout the ancient world. In his writings, he talked constantly to the early Christians about the Christ mind, once explaining: "It is no longer I that live, but Christ liveth in me" (Gal. 2:20).

In my book *The Healing Secret of the Ages*, I have explained the ancient secret teaching which shows the Christ mind in man as located at the crown of the head, while the conscious mind functions, metaphysically, from the front forehead, and the subconscious functions from the heart and abdominal region. The interesting thing about the Christ mind being located in the crown of the head is that it not only activates the superconscious wisdom found in that area but, when activated, it "opens up"—or has access to—the universal wisdom, universal good, which flows into the mind and body of man through the crown of the head.

You can greatly accelerate the awakening of the Christ mind within you by using affirmations that identify you with the Christ, such as Paul's "CHRIST LIVETH IN ME."

Recognizing and calling on the Christ mind through repeated affirmations seems especially powerful in the face of "it can't be done" or "impossible" situations. Calling on the Christ mind seems to release a superwisdom, a tremendous executive power, that sweeps through people and situations to do what "can't be done," to make the "impossible" possible.

Perhaps you saw the motion picture made from Lloyd C. Douglas's book, *The Robe*. The story is built around the seamless robe that Jesus Christ wore. For this movie, a woman and her daughter were given the task of weaving a robe that would be an authentic reproduction of the one worn by Jesus. They spent several months gathering special yarns, dyes, and other special materials and then began to weave the robe. It took them thirty-six hours. When the robe was completed, the woman and her daughter were to deliver it to the studio within sixteen hours, in order to meet the producer's deadline. But suddenly they discovered that the daughter's three-year-old son had snipped a piece of cloth from the beautiful seamless robe.

It seemed impossible that they could weave another seamless robe in just sixteen hours when it had taken thirty-six to weave the original one, but when these women got quiet and prayed, affirming that the Christ mind was showing them what to do, their guidance was to do just that: weave another robe. As they affirmed that the Christ mind was expressing perfectly through them, they finished their second seamless robe in only nine hours, or one-third the time taken on the original robe!

One might first reason that these women were able to cut their time on the second robe by as much as 75 percent because they had had practice in weaving the first one. But later these women tried twice to weave another seamless robe. Each time the task took them the full thirty-six hours! Thus, the Christ mind, in their hour of need, had helped them do the impossible: weave in nine hours a robe that ordinarily took thirty-six!

When faced with "impossible" situations, call on the Christ mind to help you by affirming: "THE CHRIST MIND IS PRODUCING PERFECT RESULTS HERE AND NOW," or "I AM LETTING THE CHRIST MIND THINK THROUGH ME NOW. I KNOW. I REMEMBER. I UNDERSTAND. I EXPRESS THE TRUTH PERFECTLY IN THIS SITUATION NOW." The tide will turn.

Early in my writing career I spent time daily affirming, "I AM THE CHRIST MIND. I AM. I AM. I AM. I AM LETTING THE CHRIST MIND

EXPRESS THROUGH ME NOW. I AM. I AM. I AM." It was as though a superwisdom was turned on within me, and I have been writing prolifically ever since! Thus, for increased knowledge, wisdom, understanding and for proficient results call on the Christ mind.

Consciously centering your mind with repeated affirmations of the Christ mind opens a channel of intelligent communication within the silent forces at the depths of your being, where new thoughts, words, wisdom, flow forth, and where entirely new sources of power are developed in you.

THE POWER OF THE PHRASE "JESUS CHRIST"

The early Christians felt that the phrase, "JESUS CHRIST," was the lost word of power for which the priests had been searching for centuries, and that this "lost word of power" could produce miracles in an instant.

One has only to experiment in prayer with the Name "JESUS CHRIST" to discover that speaking that name over and over sets up a mighty vibration, which sets into activity forces that bring results! *No person's name ever stood for such colossal achievement as the name "JESUS CHRIST."* There is power for colossal achievement along all lines—healing, prosperity, human relations —for those who call upon that name today.

Decree over and over that "JESUS CHRIST IS PRODUCING PERFECT RESULTS IN EVERY PHASE OF MY LIFE NOW," and you will be amazed at the good things that will happen to you! The words "JESUS CHRIST" are among the most powerful upon which you can ever concentrate! To meditate and affirm often the words "JESUS CHRIST" can transform your mind, body, affairs, relationships—any situation that confronts or troubles you.

If you desire to demonstrate over problems that no amount of prayer, spiritual study, medical treatment, psychiatric therapy or just plain hard work have been able to overcome—then begin dwelling upon the name "JESUS CHRIST," asking His help. As you daily affirm His name and call on His power, you will make a "major breakthrough" out of the negative thought stratum that had bound you, into higher levels of consciousness. There you will be free to claim your good.

Jesus taught his followers to pray "in His name" since He was their mighty intercessor with God. The early Christians performed mighty works by praying "in His name." "Whatsoever ye shall ask in my name, that will I do" (John 14:14), was the promise and it still applies today.

You can ask "in His name" in several ways.

CALL ON THE NAME JESUS CHRIST

Calling on the name "JESUS CHRIST" invokes a miracle consciousness.

A schoolteacher climbed a high ladder to take down holiday decorations in her schoolroom. Suddenly she lost her balance and fell head first onto a hard cement floor. On the way down she decreed, "JESUS CHRIST, JESUS CHRIST," and then blacked out. Her doctors were puzzled because, from the position in which her head hit that hard cement floor, she should have had permanent brain injuries, but she only had temporary bruises and imbalance in her equilibrium, which cleared up quickly as she continued daily decreeing that Jesus Christ was healing her. She proved that there is miracle healing power in this name.

Though we have often felt that the name "JESUS CHRIST" had spiritual and mystical meaning, we have usually doubted that it had practical, result-getting meaning in our daily affairs; and through this false assumption, we have missed many of life's daily blessings.

One of the most powerful decrees you can ever pray amid daily situations of inharmony, friction, tension, or troublesome people is the decree: "JESUS CHRIST IS HERE PRODUCING PERFECT RESULTS." In fact, it is better to prove the Christ presence in little ways in your mundane work-a-day world first, and then "graduate" into proving the power of this name in more profound ways later.

WRITE OUT JESUS CHRIST PRAYERS

I recall once sitting in my church study in the early morning hours, planning my work for that day and realizing there were not enough people to help with it. I needed a fast typist to do some special work that suddenly had to be done. I wrote out on a card this decree: "JESUS CHRIST NOW MANIFESTS THE PERFECT TYPIST TO PRODUCE THIS WORK QUICKLY."

Within an hour a lady came—not walking but running—into the church. Breathlessly she said, "Here I am. While having breakfast I suddenly had the feeling you needed me. What shall I do?"

"Can you type?" I asked, trying to sound casual.

"Can I! Before marrying my husband, I was his secretary and I am one of the fastest typists in this town." Within a few hours she had done—as a gift, free of charge—what would have taken the average typist several days to accomplish.

In another instance, I had tried for weeks to get a repairman to my apartment to make repairs. He had promised to come, but had not. In prayer about it again one night, I found myself decreeing, "JESUS CHRIST IS HERE, MAKING THE PERFECT REPAIRS NOW." Later I wrote down these words in my book of affirmations. A great sense of peace descended over me and I released the matter. The next morning quite early there was a knock at the door, and the repairman quickly did what he had promised to do weeks before!

PICTURE JESUS CHRIST

Along with calling on the name "JESUS CHRIST" verbally, and also writing out the name "JESUS CHRIST," you can invoke a miracle consciousness by picturing Him at work in any situation that bothers you, producing perfect results. There is tremendous power in picturing Jesus Christ working for you and with you.

A successful businessman was once asked the secret of his success after his business suddenly boomed. He explained that when he had a business engagement, he would always spend a few minutes beforehand quietly thinking about that appointment, declaring that Jesus Christ was in charge, producing the perfect results for all concerned. He would then behold the Christ in the people with whom he was to do business. He said he would try literally to see the Christ in the faces of the people involved.

This man said that by picturing the Christ at work in the situation and people, his success had been so marked that he had noticed that always a splendid congeniality was felt between himself and his clients. By picturing the Christ at work among them, deep friendships developed, and even with new clients it seemed they had always known each other, even at their first business meeting.

If you will spend ten minutes a day picturing the Christ at work in your business affairs, family affairs, or in other situations, or in personalities that concern you for whom you are praying, the results will amaze, delight and surprise you!

In my book, *The Dynamic Laws of Prosperity,* is the story of a housewife who restored her marriage by picturing Jesus Christ in the midst of it:

> For twenty years I had as my husband a man whom I had grown to hate. I am married now to the same husband, a man who is daily more companionable and loving. Strive as I did, I could not bring myself to love the first man. He seemed dead spiritually, was very selfish, crude, hard, careless, and unloving. It seemed like a hopeless situation, and how I longed for freedom. I had little ones to care for and was unable to work to keep them, so of course, I had to stay with my husband. Then I began to think of the presence and power of Jesus Christ, and decided to prayerfully image Jesus Christ at work in the situation.
>
> Daily I began to think of Jesus Christ going to work with my husband. I saw the Christ working in and through him, working with him, even having lunch with him. I visualized my husband and the Christ with him, coming home to his wife and family to well-cooked meals, happy and contented.
>
> Now, as a result of this, although I am still married to the same man, he is truly a different man, one who is kind, thoughtful, happy, and loving. At this very moment, he is sitting out on the back veranda happily whistling 'Rock of Ages' as he mends his leather jacket in preparation for work tomorrow. *Through prayerfully bringing Jesus Christ into the situation, I have found the companionship I longed for.* Truly I love my husband. I feel like telling other wives who continually quarrel with and condemn their husbands just to try my prescription.

If it is hard for you mentally to behold the Christ at work in a situation, then get a literal picture of Jesus Christ and look at it. Anytime you feel upset, confused, disturbed, look at a picture of Jesus Christ, and you will begin to feel peaceful and powerful again.

Genevieve Parkhurst, the wife of a minister, once described in her book, *Healing and Wholeness Are Yours*,[2] how she was healed of cancer of the breast by doing this. One afternoon she was propped up in bed reading a book by Dr. Frank Laubach, which contained beautiful pictures of the Christ. She was studying these pictures carefully when suddenly the physical presence of Jesus Christ appeared in the room before her. He was standing in profile with His face lifted—just as in the picture she had been studying. She held her breath while the visible form of Jesus Christ turned slowly and looked straight at her. As she studied this visible form of Jesus Christ, suddenly a sharp stab of pain went through her diseased, painful breast. The pain ran down her arm and out at the elbow. She quickly discovered that the lump was gone.

BEHOLD THE CHRIST IN OTHERS

This is a marvelous way to pray for other people. Instead of dwelling upon their problems and failures, behold the Christ at work in them and within their problems. A retired businessman found himself in a deep state of depression. His wife had passed on, leaving him very lonely, as well as sick in mind and body. He had a small house in Florida and grove of mango trees, which were his only means of livelihood. In his depression he had let them become run down and unkempt, so he was suffering from financial problems too.

Feeling he could no longer go on, one day he went out to the end of the pier and jumped in the bay, expecting to "end it all." But instead of being the end, this experience opened the way to a

---

[2] Genevieve Parkhurst, *Healing and Wholeness Are Yours* (St. Paul, Minn.: Macalester Park Publishing Company, 1957).

whole new wonderful beginning. This man was rescued by an early morning swimmer, who then went on to breathe new life and hope into him. The neighbor fixed up this depressed man's house and run-down grove, teaching him how to love, praise and bless his house, fruit, health and life.

Later when this formerly depressed man was leading a prosperous, healthy, contented life again he explained, "My neighbor is responsible for all this because he knew how to behold the Christ in me when I was at my lowest ebb, and by seeing the Christ in me, he wrought a miracle."

You may expect and look for wonderful things to happen whenever you behold Jesus Christ at work in a situation or person. You may even expect the "impossible!"

I like to take little pictures of the Christ and place them around the picture of anyone for whom I am praying. I like to write out any situation that I am concerned about, then around the written words describing that situation, paste pictures of the Christ. This helps me literally to behold the Christ in people and situations that I am concerned about, and it works.

When anyone gives you a "hard time" take his picture or his name, and place it on a sheet of paper. Around the name or picture place pictures of Jesus Christ. You will be amazed at the results that come, sometimes slowly but surely, sometimes quickly. Sallman's famous picture of the Christ has been reproduced in small pictures and is ideal for placing on your prayer list.

HOW TO BEHOLD THE CHRIST IN YOURSELF

Also, don't forget to behold the Christ in yourself! Once when I had prayed and prayed about a difficult situation, apparently to no avail, the "still, small voice" within me whispered quietly, "Why don't you behold the Christ in yourself, as well as in this situation? Pray for yourself for a change!" I did so by calling my name often and affirming, "CATHERINE PONDER, I BEHOLD THE CHRIST IN YOU. I BEHOLD THE CHRIST AT WORK IN YOUR LIFE, PRODUCING PERFECT RESULTS." I also placed a picture of Jesus Christ near my own picture and viewed the two together often. These acts proved to be the turning point toward answered prayer in that particular situation.

It is also good when you have prayed for yourself, apparently to no avail, to just release yourself to the "Christ within," to cast the whole burden of answered prayer on the Christ within you. This often brings the right results quickly. A series of affirmations such as the following can help you to do this:

"MY LIFE CANNOT BE LIMITED! CHRIST IN ME IS MY FREEING POWER."

"CHRIST IN ME IS MY FORGIVING POWER. CHRIST IN ME IS MY RELEASING POWER."

"CHRIST IN ME NOW FREES ME FROM ALL ATTACHMENTS TO PEOPLE, PLACES OR THINGS."

"CHRIST IN ME IS MY HEALING POWER. CHRIST IN ME NOW RAISES ME UP TO PERFECT HEALTH."

"CHRIST IN ME IS MY PROSPERING POWER. CHRIST IN ME IS ALWAYS WORTHY."

"THROUGH THE CHRIST WITHIN, I GIVE OF MY BEST AND I RECEIVE THE BEST AND ONLY THE BEST IN RETURN."

"CHRIST IN ME NOW REVEALS ANY BLOCK TO BE REMOVED MENTALLY OR EMOTIONALLY, SO THAT I AM RECEPTIVE TO ALL HEALTH, WEALTH AND HAPPINESS."

"CHRIST IN ME NOW GUIDES ME INTO MY TRUE PLACE IN LIFE WITH THE TRUE PEOPLE, AND I REJOICE!"

"CHRIST IN ME IS PRODUCING PERFECT RESULTS IN EVERY PHASE OF MY LIFE NOW AND ALL IS WELL. I RELAX, LET GO AND LET HIM!"

"I RELEASE MY LIFE (THIS SITUATION, THIS PERSON) TO THE PERFECT OUT-WORKING OF THE CHRIST CONSCIOUSNESS NOW."

HOW INVITING THE CHRIST WITHIN HEALS ONE

Paul pointed out that this "Christ in you" is your hope of glory (Colossians 1:27). He said this is the mystery that has been hidden for generations. The word "Christ" means "anointed one." It describes your spiritual nature. When you use words or affirmations that identify you with the Christ, you awaken, arouse, bring back to life the Christ child, the Christ within you.

Sometimes it is good to talk directly to this Christ nature within yourself. It is wise to invite the Christ within you to heal, harmonize, guide, prosper or bless you. *The Christ within you awaits your attention and recognition. The Christ within you is very polite. It waits to be asked, invited or noticed. But when it is, how quickly it responds! Just as you awaken a child by calling his name, you awaken the Christ Child within you by calling His name.*

During World War I, an American soldier was badly gassed on the battlefields of Europe and was expected to die. For months he lay in an Army hospital, near death, and was finally given three months to live.

As he lay near death in that hospital, he began to remember that at the age of twelve he had met a spiritual healer who had been an Essene. (Jesus may have studied with the mystical Essenes.) For one year this man, now sick, had received instruction from the Essene healer, after which he had studied many phases of truth.

Now, with death hovering over him, he remembered a great healing secret he had learned at the age of twelve, about the Christ being within him. He said to himself, "Within me lives One who has overcome death, so what have I to fear?"

Then he began to talk to this living presence and power within himself: "Forgive me, Friend and Lover of my soul, for being so long unaware of Your presence within me. I cast the whole burden of this body upon Your love and I go free to perfect health now." Not only did this previously dying man recover, but he lived to become an outstanding spiritual healer of the 1920's and '30's.

This man later said, "Regarding the effect upon your practical business life, this technique of inviting the Christ within to participate in it is as potent and effective as it is in healing the body. There is a great adventure awaiting you—the greatest adventure any human being can have! It is in seeking, finding, arousing, and activating the previously hidden Christ within!"

HOW TO INVOKE THE PEACE OF JESUS CHRIST

One of the most powerful ways to invoke the miracle consciousness is to affirm "the peace of Jesus Christ."

A prayerless person usually repels his good by his repelling vibrations. He scares away his good with a sense of rush, worry, force or agitation, whereas a prayerful person attracts his good by his quiet, peaceful, powerful vibrations. A prayerful person is magnetic to his good and unconsciously draws it to him. A tranquillity of bearing, a facial and bodily repose, are usually observed in those whose inner lives are enriched through prayer. Prayer quiets your mind, body, emotions, vibrations. In that peaceful, prayerful state of mind, you unconsciously draw your good to you.

If prayer has not had this effect on you, perhaps it is because you should deliberately invite it by affirming "the peace of Jesus Christ."

When you battle life, people and circumstances, your soul gets twisted out of shape. Decrees of "peace" take away your spirit of fuss and give you a gentleness of pace. If there is one experience which marks true prayer, it is the deep peace which it brings to the soul. Decrees of peace slow you down to your good and give you a gentleness of pace that really get the job done. Decrees of peace help you to pray things through rather than trying to force them through. Peace is the forerunner of victory and prayers decreeing the "peace of Jesus Christ" give you that peace and that victory.

You will soon notice that the first thing that happens when you begin to think about Jesus Christ is that a great calm descends upon you. You immediately begin to feel better about everything in your life. I know someone who healed insomnia after many sleepless nights by affirming, "THE PEACE OF JESUS CHRIST IS POURED OUT UPON ME NOW AND ALL IS WELL."

I know of a human relations problem filled with confusion, inharmony and conflict that was resolved after someone affirmed

for it, "THE PEACE OF JESUS CHRIST IS POURED OUT UPON THIS
SITUATION NOW, PRODUCING PERFECT RESULTS."

A fine Negro schoolteacher was placed in an integrated school
for the first time. At first there were grave behavior problems.
This was the first time most of the children had had a Negro
teacher, and the Spanish students seemed especially resentful.
This teacher was rather frightened and upset over this challenge
until she began to affirm, "JESUS CHRIST IS TEACHING THIS CLASS.
THE PEACE OF JESUS CHRIST REIGNS SUPREME IN THIS CLASS. I BLESS
EACH STUDENT WITH THE PEACE OF JESUS CHRIST AND ALL IS WELL."
Everything quickly calmed down and harmony was restored. A
happy teacher with a class of happy students was the ultimate
result.

It has been estimated that 80 percent of all illness results from
suppressed emotion. We see it happen all the time: headaches,
colds and many common ailments appear after an emotional
conflict. The Christ consciousness is very powerful in healing
because the first thing it does is give peace of mind. In that peace
of mind comes healing from the hurts, fears, resentments, jealousies and other emotional conflicts, which just fade away in that
peaceful Christ consciousness.

Thus, affirming "the peace of Jesus Christ" is a marvelous
prayer decree for bringing fulfillment to all phases of your life—
and the lives of others. The marvelous thing about affirming "the
peace of Jesus Christ" is that everyone around you responds to
that prayer unconsciously, slows his tempo, becomes happier and
more efficient. Tension, stress and strain just fade away in this
prayer consciousness of peace. One person decreeing "the peace
of Jesus Christ" in a situation can quiet the whole atmosphere
and produce harmony.

HOW TO AFFIRM THE FINISHED WORKS OF JESUS CHRIST

Something often transpires in the way of a miracle when you
affirm "the finished works of Jesus Christ," or that "the finished
results of Jesus Christ" now manifest in some situation or condition. When I have more to do than it seems I can, often it gets

done in half the time as I affirm "the finished results of Jesus Christ now manifest." Ideas flow, helpers appear volunteering their services. Events occur unexpectedly. The job gets done.

Often you will pray and things will begin to unfold which point the way to answered prayer, but never quite materialize and you wonder why. This is the time to affirm, "THE FINISHED RESULTS OF JESUS CHRIST NOW MANIFEST IN THIS SITUATION FOR THE GOOD OF ALL CONCERNED. THIS IS A TIME OF DIVINE COMPLETION."

Often, prayers are *almost* answered that never quite get answered, simply because no one spoke the word of completion. Don't miss your good by praying a situation almost all the way through and then become discouraged when it doesn't quite materialize. It is simply waiting for you to seal the results by affirming "the finished works of Jesus Christ." This is the miracle prayer that can quickly "wrap up" situations that have lingered on the brink of results. *Often the decree of completion is all that has stood between you and answered prayer!*

WAYS TO INVITE THE UNIVERSAL CHRIST PRESENCE

Along with the innate Christ mind, Christ consciousness, or Christ nature within you, there is also the resurrected universal Christ presence that is available to you!

After the disciples of Jesus saw this resurrected Christ Jesus presence in their midst, these previously downtrodden, defeated, helpless men were transformed into the fearless, undaunted, inspired apostles, who then uplifted and converted thousands of people to the Christ message in a way that no one has ever been able to equal since. Because of their sudden transformation, this previously confused, discouraged, insignificant group converted three thousand people at their first public meeting and caused Christianity to spread quickly throughout the ancient world and to continue to spread for twenty centuries.

The same resurrected Christ presence that was seen by Jesus' followers after His crucifixion and which transformed them and their followers so thoroughly is in the ethers of this planet and longs to help you transform your problems into solutions in this modern age as well! "Lo, I am with you always," was the promise (Matthew 28:20). Many have seen the radiant resurrected Christ presence in their midst in modern times, as it lovingly ministered to them. Jesus Christ is still Lord of this planet!

Like the Christ within, this universal Christ does not press upon you, but awaits your attention and recognition. The Christ presence is polite. It longs to be invited into your life to help you and quickly responds when it is. After the time of Jesus, His followers often invited His resurrected presence into their midst by calling, "Come, Jesus Christ!" They knew that spiritual man had been given power of choice and dominion over his world, so that it was up to him to invite the Christ presence into His midst if he wished the benefits of its spiritual power.

Recently, when lecturing in a hotel ballroom, I mentioned that I would soon be giving a series of lectures on the Christ consciousness. At the close of that lecture, as I gave the benediction, a lady attending felt a presence near her right shoulder, looked up and saw the literal figure of Jesus Christ standing in the midst of the ballroom.

In another instance, I had a health problem which I had not been able to overcome through prayer. One afternoon I sat quietly while another minister prayed with me about my health, and in her prayer she invited the healing presence of Jesus Christ to make me whole again. After her prayer for me, I felt relaxed and peaceful, and took a nap. As I was awakening I was aware that the filmy figure of Jesus Christ had been standing over me with outstretched hands, as though in blessing. It was only for a fleeting moment that I saw Him, but I knew then our prayer had been answered. In due time my health problem resolved itself.

Inviting the living presence of Jesus Christ into your mind, body or affairs brings it! Your invitation also invites its quiet, peaceful, miracle power.

A woman who was suffering from the shingles was unable to attend church one Sunday morning and was listening to the radio broadcast of the Sunday morning service at Christ Church, Unity, Los Angeles. Her minister, John Hinkle, was speaking of the healing power of Jesus Christ. Suddenly as he described one of Jesus' healings in his sermon, the literal presence of Jesus Christ appeared to this woman in her home.

As she looked at the Christ, with His eyes filled with love for her, she noticed that He wore an exquisite robe, too beautiful to describe. Then He spoke saying, "Thank you for loving me. Go, tell John" (her minister). The next day when she described her experience to the Reverend Hinkle, he explained that he had been praying for an appearance of the living Christ, feeling it would strengthen his faith and that of his congregation. Her experience was the answer to his prayer. As she sat describing her experience to him, she realized for the first time that the painful case of shingles from which she had suffered was gone, having been healed by the resurrected Christ Himself!

Whoever you are, wherever you are, Jesus in His spiritual consciousness is waiting for your mental recognition. Whatever your objective, He will show you how to attain it, if you will only invite His help and presence into your life.

The early Christians proved this. As you read the Book of Acts of the Apostles, you discover that that book is not so much a record of the acts of some of the aspostles as it is a record of the acts of the Holy Spirit *through* the apostles. Thus, historians have described the Acts as "The Gospel of the Resurrected Christ" acting *through* the apostles.

It is very interesting that the physician Luke wrote both the Gospel of Luke and The Book of Acts. His first book (Luke's Gospel) related the results of Jesus Christ's spiritual power while on earth. His second book (Luke's Acts) related the resurrected Christ's spiritual power as this Christ presence poured forth His power from the ethers *through* the early apostles.

Is it any wonder those early apostles seemed filled with an indescribable electrifying, intoxicating power which quickly ran the gamut of the entire ancient world?

Isn't it exciting to realize that that same indescribable, electrifying, intoxicating power is available to you and to me today? That it only awaits our mental recognition in order to pour forth through us as healing power, harmonizing us and our world?

How a Sophisticated Woman
Was Healed

A very sophisticated woman—hardly the type one would expect to be in communion with the resurrected Christ—recently told me how she was healed a few months ago: As she lay in pain she cried out, "Oh Christ, You promised that if we asked anything in Your Name, you would help us. Please heal me now of this pain."

A sense of peace first descended upon her troubled spirit. Then she saw the hand of Christ as it was extended to her from the ethers. She unhesitatingly placed her hand in His and an electric shock went through her body, carrying with it all former pain. Just that quickly and simply, she had been healed.

HOW TO BE BLESSED WITH THE FORGIVING POWER OF JESUS CHRIST

If decrees of "the peace of Jesus Christ" and "the finished results of Jesus Christ" do not give you the peace and completion in your life you think they should, it may be that you have unfinished business in the department of forgiveness.

Often just affirming, "THE FORGIVING LOVE OF JESUS CHRIST NOW SETS ME FREE IN MIND, BODY AND RELATIONSHIPS FROM ALL MISTAKES OF THE PAST OR PRESENT" will cleanse and free you. Or "THE FORGIVING LOVE OF JESUS CHRIST NOW SETS ME FREE FROM ALL FINANCIAL MISTAKES OF THE PAST OR PRESENT" will clear up financial problems. Or a cover-all forgiveness decree such as "CHRIST IN ME IS MY FORGIVING POWER. THE CHRIST IN ME FORGIVES THE CHRIST IN YOU. THE CHRIST IN YOU FORGIVES THE CHRIST IN ME. THE CHRIST IN THIS RELATIONSHIP (SITUATION, CONDITION) IS ITS FREEING, FORGIVING POWER" will bring peace and relief.

If it does not get the job done, it may be because you should invite the living presence of Jesus Christ to help you forgive. Agnes Sanford, the wife of an Episcopalian minister, has explained in her fine books, *The Healing Gifts of The Spirit*,[3] and *Behold Your God*,[4] how she helped a number of people find healing by inviting the living presence of Jesus Christ into the memories of the past. As they did, Jesus Christ healed the unhappy memories of hurts, disappointments and frustrations that had filled their past. But He did so in the present. They actually felt His healing power as it went to work in their subconscious minds, clearing out those hurts—often with a rush of emotion—then producing peace. Thereafter, when they later remembered those old hurtful experiences, they realized the bitterness was now gone.

I agree with Mrs. Sanford that Jesus Christ came to heal not only the conscious but also the subconscious mind, which contains all the memories and emotional blocks that stop our prayers from being answered. Since there is no human time element on the spiritual plane, you can invite Jesus Christ into your childhood, into your prenatal life even, into your teens, young adult years, etc., to heal and comfort whatever unhappy or bitter memories linger there: "COME INTO MY LIFE, JESUS CHRIST. I INVITE YOU, JESUS CHRIST, INTO MY SUBCONSCIOUS MEMORY TO HEAL WHATEVER NEEDS TO BE FORGIVEN, RELEASED, REDEEMED. CLEANSE ME AND FREE ME FROM IT NOW!"

Then picture the living presence of Jesus Christ going back into your childhood, taking your hand, comforting, loving, forgiving, healing you and those bitter experiences. Thereafter, whenever you think of the process that is taking place, just say, "THANK YOU, JESUS CHRIST. THE FORGIVING LOVE OF JESUS CHRIST HAS NOW SET ME FREE FROM THE UNHAPPY EXPERIENCES OF THE PAST OR PRESENT (or get specific, "THAT UNHAPPY MARRIAGE, THAT HEALTH PROBLEM, FINANCIAL LOSS, ETC.") AND I NOW GO FREE TO BE HAPPY."

You will be amazed at the mental, emotional and physical blocks that will be removed, at how happy and cleansed and

---

[3] Agnes Sanford, *The Healing Gifts of the Spirit* (New York: J. B. Lippincott Co., 1966).

[4] Agnes Sanford, *Behold Your God* (St. Paul, Minn.: Macalester Park Publishing Company, 1958).

relieved you will feel. Your prayers will probably then be answered in a rush of happy events!

THE MIRACULOUS WORD POWER OF CHRIST JESUS

The early Christians invoked the miracle consciousness by intoning the name "Christ Jesus." In reading the Acts and the writings of Paul and his co-workers, you find that they described the living presence of the resurrected Christ not so much as "Jesus Christ," who was the man of Nazareth, but as "Christ Jesus," who was the universal resurrected Christ presence (who had been the man of Nazareth while on earth) but who had become Lord of this planet when making His ascension.

When the early Christians realized that Jesus was not dead but had ascended into a powerful universal presence that could appear and disappear to help them as needed, they gathered in an upper room in Jerusalem and remained there for many days, calling on His presence and intoning His name over and over. It was after tuning into His miracle presence and power that they then went forth to establish Christianity in the entire ancient world—a magnificent feat by any standard.

These early Christians produced miracles by calling on the name "Christ Jesus." Thus, along with affirming the name "Jesus Christ" which awakens within you the same healing, prospering miracle power that Jesus the man of Nazareth had—you can invite into your midst the universal Christ presence that fills and surrounds this planet by affirming the name "Christ Jesus" as did Paul and the early Christians. You will find a far different vibration is aroused by intoning these two names.

When you affirm over and over "Jesus Christ, Jesus Christ, Jesus Christ," a vibrant, alive, warm, electric feeling comes alive within you and within your circumstances, producing almost instantaneous results of good. Whereas, when you affirm over and over the name "Christ Jesus," you will find it invokes a far more impersonal vibration, which seems to work more quietly, more slowly, and more universally. At some levels of your spiritual growth you will find soul satisfaction in decreeing one name; in

other phases of your growth, you will be spiritually fed and satisfied only by decreeing the other name. Either has miracle power
and contains great soul satisfaction and opens the way for great
soul growth.

Emma Curtis Hopkins described the power released in decreeing the name "Christ Jesus" in her book, *Resume*:[5] "The Christ
Jesus name is an embodying name, causing one to see embodying
of beauty, wealth, strength, fresh life." The word "embody,"
which Mrs. Hopkins made a significant point of using twice in
this one short sentence, means "to give bodily form," "to give
definite, tangible, or visible form," "to collect." By affirming over
and over the name "Christ Jesus," you can give definite, tangible,
visible form to your prayers! You can collect your good!

I know of a small prayer group whose members had spent years
dwelling upon the name "Jesus Christ" and felt the time had
come to begin meditating upon the name "Christ Jesus." As they
did so, they literally saw the embodying of beauty, wealth, fresh
life. Many changes came in their affairs and relationships:
changes of jobs, places of residence, the acquisition of new cars,
clothes, homes. Also a much deeper spiritual insight seemed
theirs in facing the challenges of life and how to meet them
victoriously through intoning the Christ Jesus name. Their prayer
consciousness noticeably deepened and strengthened. It can
prove so for you too!

THE WHITE MIRACLE LIGHT OF THE CHRIST

Along with intoning the various names for the Christ consciousness, another way to invoke its miracle consciousness is by
meditating upon and picturing the "white light" of the Christ.
The mystical followers of the Christ, down through the centuries,
saw and wrote about the "white light" of the Christ. As Dr. Bucke
pointed out in his book, *Cosmic Consciousness*,[6] Moses, Jesus,

---

5 Emma Curtis Hopkins, *Resume* (Cornwall Bridge, Conn.: Emma Curtis
Hopkins Fund, 1928).
6 Richard Maurice Bucke, *Cosmic Consciousness* (New York: E. P. Dutton &
Co., Inc., 1901).

Paul, many of the great saints and mystics of the early church,
knew about this light within. George Fox, of the Quakers, constantly spoke of the inner light. Among modern mystics, Dr.
Albert Schweitzer was prominent in writing about the light
within.

Whether there seems to be a light within or not, you can invoke
the pure, white light of the Christ and its protecting, miracle-
working power, by deliberately picturing it around people and
situations for whom you pray. Decree that it is there whether you
can visibly see it or not.

In his book, *You Try It*,[7] Dr. Robert Russell writes of this light:

> This is an age of light. Electric light, violent light, neon
> light, black light, X-rays, Beta rays and light in countless
> other forms serve man. But there is another light that tran-
> scends in power every form of material light. It is the benefi-
> cent and protecting power of the luminous energy flowing
> directly from God that illumines the lives of those who ac-
> cept the promise, "Christ shall give thee light."
>
> "Ye are the light of the world," said Jesus. The mystical
> light is in you; it is at the very center of your being now. It
> is the same light that led Moses and his people through the
> wilderness, that blinded St. Paul on the highway to Damas-
> cus . . . God brought order out of chaos with the creative
> phrase, "Let there be light." The "children of light" referred
> to in the Bible are those who have surrendered personal con-
> sciousness for Christ consciousness. Christ consciousness rep-
> resents spirit in action. If one dwells in spiritual consciousness
> (walks with the indwelling presence), he is secure. The
> spiritual man, then, is distinguished from other men by a cer-
> tain light that shines through him.
>
> When you look to the source of light, you find a great
> change coming about in your life and affairs. You feel more
> alive than ever before. Commonplace things are glorified.
> Difficult tasks become easy. Everything in your world is
> transformed for the better. One of the amazing things about

living in the light is that we are so often guided into the things we have subconsciously wanted to do all our lives.

Are you failing in the business of living? Then step into this light and it will send you forth with new life, new faith, new hope, new affections, and new ideas. How, then, do we magnify the light? By consciously recognizing it. When we identify ourselves with the light, our prayers flash forth like lightning and open the way for us. Demonstrations, demonstrations, demonstrations follow—so many we cannot count them. With such speed does the light operate in our affairs that we are astounded.

I know of a tangled human relations problem, filled with conflict and confusion, that cleared up quickly when a praying onlooker quietly surrounded the situation and all the people involved with the pure, white light of the Christ. Though this was a situation that had been filled with confusion, hard feelings and conflict for several years, within a matter of weeks it had been quickly resolved as the white light of spirit was released to penetrate it.

In another instance, it seemed that a dominating personality was going to overpower a small organization and gain a willful foothold for selfish, personal reasons. But one of the members of this organization began decreeing that it was surrounded by the pure white light of the Christ, into which nothing negative could penetrate and out of which only good could come. The domineering personality soon began to lose interest in that organization and later disassociated from it completely—to the relief of everyone concerned.

Instead of thinking of yourself or others as problem-ridden, downcast, limited and bound to unhappy conditions, begin to surround yourself in your prayerful meditation periods with the pure white light of the Christ. Mentally saturate yourself with the light. Affirm, "LET THERE BE LIGHT" or "I AM A CHILD OF THE LIGHT AND I WALK IN THE LIGHT." This decree has been known to heal those who appeared to be dying. Fill yourself and your world with "the light" and, as Dr. Russell promised, the miracle of answered prayer will begin coming your way!

HOW TO INVOKE CHRIST CONSCIOUSNESS THROUGH WORDS OF JESUS

Another method of invoking the Christ consciousness is to meditate upon the words of Jesus from the Four Gospels. When you have a healing need, meditate upon Jesus' healings and you will tune in on that same healing consciousness.

Why? *Because words of truth have life in them. The words of Jesus Christ have moved men for nearly two thousand years to dare to demonstrate as have no other words ever uttered on this planet!*

He who meditates upon Jesus' words, turning them over and over in his mind, using them as his own, studying the very essence and spirit of them, he will receive new thoughts, new revelations and inspirations each day of untold value. This method leads to a life of infinite satisfaction. Eat and drink the words of Jesus!

I know a lady who was once healed of a chronic, nagging ill by writing out one of the healing promises of Jesus and wearing it next to the skin over the diseased area of the body. Sleeping with one of Jesus' promises under one's pillow has been known to heal others. *There is fantastic power and vitality in the words and promises of Jesus now, as in His time.*

There was formed at Jerusalem, about the year 40 A.D., a school whose whole purpose was to understand the sayings of Jesus. The early Christians who studied in that school and who invoked the Christ consciousness by studying the sayings of Jesus went forth repeating His words and parables with such powers that they were transformed, and they also transformed the lives of those to whom they ministered. One had only to touch them to be healed.

Why did they have such power? Because, in addition to other spiritual techniques which they used, they prayed over and over the Lord's Prayer. H. B. Jeffery in his book, *Mystical Teachings*,[8] has written:

---

[8] H. B. Jeffery, *Mystical Teachings* (Fort Worth, Texas: Christ Truth League, 1954).

The Lord's Prayer is all command. To speak authoritatively is to renew and strengthen one's courage. We learn to speak authoritatively by repetition of the Lord's Prayer. Repeat the whole prayer over and over. *The repetition of the Lord's Prayer has a certain energizing effect, like eating and drinking. Let it fire the whole being with energy.*

Instead of taking for granted the Lord's Prayer and ripping through it in fifteen seconds, begin to speak it over and over slowly, deliberately, authoratively (preferably in a loud voice) and you will feel its electrifying, energizing, transforming effect upon your life. Such use of the Lord's Prayer is another way to invoke the words and consciousness of the Christ. In doing so, the Lord's Prayer may literally shock you into greater good than you have ever known. Jesus was quite positive and determined in the big claims He made on God. The Lord's Prayer is a series of determined affirmations.

The early Christians discovered that when they affirmed over and over the most powerful prayer Jesus ever uttered—the Lord's Prayer—the hidden Christ within each one of them was called into action. They further discovered that by affirming the prayer over and over as many as fifteen times, hard conditions, diseases and tribulations faded away. This same prayer technique later proved powerful at the Healing Shrine of Lourdes, too.

Praying over and over the Lord's Prayer is a great success formula for invoking healing, peace of mind, vitality, right action in one's affairs, prosperity, and guidance, as well as a great power for breaking up and dissolving hard—even "incurable"—conditions quickly. Use it often as another way of invoking the miracle Christ consciousness.

HOW TO RELEASE YOUR MIRACLE ENERGY POWER

Regardless of which of the foregoing prayer methods you develop for invoking the miracle consciousness, call on the Christ consciousness often. When you do so, you release into your mind, body, affairs and relationships a spiritual force, a spiritual energy, an atomic vibration, that shatters fixed states of mind. *When you*

*call on the Christ consciousness to help you in any way, you
release a high-powered energy to do for you what you cannot do
for yourself!*

If you do not at first seem to get results, after invoking the
Christ consciousness, do not fret. Just keep on. Practice makes
perfect and repetition is the mother of wisdom. It is through
repeated affirmations of the Christ consciousness that miracle
power is released. When you keep calling on the Christ consciousness to help you, the Christ power goes to work for you,
helping you break out of the negative thought strata that have
bound you. You can prove to your own satisfaction that through
the Christ within, your life cannot be limited and that Christ in
you is your miracle power!

SUMMARY OF CHAPTER 7

1. The prayer for miracles is the one that decrees the Christ
   consciousness for yourself.
2. The previous methods of prayer heretofore described usually
   work through the conscious and subconscious phases of your
   mind, clearing the way for answered prayer. However, the
   miracle decrees that release the *Christ consciousness*, go deeper
   in your thoughts and feelings and crash through negative
   thoughts that have bound you, raising you to higher levels of
   consciousness quickly, where you become attuned to divine
   energy that floods you with power.
3. If the people and situations for whom you pray do not respond,
   their lack of cooperation need not stop your prayers from being
   answered. The Christ consciousness simply helps you overcome or "come up over" them and be freed from them as you
   rise into higher levels of understanding and into higher levels
   of living.
4. Man has not only a conscious mind with which he thinks and
   a subconscious mind which contains his memory and emotions,
   but a third level of the mind—the superconscious level—in
   which resides an infinite intelligence that longs to work for and

through the conscious and subconscious phases of the mind to produce fantastic good in man's life quickly.

5. This third level of the mind, referred to by psychologists as "superconsciousness," "infinite intelligence," or "divine mind," is referred to by practical Christians as "the Christ mind," or "the Christ consciousness."

6. Jesus Christ seemed to know about and to have developed this miracle level of the mind, as is reflected in His life, ministry and teachings. He knew that all men had the same Christ mind within them, which, when activated, could produce apparent miracles for them quickly.

7. That Jesus did re-establish this miracle consciousness, which man can tune in on, is evident in the miracle power that the early Christians had. They were able to do the works of Jesus for several centuries. Therefore you and I should also be able to do these works.

8. When you invoke the Christ consciousness, you accentuate your prayer power, you speed up results.

8

The Prayer of
Concentration and Meditation

When I think about concentration, I am always reminded of the famous Longhorn Band at the University of Texas. For five years I heard practically every practice session members of the band conducted, because I lived near their practice hall.

During all those years they followed the same routine: When they gathered to practice their music for the next football game, they invariably began by playing "The Eyes of Texas Are Upon You," as though they had never played it before.

Then at the close of each practice session, they concluded the same way: by again playing "The Eyes of Texas Are Upon You"— as though they had never played it before. Day in and day out, month in and month out, football season in and out, they practiced that song over and over. Those musicians concentrated!

It has been estimated that what usually takes six hours to do could easily be accomplished in only one hour by the person who knew how to practice concentration; that absolutely nothing is impossible to the one who knows about the power of concentration. I believe it!

Psychologists have estimated that you use only 1/10 of 1 percent of your energies and powers. The rest of your forces are lost, because they have been expressed outward through scattered thought and action, instead of inward through deliberate concentration.

Your forces have been expressed outward, instead of inward, because you have not known the fantastic power of deliberate concentration—which could help you dwell upon all the right things in life, thereby drawing your forces inward and upward so that they would produce fantastic good for you and through you.

"But," you may object, "I have neither the time nor the energy for concentration." Or perhaps you are thinking, "I do not have a strong enough mind to concentrate."

Nonsense!

There's nothing hard, complicated or forceful about concentration. You do not grit your teeth, get into a rigid body position or do some kind of mental gyrations in order to concentrate. *No force or hard mental effort is involved in true concentration.* The act of concentration is meant to be a normal, pleasant activity to the mind.

The word "concentrate" means "the act of drawing to a center." To concentrate is to rest the mind on an idea, to draw the mind back again and again to an idea. *You are concentrating all the time!*

The normal action of the mind is to concentrate as it dwells upon and feeds upon ideas. Every time you think about all that is wrong in your life and dwell upon your problems, you are concentrating. Every time you think about all that is good and right in your life, you are also concentrating.

Often you have concentrated as you have rested your mind on ideas, drawn your mind back again and again to certain subjects that interested you. But usually you have concentrated in a scattered way as your mind flitted from one subject to another. Since what you concentrated upon, you became one with—you simply became one with a lot of scattered, helter-skelter results; whereas, in deliberate, constructive concentration, you draw your thoughts to a common center and they then have the power to manifest deliberate, constructive results in your life.

There is a saying: "What you look to, looks to you." That's concentration.

THE HISTORY OF CONCENTRATION

There is no great world religion but has its method of concentration. What the Hindu calls "yoga" or the prayer of concentration, the Christian simply calls prayer.

The importance of concentration is an ancient teaching. The people of Rome, Greece, Persia, Egypt, India all knew that in order to experience anything worthwhile in life, they had to concentrate upon it.

The great teachers of the Bible emphasized the importance of prayers of concentration. Jesus referred to the prayer of concentration in healing when He said: "If thine eye be single, thy whole body shall be full of light" (Matthew 6:22). Concentration played a big part in many of His healings as well as in His prosperity miracles. Paul's powers of concentration had much to do with the successful establishment of early Christianity in a hostile world.

Among the spiritual giants of the Old Testament, the prophet Elijah was among the more obvious in his use of concentration; by the power of his thought, Elijah penetrated the atoms and precipitated an abundance of rain. By the same power he increased the widow's oil and meal.

Madame Guyon, a Christian devotee of the 17th Century, was an adept at concentration and described it in her treatise as "a simple method of prayer."

The Hindus regarded concentration as being "one-pointed." They felt that concentration was the basis of all success in life. The masters of the East have long felt that the man who was truly "one-pointed" was destiny's darling and was bound to succeed.

The Hindu philosophers, who are among the deepest students of psychology, called the practice of spiritual concentration "yoga," which means "union." In Raja yoga, or the yoga of mental development, the second step is concentration. The Hindus felt that, through the prayer of concentration, man united with his indwelling spiritual nature and literally got "turned on," so that all things were then possible to him.

Hindu devotees have spent whole lifetimes in the study and practice of concentration because they felt that, through constructive concentration, every good thing would come to them in life: power, knowledge, bliss. They also felt that through the practice of concentration they would be delivered from every ill.

THE INCREDIBLE POWER OF CONCENTRATION

"One-pointed" concentration releases extraordinary powers within you as it unites the conscious, subconscious and superconscious phases of your mind, bringing heretofore undreamed-of powers and energies into play in your behalf.

In the simple act of concentration, you draw the mind back again and again to an idea, which taps and releases deeper potent energies of the mind not ordinarily touched. Those deeper, finer, more penetrating currents have the capacity to produce extraordinary results because it is those finer, more potent currents that give the mind the power to exercise complete control over all the actions and forces of the mental world.

Furthermore, *the emotional blocks that exist in the minds of most people, keeping them from getting what they want, are eliminated in the minds of people who know how to concentrate. Thoughts of doubt, fear, fatigue, discouragement can be completely dissolved through concentration.*

Thus, *concentration is more than a mental action. It is also an emotional one as it purifies, calms and stills surging emotions.* According to the psychology of the Hindus, prayers of concentration can help you gain control of your emotions. They even felt that three distinct types of emotional personalities were especially helped through prayers of concentration. These types, which will be handled separately in turn, are as follows:

The First Type were those suffering from ignorance, dullness, inertia, laziness. This type took no step forward toward progress.

The Second Type were those who expressed their passion in hurry, struggle, strife, worry, agitation, and in other emotional disturbance. This type is easily upset and overreacts.

The Third Type were the over-proud, self-assertive, selfrighteous, often feeling they have been wronged, misunderstood, filled with thoughts of their personal rights, egotistical, egocentric. This type is inclined to battle and fight life.

A Housewife's Experience

A housewife recently used the power of deliberate concentration to calm the emotions of those around her and to bring deliverance from an unhappy situation:

"My husband and I were on our way home from a Christmas trip. We had our seven-month-old baby with us. In the mountains of Pennsylvania, miles from anywhere, our car just quit running. It was getting dark, the baby was crying, and my husband was mad. He got out and looked under the hood and could find no reason for the car trouble.

"In the meantime I remembered an affirmation from one of your books and started dwelling upon it: 'DIVINE SUBSTANCE APPROPRIATELY MANIFESTS FOR US HERE AND NOW.' I did not understand what it meant, but I used it anyway.

"In a little while, the baby calmed down and so did my husband. He got back in the car, tried the ignition and the car started. After that we had no more trouble. All the way home as we drove along, he kept saying, 'I sure don't get it.' "

Through concentration, you create what you want mentally first. Then through continued concentration, you bring into play the incredible powers of your conscious, subconscious and superconscious mind powers. Next, you gain control of them and make them work for you in a constructive, productive way. Through this process you become master instead of slave, victor instead of victim.

Until deliberate, constructive concentration is practiced, all your other prayer efforts are like scattered forces that have little visible effect.

THE NECESSITY OF CONCENTRATION IN PRAYER DEVELOPMENT

There are those misguided souls who say, "I do not need the preliminary types of prayer such as relaxation, release, forgiveness, decree or concentration. I pray in an 'advanced way.' My method of prayer is meditation and the silence." Those confused people then often let it slip that their prayers are not being answered.

You have got to get ready for the deeper phases of prayer such as the prayers of meditation and the silence by first taking prayer's preliminary steps. The prayers of relaxation, release, forgiveness, decree lead you into the prayers of concentration and meditation.

There is a great difference between the prayers of concentration and meditation. In concentration you are resting your mind on one basic idea of good. You are calling your mind back again and again to that idea of good; whereas, in meditation you let your mind roam and you let it consider many ideas. Meditation is a mental analysis, where you consider many ideas mentally. But before you can practice successfully the art of meditation where your mind can roam freely in a constructive, productive way, *you have got to have control of it.* You gain that control only through developing the preliminary types of prayer: relaxation, release, forgiveness, decree and concentration.

There are two basic methods of concentration, and the first method prepares you for the second, more advanced, inner method; and this second or more advanced method of concentration then leads you into meditation.

Before trying to arouse your innate spiritual powers within through the formal prayer of concentration and meditation which will be described later in this chapter, it is wise to begin by developing the first method: that is, by beginning to develop the art of concentrating upon what you want to experience in your life through the definite physical-mental methods of list-making, imaging and decreeing it. As you use these definite physical-mental methods of concentration, they will naturally lead you into the formal prayer of meditation.

HOW TO INDUCE CONCENTRATION THROUGH LIST-MAKING

Another name for concentration is "attention." *What gets your attention, gets you!* It is a well-known axiom that *what you concentrate upon, you bring into your life.*

Among the delightful methods that induce concentration as it "focuses" your thoughts, drawing them to a center, giving them power to produce results for you, is that of list-making.

Your First List

Your First List should be a list of the things or conditions you want to *eliminate* from your life. Often you have been so busy concentrating on these undesirable problems, conditions and things, that you have spent all your mental and emotional energy dwelling upon them, thereby unwittingly inviting them to multiply in your life. And so they have!

Sit down with a pencil and paper and write down that which you wish eliminated and removed from your life. Be definite and specific. At the bottom of your list write: "I NOW RELEASE WORN-OUT CONDITIONS AND WORN-OUT RELATIONSHIPS. I RELEASE THEM AND BLESS THEM TO THEIR TRUE PLACE NOW. THEY RELEASE ME AND BLESS ME TO MY TRUE PLACE NOW. I LET THEM GO, AND LET GOD GUIDE ME INTO MY NEW GOOD, WHICH IS MY TRUE GOOD NOW!"

In the future, instead of concentrating on these problems, secretly fighting, resenting and sulking over them—thereby concentrating upon them and holding them to you—call your mind back again and again to the foregoing words of release and blessing.

How a Businessman Made a
Special List

I know a businessman who had tried and tried to demonstrate greater prosperity in his life. He had affirmed and prayed and made a list of the blessings he wanted to experience. *But nothing happened until he made a list of the things and conditions he wanted to eliminate from his life.*

Within a matter of weeks, a business he no longer cared about had been sold at a profit. Several pieces of property had been sold. And a job in a new field of work opened to him, though he was supposed to be "too old" to qualify. That man is happy and successful today because he finally made a list of what he wanted to be rid of in his life and started declaring release from worn-out conditions and relationships, rather than continuing to dwell upon and mentally battle with them.

To make such an elimination list, blessing worn-out situations and relationships to their true place, helps you to withdraw your attention from that which you no longer want in your life. When you pull your attention out from under that which is undesirable in your life, it no longer has anything to feed it emotionally and so it fades away for lack of attention.

Your List of Choice— The Second List

Your Second List should list the things and conditions you *wish* to manifest in your life. Remember that the word "choice" is a magic word to the mind. Choice produces results. Your mind constantly works through what you choose.

If you drift along without any definite goals for better experiences in life, you become the helpless victim of circumstances. Furthermore, if your desires are passive and not clearly defined, you become subject to the dominant mentalities around you, and often manifest what *they* want in your life. Haven't you bought the car, house, clothes, or taken the vacation that somebody else thought you should? You became the victim of their concentrated desires when you had none of your own.

The way to overcome difficulties in life is to set a goal. If you do not know what you want and have no set purpose, your subconscious mind just produces a conglomeration of circumstances.

By writing out your list, your definite written words dissolve all obstacles and barriers on both the visible and invisible planes of life. Your written words go out into the ethers of the universe to work through people, circumstances and events, and open the way for the items on your list to come to pass.

Psychologists tell us that all things are done by choice. Choice produces results, but it is up to you to make your choice!

A Healer's Secret Formula
of Success

A very successful doctor of chiropractic recently told me that for twenty years this had been his secret formula for success. At the time this chiropractor went into practice two decades ago right out of college, he had nothing. But he and his wife believed that, if they concentrated on what they wanted in life, they would get it.

At the beginning of each New Year, instead of making New Year's resolutions of what they hoped the year might bring, they made a list of what they definitely expected the year to bring. The first year they listed nice rental offices and a thriving practice. The second year they listed the purchase of business property on which they planned to build their own offices. Later they listed the purchase of a home and the birth of their first child. Another year their list included the acquisition of stocks, bonds, and other investments. Still later they listed a larger professional practice. Then their list included the purchase of a private plane, more cars, a boat.

From the very first New Year's list this couple made, this method began to work for them! Once they had written down their desires for that particular year, they placed the list in their Bible, and simply gave thanks for the perfect results throughout the year. In several instances by midyear the major desires on their list had manifested. At other times it was as late as December before the list began producing results. The year they listed the desire for their first child, she was born in October. Invariably the list-making method worked!

Today this couple has all the blessings they have put on their New Year's lists over the years: a fine professional practice and their own business property on which they have built beautiful offices; they now enjoy a lovely home, several cars, their own private plane, additional financial assets such as stocks and bonds, and several healthy children who had first been on their list! The result is a healthy, happy, prosperous, spiritually oriented family.

"List-making is the simplest success technique in the world, if people would just do it!" declared this doctor of chiropractic.

Top Executives Prove Value of List-Making to Themselves

After I had written about the power of listing your desires in my books, *The Dynamic Laws of Prosperity* and *The Prosperity Secret of the Ages,* a businessman from Philadelphia wrote confirming the success power of this method. He had recently given a success course to ninety-two top corporation executives for which their company had paid him a high fee.

In this success course, these ninety-two executives were asked to write out the things they wished to experience in life, as well as to list the problems they wished to eliminate from their lives. This man reported:

"Miracles happened. Everyone was healed of health problems, even of "incurable" diseases. Out of these ninety-two men, all but two said they had gained immeasurable good. All got raises in pay of from $2,000 to $20,000 a year from this method. One man was an atheist, another an agnostic. Their friends at work said they had been impossible to work with. After this course, the co-workers reported that these executives were much more pleasant. Problems of health, prosperity and personality were all resolved by using this list-making method. Ninety out of ninety-two admitted to results."

A business executive from Illinois recently wrote a long, happy letter in which he said:

"This business of writing a list of those things you feel you need in your life works! I have done just that and success became apparent almost instantly. Since then, everything I had on my list has come to me. Some of them were tremendous things, such as retirement early so that I might become a public speaker. I also listed an adequate income, so that my life might continue normally as before retirement. I now am a lecturer for business groups, from which I get several hundred dollars per lecture.

"Even such things as an expensive travel trailer, a fine motion picture camera, and other such items have come easily. I have proved beyond all doubt that God intends us to have whatever we want that will advance His work on earth. But it's up to us to mentally claim those blessings. List-making helps us open our minds to the good things we want in life, rather than fretting and fuming about the problems we don't want."

Your Third List

Your Third List should include the things you are now experiencing in life for which you are *thankful:*

List your talents, skills, friends, family, possessions, health, happiness, progress, understanding . . . blessings tangible and intangible. List them all. Nothing is too trivial to give thanks for. This simple act of thanksgiving has miracle power, because *words that express thanks release certain potent energies not otherwise tapped. Thanksgiving releases dynamic forces for good.*

Along with being thankful for the good you are already enjoying, it is also good to place on your list the things that have not yet appeared. Just thank God for them anyway. Your act of thanksgiving opens the way for those blessings to appear.

A businessman had been transferred out of state and had tried for months to sell his house. He had prayed to no avail. Then a friend said, "Try giving thanks that it is already sold." He listed this sale on his "Thank you, God" list. Within a few days the house he had prayed about for months sold! (More about the miracle power of thanksgiving in the Epilogue of this book.)

After making your three lists—(1) what you want to *eliminate* from your life; (2) what you want to *manifest* in your life; and (3) what you are *thankful* for—go over your lists daily, revising them as you are guided to.

Think about what you really want, not what somebody else wants you to have. Try to please only the Christ within you when making your list. "The highest is the nearest." If you try to compromise, you stop your good and bring on confusion.

This act of concentration helps clarify your thinking about what you want and don't want in your life. That very act of concentration then goes to work to manifest your desires for you.

Protect your list and your desires by declaring, "THIS OR SOME-THING BETTER, FATHER. LET THINE UNLIMITED GOOD WILL BE DONE." Or "I RELEASE MY DESIRES TO THE PERFECT OUTWORKING OF THE CHRIST CONSCIOUSNESS NOW." Or "I SURROUND MY DESIRES WITH THE PURE WHITE LIGHT OF THE CHRIST, INTO WHICH NOTHING NEGATIVE CAN PENETRATE AND OUT OF WHICH ONLY GOOD SHALL COME."

As you give thanks for "divine results" which are sublime results, they will manifest with perfect timing—that which you had in mind or something more appropriate.

HOW TO INDUCE CONCENTRATION THROUGH IMAGING

You can practice the art of concentration through the deliberate use of the picturing power of the mind.

There is nothing new about this simple, delightful form of concentration that often produces the desired results quickly. Prehistoric man carved pictures of the food he desired on the walls of his cave. He believed that as he looked often at those pictures, an unseen power would attract the food near him in the form of game, fish, fowl. It happened repeatedly.

Later the ancient Egyptians, who were versed in all the occult success teachings, used the picturing power of the mind in their Egyptian tombs. As soon as a child of royalty was born, a tomb was started for him. On the walls of the tombs were painted pictures of his life up to his death, showing all the desired experiences he would have throughout his lifetime: the winning of war, the capturing of large numbers of prisoners, and the living of a happy, victorious life were depicted. The Egyptians expected these pictures to come to pass in the life of the royal child.

Only 2,400 years ago, during the Golden Age of Greece, the cultured Grecians took advantage of this mental law and surrounded their prospective mothers with beautiful pictures and statuary in order that the unborn children might receive from each mother's mind pictures of health and beauty.

The Tibetan Buddhists have combined affirmations and the

picturing power of the mind and used them for centuries in the form of "prayer wheels."

They feel that prayer wheels are a spiritual device whereby man may expect miraculous benefits from his frequent recitation of religious formulas or affirmations. Cylinder-shaped boxes containing sacred texts or prayers are spun in the hands, and wheels are hung up in temples where visitors can turn them. Each revolution of the prayer wheel is believed to bestow as many benefits as would be gained by reading the texts or reciting the prayers, thus setting up the picturing power of expectancy of good.

The picturing power of the mind is one of the oldest devices known to man for concentrating upon the good, thereby manifesting it!

Concentration functions best through imagination. Through deliberate, constructive use of the imagination, you bring together the many creative energies of the mind. Imaging is an invaluable aid to imagination. Concentration can, by working through the imagination, bring together into one powerful line of mental action all the best ideas of the mind and all available creative energies. A vivid, well-trained imagination tends to "light up" your entire mental world.

How much better you can concentrate when you have a distinct picture in view. Imagination has the power to take the lead in the mental world. Whenever you image a certain thing being done in the mind, you release a majority of the energies of the mind to go and do that very thing! To help achieve this purpose, make a prayer wheel.

THE GRAND RESULTS OF MODERN PRAYER WHEELS

In connection with the prayer of concentration, I suggest that you make a modern "prayer wheel" which not only contains words describing the good you wish to experience in life, but also contains pictures of your desired good.

Such a prayer wheel is a "prayer in pictures" and is a simple way of praying and then mentally accepting the answer to your prayer through the art of concentration.

As a spiritual being made in the image of God and containing His divinity, *man is the only creature on the face of the earth that looks up. When the forces of nature move upward, through the picturing power of prayer, they always move with great energy and power. When your doubts leave, your dreams come true. A prayer wheel wipes out your doubts!*

There is an old axiom: "If you look up, you will always be provided for." Through picturing your prayers as already answered, you are invoking the highest form of faith, because you are saying, "It is already done, and it now manifests in my life as satisfying, tangible results." *Picturing your prayers as already answered* (as is done when you make a "prayer wheel") *is often the turning point to answered prayer.*

How a Businesswoman Worked Out a Happier Life

A businesswoman was lonely and desired a more balanced life. She made a prayer wheel, picturing the happy, balanced life she wished. Each night before retiring she would view her prayer wheel, quietly resting her mind on the pictures of good she saw there. Over and over she drew her thoughts to a common center. As she did, they gained power to produce results for her.

One day she was suddenly called out of the city on a business trip. While away, she met her future husband and soon was established in the happy way of life pictured on her prayer wheel. But none of these happy events occurred until she practiced daily concentration, resting her mind on the pictured results; through drawing her thoughts and attention often to a common center concerning that pictured result she then fed her mind constantly on that idea.

The law of concentration is: *picture a thing and bring it through, rather than trying to force it through.* Often you have cut off your good by thinking in strained terms of wishing, needing, wanting. Through the imaging power of the mind, you begin to think in terms of having, being, and experiencing present fulfillment. This mental action releases to you the results you have been picturing. It is a mental law.

My Own Experience in Completing an Assignment

Once when I had been unable to complete a writing assignment, due to lack of time and many interruptions, I was in a state of despair until I remembered the picturing power of the mind: that *generalities do not produce results because they lack substance and power. Vague hopes and indefinite goals are not convincing to the mind, whereas a clear-cut picture of the good you want to experience motivates people, places and events to cooperate with your pictured desires and unconsciously produces those results for you.*

I quickly made a prayer wheel showing the book as already completed and placing on it these words in big bold print: "Get things done! Inspired manuscript. Easy success in writing. The good work hurries on. Editors glad." It worked! Suddenly the tempo changed and within a short time my manuscript was completed and everyone was glad.

How a Prayer Wheel Served a College Professor

A college professor wished to change his field of teaching but needed another degree in order to do so. For three years he longed to make the change, but just worried and fretted about it. Nothing happened until he learned of the fantastic power of the imagination, and made a prayer wheel picturing himself with the additional master's degree, teaching in the new field of work.

Suddenly, after he made his prayer wheel, everything and everybody seemed to tune in on his pictured prayer and co-operated to help bring it to pass. His teaching schedule on campus was light that next year; his students were more mature and less demanding of his time; less of his time was taken in campus student activities; he discovered that he already had certain college credits that would apply toward the desired degree; and the subject and research for his master's thesis unfolded easily.

Within a year, this professor had that additional master's degree that he had spent three years worrying about! It all came quickly after he stopped fretting about *how* it could happen, and just dared to picture it anyway in faith. The image made the condition, but only after he had made the image.

Solomon described the power of the imagination: "He that hath a bountiful eye shall be blessed" (Proverbs 22:9).

The picturing power of the mind turns your thinking from "I cannot have this," or "It will never happen" to the thought of hope, belief, and finally to mental acceptance.

You are using the picturing power of the mind all the time anyway, so begin deliberately to picture what you want, or you will unconsciously continue to get what you do not want.

In my book *The Dynamic Laws of Prosperity* is the story of the engineer who demonstrated great success professionally after picturing it. In my book *The Prosperity Secret of the Ages* are stories of countless people who experienced prosperity and success after developing their master plan and picturing it. In my book *The Dynamic Laws of Healing* are numerous stories of people who overcame all kinds of health problems through picturing health. And in my book *The Healing Secret of the Ages* you find detailed instructions for making a prayer wheel, including occult instructions on the science of color and how it affects the results of your prayer wheel.

How a Tenement Family "Graduated" from Their Tenement

An overworked housewife, the mother of nine children, was despondent because her husband's job as a day laborer was grossly inadequate to meet the needs of their family. They were living in a crowded tenement in a slum area of their city. Upon learning of the power of prayer wheels, this housewife made one showing her husband in a well-paying job. Other pictures on her prayer wheel showed them living in a comfortable house with adequate bedrooms for all the children, and with a nice car parked out front. Other pictures showed ample outdoor space in which the children could romp.

An impossible dream for one in her poverty-stricken circumstances? It would seem so, until the prayer wheel began to work. Then one day her husband was offered the job of overseeing a large ranch. On this job he was provided with a nice house and car, and there were hundreds of acres of ranchland on which his children played!

Imaging Creates and Concentration Hastens Desires into Manifestation

After making your prayer wheel, you should spend at least 30 minutes a day quietly studying your pictured desires. Concentrate by looking at them lovingly, intently, mentally enjoying the pictured results as though you are experiencing them. The quicker your feeling nature responds, mentally accepting those pictured results, the sooner they will manifest as a reality in your life

INDUCE CONCENTRATION THROUGH DECREE

In previous chapters, you have been given numerous types of prayer decrees to use as a simple method of prayer.

Prayers of decree are also another way to induce concentration. The Tibetan Buddhist's prayer wheel included sacred texts or prayers which they chanted. By affirmation they claimed and appropriated that which was already theirs on the invisible plane. You can too!

You can invoke concentration through listing your desires and picturing them on your prayer wheel. But *you may speed up the results of your list-making and prayer wheel as much as 80 percent just by speaking forth definite decrees about your desires.* "Thou shalt decree a thing and it shall be established, and the light shall shine upon thy way," promised Job, who went from rags back to riches through the power of decree (Job 22–28).

Prayers as "Mantrams of Power"

Knowing about the power of words, the yogis have their verbal prayers they describe as "mantrams of power." These are nothing more than affirmative decrees. The people on the lost continent of Atlantis apparently knew about the creative power of decree and used it selfishly, bringing about their own destruction. For many centuries, the power of decree was a secret teaching shared with only a select few, but in this century it has been rediscovered by the masses.

Too Old to Get a Job?

About a year ago, a man telephoned me from Southern California for prayers for work. He had been jobless for four years, was fifty-five years of age, and had been informed he was "too old" to get another job. He had studied metaphysics for thirty years, but had been unsuccessful in applying it to his job situation.

When I asked what affirmative decree he was using he said, "I have been reading inspirational books, but have not used any specific prayer decrees."

We talked about the fact that for every fifteen minutes of inspirational study, he should spend at least five minutes speaking forth definite decrees for work. He began following this formula and declared aloud at least five minutes each day: "I AM A DIVINE IDEA IN THE MIND OF GOD, AND I AM NOW GUIDED INTO MY TRUE PLACE WITH THE TRUE PEOPLE AT THE TRUE PROSPERITY."

I heard no more from him until about six months ago when a letter arrived from South America, saying he was now manager of the South American division of one of our fine American companies, that he was happy, prosperous, and doing well. He wrote: "I can attest to the fact that spoken decrees get your prayers answered. Affirmative decrees turned the tide from failure to success for me when I had been out of work four years, was heavily in debt, and when just reading inspirational books had done no good."

True Cases of "Rags to Riches"

A widow who went from rags to riches within twenty years attributed her success to the daily use of one prosperity decree: "GOD IS MY SUPPLY AND MY UNLIMITED ABUNDANCE OF EVERYTHING NOW." After beginning to use that decree she went into business on a shoestring and for a time had to pray for her daily supply. Once when she desperately needed $100, she walked the floor and spoke her prosperity decrees aloud. As she was doing so, her secretary opened a file cabinet and found five very old $20 bills stuck in an order pad!

Another time when she was affirming God as her unlimited abundance in an attempt to meet the payroll for her employees, a stranger walked into her store and offered to buy a piece of property he said she owned down the street. She exclaimed that she only wished she did own that piece of property! But when the stranger explained that her father (now deceased) had bought the property for her many years previously, her attorney verified this. This businesswoman then sold the piece of property she had not even known she owned a few hours previously, met her payroll, and had an abundance left over.

During the depression years, a lady daily gathered her little daughters around the kitchen table where they said prosperity decrees for the head of the house, who was out of work: "YOU HAVE A WONDERFUL JOB WITH WONDERFUL PAY. YOU RENDER A WONDERFUL SERVICE IN A WONDERFUL WAY." It worked.

At the height of the depression this man was offered a job in the bonding business, if he could raise just $25 to get him started. He raided the sugar bowl and went into business. His wife recently stated that they are now worth $250,000! She commented: "That $25 became a quarter of a million dollars, because I have continued to speak forth prosperity decrees every day over the years." Furthermore, the daughters that helped her with the affirmations years ago are now all married to prosperous men and are busy leading happy lives.

INDUCE CONCENTRATION THROUGH SECRECY

When you write out your list, make your prayer wheel, and speak forth your daily decrees concerning the good you want to manifest in your life, you are practicing the art of concentration and remarkable things will happen!

However, remember that concentration has been described as being "one-pointed." Secrecy, silence, keeping quiet about what you are concentrating upon are necessary.

Many people fail in concentration because, although they draw their thoughts to a common center, they dissipate that thought force by talking about their desired good, and thus do not get results. If you talk about your lists or show your prayer wheel to others or discuss the affirmations you are using, you can dissipate their results. "In quietness and in confidence shall be your strength," cautioned the prophet Isaiah (Isaiah 30:15).

The word "sacred" and the word "secret" have the same root meaning. The good you desire in life comes from God and is thereby sacred. It should also be dealt with in secret.

Another name for concentration might be "loving attention." So persist! *List-making, picturing, and decreeing the good draws it together on the invisible plane, but the act of concentration, where you repeatedly dwell upon it, hastens the good into manifestation.*

By concentrating in a superficial manner, you may secure some slight results *temporarily*. Yet it is those deeper, finer, more penetrating currents of thought and feeling that produce permanent results and that have the capacity to manifest extraordinary good for you.

HOW A WOMAN HEALED HERSELF THROUGH CONCENTRATION

The use of concentration for improvement in one's life can be a delightful process. As related in my book, *The Dynamic Laws of Healing*, a woman had long suffered nagging health problems which the finest of medical treatment had been unable to clear up. Finally she began to read inspirational books on self-improvement and realized that her health could be restored only after she concentrated upon the picture of health. She decided to test the validity of the quip: "To be the picture of health, one must get into a good 'frame of mind.'"

She invoked concentration in a number of ways:

First, she stopped talking about her aches and pains and began to read various books on healing. She began taking physical exercises, tried a new diet, and resumed taking the vitamins previously prescribed by her physician. In this regard she followed carefully the instructions given by a competent nutritionist.

This lady then sought healing, even concentrated upon it, by deliberately leading a more balanced life of work, play, and rest. She started working in her flower garden daily, took sun baths, and enjoyed the fresh air.

Next, she made a prayer wheel, which pictured an active, healthy life. As she viewed her prayer wheel daily, she decreed: "I AM THE RADIANT CHILD OF GOD. MY MIND, BODY AND AFFAIRS NOW MANIFEST HIS RADIANT PERFECTION."

She began to praise her body. She also made it a point to praise other people, rather than dwelling upon their faults. She began associating with friends and relatives who were healthy, who spoke in terms of health. She deliberately terminated her membership in one organization whose members spent most of their meeting periods discussing their aches and pains.

She made it a point to plan ahead for special events she could look forward to: plays, movies, concerts, art exhibits, dinner parties, church events. This helped her to picture herself as healthy enough to attend those anticipated events.

She constantly blessed her body with health and her life with "divine activity." She daily gave thanks that she was whole and well, through and through.

As she worked in all these ways to deliberately set up the mental picture of health, life, and activity to replace the former beliefs in fatigue, ill health, old age, and inactivity—her mental pictures began to take control of her thoughts, emotions, body and life. She became "pregnant with the image of health."

In only a matter of weeks, her life began to reflect the beautiful images of health and happiness pictured on her prayer wheel. Later she went on to a new career. Though this lady was more than seventy years "young" when she began concentrating upon a healthy way of life, she proved that you can produce wonderful changes in your body through the act of concentration.

HOW TO INDUCE INNER CONCENTRATION AND MEDITATION

The foregoing methods of concentration are ways of inducing it informally amid daily living, combining mental and physical power.

However, there is the definite formal prayer of concentration that releases inner spiritual power. And it is worthwhile in your prayer development to unfold this inner method, because the prayer of concentration helps you still your unruly thoughts so that one basic thought can rest in your mind. As it rests in your mind, it penetrates, permeates, saturates your thought and feeling nature, going deeper and deeper within, until your whole being responds and goes to work to make that idea a reality. When this happens you are then experiencing the art of meditation.

The prayer of concentration is powerful because it penetrates not only the thoughts of your conscious mind, but also the tremendous feeling nature of your subconscious mind. Since the subconscious supply of latent energy is enormous, the possibilities of concentration begin to assume enormous proportions.

When concentration penetrates the subconscious, it releases latent energies, undreamed of powers, potent forces from all phases of the mental world, and suddenly the impossible becomes possible and happens!

As concentration penetrates the enormous latent energies of the subconscious mind, it has the power to get beneath the surface and dissolve all kinds of blocks and obstacles, which simply melt away under its penetrating power. Because of the obstacle-solving power of concentration, the ancient people had a saying: "The penetrating power of the mind is the freeing power of the mind."

*You will find that the times you practice this inner concentra-
tion are times of your greatest accomplishments!*

Formal prayers of concentration also tap and release powers of
the superconscious spiritual nature within man.

HOW CONCENTRATION LEADS INTO MEDITATION

As stated previously, concentration is centering the mind upon
a single idea, calling the mind back again and again to that idea.
This process of concentration induces meditation, which is more
of a mental analysis. In the process of meditation one ponders
ideas and lets those ideas reveal their truths to the mind.

In concentration you feed the mind ideas. This process
awakens the deeper levels of the subconscious and superconscious phases of the mind. Then those deeper phases of the mind
come alive and begin to feed your conscious mind a flow of ideas
or impressionable feelings. That is meditation.

The goal of concentration is to rest the mind on an idea long
enough to quiet and still the conscious mind and penetrate the
deeper levels of the mind. When this happens concentration becomes meditation in a flow of ideas that wells up from deep
within.

The goal of meditation is to turn man to the light within him
and let it come alive like a lamp gradually lighting up his whole
being. It is in meditation that man gradually makes contact with
his own indwelling Lord, whose whole business is to care for him.
*Whereas, the previous phases of prayer are a means of getting,
meditation is a means of letting.*

In meditation you are not trying to make anything happen.
There is no hurry or force. In meditation your attention is not
directed "up" or "out" but "in." You are only attempting to contact your own indwelling Lord and then let divine ideas and
energy flow forth from the center of divinity deep within you.

However, all the foregoing prayer methods are necessary to
develop first, because *the art of meditation comes only to the
controlled mind and relaxed body*. When you are ready for meditation mentally and emotionally, it is an easy, natural phase of
prayer. Something within seems to draw your attention inward

and hold it there in meditation, feeding you new energy and ideas. Because of the tremendous energy generated in meditation, it could be dangerous for a person to have deep meditation powers that he had not developed gradually. The mind and body would not be prepared for them.

Prayer is possible to all. Meditation is possible only to the mentally polarized man. The prayer of concentration naturally prepares you for its twin prayer power of meditation. Concentration leads into meditation. First you feed the mind ideas (concentration). Then the mind feeds you ideas and energy (meditation). As you gradually unfold your concentration-meditation powers, you will meditate more and rush around less. You will discover that more meditation leads to less medication—on all levels of life!

HOW TO DEVELOP YOUR CONCENTRATION AND MEDITATION POWERS

You can begin developing and releasing this tremendous power of inner concentration and meditation by selecting a time and place where you will not be disturbed. Seat yourself in a comfortable position, or even lie down, loosening and removing items of clothing that restrict you.

Then speak words of relaxation to the mind and body: "RELAX AND LET GO."

When you begin to feel relaxed and at ease, take a definite statement and rest the mind upon it. Keep calling the mind back again and again to that thought. You may wish to begin by writing down a prayer decree, looking at it, filling your mind with it. You may wish to speak it aloud to help you become attuned to it. Then silently rest your mind on that idea.

Confucius said, "I do not talk of God but of goodness." The word "good" might be the subject of your prayer of concentration: "THE GOOD IS ALL THERE IS IN THIS SITUATION. ONLY GOOD SHALL COME FROM THIS EXPERIENCE. LET THE GOOD NOW BE REVEALED. LET THE GOOD NOW MANIFEST AS PERFECT RESULTS."

The decree you concentrate upon might be "GOD IS LOVE." It might be "PEACE," or "PEACE, BE STILL" for some troublesome situation. Any of the attributes of God's goodness might be the subject of your prayer of concentration: "LIFE" for health; "LOVE" for happy relationships; "WISDOM" for guidance, right action, right results; "POWER" for dominion and authority; "SUBSTANCE" for success and prosperity. (The ancient people felt that the word "substance" was one of the strongest words upon which to concentrate because it contains every element of good. Concentration upon this word seems to stimulate that good in all its parts.)

You might wish to dwell upon a Bible promise or a passage in a book that inspires you. It is wise to take the particular word or phrase, repeat it over and over a number of times until your whole being "feels" it and responds. Repeatedly speaking the Lord's Prayer, the name "Jesus Christ" or "Jehovah" often induces this feeling. To dwell upon the phrase "I AM," focusing the attention within one's self, gathers the mental energies together, instead of allowing them to remain scattered and ineffective. This is a powerful ancient prayer technique as discussed in my book, *The Dynamic Laws of Healing*. The phrase "I AM" arouses the inner spirit in man and releases its superconscious power to work through him.

When your whole being has responded with inspired feeling, then let your mind relax, quietly dwell on the ideas you are holding, bringing the mind back to them again and again. When the flow of ideas and energy subsides, your meditation has been concluded. Then you feel a sense of peace and release about it, your mind has become centered and poised upon your idea of good; your mind has accepted and absorbed it, and will go to work to produce a perfect result for you.

When you want to know a thing, or need certain guidance, practice the prayer of concentration: Simply center your mind steadily on that subject saying, "WHAT IS THE TRUTH ABOUT THIS SITUATION? LET THE TRUTH NOW BE REVEALED."

Presently the subject will open up to you. You will find yourself knowing or "feeling" the answer, without the ordinary efforts of getting information. The word "let" is a much more powerful word than "get." In meditation, you "let" the mind reveal to you its truths. This the mind has the power to do since it is filled with the omnipresent intelligence of the universe. All the extra-sensory powers begin to unfold in the one who practices concentration and meditation: telepathy, clairvoyance, clairaudience, etc.

The prayers of concentration and meditation are all-powerful because they slow the mind down to the point of revelation. Many people miss their good because, after praying prayers of denial, cleansing and decree, they rush off to further outer activity. They do not take time to slow the mind down to the point of revelation and then wait and listen. Through the process of concentration and meditation you'll take time to be holy, to become whole in mind, body, affairs, and in every phase of your world.

In his book *Teach Us to Pray,*[1] Charles Fillmore has written:

> We have found that very definite changes occur in our mind and body when we practice concentration in the silence.

Even fifteen minutes a day spent in this practice of the prayer of inner concentration and meditation would bring vast improvement in your life within a matter of weeks. Those who practice concentration and meditation evolve quickly! (You will find my meditation method described in Chapter 10.)

HOW TO CONCENTRATE REGARDING TROUBLESOME PEOPLE

In regard to troublesome people, concentrate upon this great truth:

Everything and everybody that come into your life are there for one of two purposes: either to heal you or to be healed by you of some wrong attitude of mind, body or affairs. Everything and everybody in your life are there to press you into more good, or so that you may draw out of them more good. As Emerson said, "A weed is only a flower whose use has not been found."

As you practice the prayer of concentration and meditation, you will learn not to try to run away from troublesome situations or people, but to call forth the good in them. As you do, a blessing

---

[1] Charles Fillmore, *Teach Us to Pray* (Lee's Summit, Mo.: Unity School of Christianity, 1941).

for all concerned takes place, and then the picture changes. Decree often, "THE GOOD IS ALL THERE IS IN THIS EXPERIENCE. I PRONOUNCE IT GOOD. I AGREE WITH THE GOOD IN THIS SITUATION, AND THE GOOD IN THIS SITUATION AGREES WITH ME."

Such prayers of concentration upon the idea of "good" give you emotional stability and control of your world. With that stability comes every blessing, since most of one's problems have an emotional basis.

THE ART OF CONCENTRATION DEVELOPS SLOWLY

Concentration is a bridge between the inner and outer phases of prayer. Concentration leads you into the mystical phases of prayer: meditation, the silence, illuminative realization. *But concentration must come first since it gives you the mind control needed before meditation can become deep and satisfying.*

Indeed, concentration is the first step in meditation.

The thing you concentrate upon is the thing you draw to yourself. Your prayers will be answered to the extent you can hold one thought in the silence. Developing this ability takes time. Do not become discouraged if at first you do not succeed. Practice makes perfect.

The art of concentration is not acquired in a short time, but is a matter of growth and practice. Nevertheless it is worth the effort, because the regular practice of concentration will greatly quicken your powers, and enable you to do speedily and efficiently everything you undertake. Both Sir Isaac Newton and Thomas Edison proved this.

Indeed, you gain this interior hold upon the deeper forces of the mind through *continuous practice.* As you continue to practice concentration, you awaken latent forces, develop new talents, and arouse increased power in every faculty and talent you are already using.

Concentration can lead the mind further and deeper in every direction. Concentration leads you into meditation and into the more interior phase of prayer, which is described in the following chapter as the prayer of silence.

SUMMARY OF CHAPTER 8

1. It has been estimated that what usually takes six hours to do could be accomplished in only one hour by the person who knew how to practice concentration; that absolutely nothing is impossible to the one who knows the power of concentration.

2. Most of your forces have been lost because they have been expressed outward through scattered thought and action, instead of expressed inward through deliberate concentration. There is fantastic power in deliberate concentration in which your forces are drawn inward and upward, so they are then focalized and have the power to produce great good for and through you.

3. No force or hard mental effort is involved in true concentration. To concentrate is to rest the mind on an idea, to draw it back again and again to that idea. You are concentrating all the time.

4. "One-pointed" concentration releases extraordinary powers within you as it unites the conscious, subconscious and superconscious phases of your mind, bringing heretofore undreamed of powers and energies into play in your behalf.

5. The emotional blocks that exist in the minds of most people, keeping them from getting what they want, are eliminated in the minds of people who know how to concentrate. Concentration is more than a mental action. It is also an emotional one as it purifies, calms and stills surging emotions.

6. Until deliberate, constructive concentration is practiced, all your other prayer efforts are like scattered forces that have little visible results.

7. Through concentration you create what you want emotionally first. Through continued concentration, you bring into play the incredible powers of your conscious, subconscious and superconscious mind powers; you then gain control of them and make them work for you in a constructive way. It is then that concentration becomes meditation, as those incredible powers of your mind begin to feed you ideas and energy. And this is the purpose of meditation, to feed you ideas and energy.

8. There are two basic methods of concentration—the outer and inner. The first method prepares you for the second, which includes meditation.

9

The Might of the Prayer of Silence

There once was a country banker who practiced the prayer of silence. His bank needed to borrow what it considered a large sum of money and he went to New York City to negotiate for the loan, but without success.

While he was talking over the matter with a city bank executive, his customary "silence hour" approached and he was puzzled about what to do. He finally decided to be honest, and in the midst of the apparently unfavorable discussion, this country banker quietly announced that he always devoted a few minutes to prayer at that hour, and begged to be excused.

The attitude of the city bank executive immediately changed. He recognized in his client something he did not have: peace, poise, and trust in the face of defeat. The city banker haltingly replied that he also liked to observe daily periods of prayer and would be glad to join in.

Together these men entered the silence and experienced a high realization of God's presence and power. At the conclusion of their prayer period, the city banker informed his country client that he was satisfied with the securities offered and that the loan would be granted without delay.

There is an occult formula for success: *Think. Act. Wait.*

Many praying people dissipate their prayer powers because they think and act, but do not complete the last part of the formula *by then waiting*. The prayer of silence *helps you to wait*.

In my book, *The Prosperity Secret of the Ages*, the importance of this silence period of waiting is discussed in connection with the Sabbath, or seventh day of creation, in which God finished His work and rested. It was thereafter that it manifested as a visible result. The success symbology is that you should do all that you can mentally and visibly to make a situation right. Then you should "let go" and let it work out completely in God's own way. While it is working out in God's own way, you observe a silence. And unless, and until, you observe a silence, it never works out because you haven't released it to do so!

Why is the silence so powerful? Why is waiting necessary in order to get your prayers answered? Why did everything change for the country banker after he practiced the silence?

Everything changed because the silence creates. The reason the silence creates is because in it you still your surface mind, so that the deeper levels of the mind may be free to function. In the silence, when your conscious mind becomes quiet then the subconscious phase of the mind which is the seat of memory and feeling is free to function. In the silence as you are still, the highly sensitive superconscious phase of the mind begins to function, revealing fresh inspiration and new ideas. *Though the silence appears to be a "do nothing" state of prayer, plenty happens in that state, so that it is one of the most powerful and creative. Indeed, everything comes out of the silence!*

The silence is the simplest operation of which the mind is capable. There is no mystery about it. *In the silence you gather together your spiritual forces and creative energies necessary for the expression of your good.* Within you is a mighty quietness in which lies all power. By going into the silence, you tap that power.

The silence is the workshop of God. "Silence is the element in which great things fashion themselves together," explained the Scottish writer, Carlyle.

The silence is the key to greater power, dominion, harmony, health, to perfection of every phase of your world. *Whatever your heart craves, whatever your life needs, may be contacted in the silence. Practicing the silence is the secret of all attainment, because it is the secret of all creative power.*

WHY THE LACK OF SILENCE IS ABNORMAL

Most people think that unless you stay busy every minute, something is wrong with you. Just the opposite is true: It is only *if* you stay busy every minute that something is wrong with you! People usually seek outside themselves for the calm, peace, and creative power that can only be found within themselves, in the silence.

People who condemn the practice of repose, stillness, quietness do not realize that the silence is the "power behind the throne" of all results. Meister Eckhart, the 13th Century German mystic, described the silence as "that immobility by which all things are moved." People who sit with folded hands, apparently doing nothing, may not be lazy or idle but just may be in the process of bringing forth a great and wonderful stillness out of which new good will be created. The difference between laziness and quiet contemplation is that the contemplator is taking time to be holy, or to become whole.

Unfortunately, a number of our useless life activities arise from the erroneous belief that we must be doing something all the time and that, if we are not busy, something is wrong with us. Yet the practice of the silence is a more powerful cause of results than many of the activities we see about us that have no principle.

In his fine book, *Commonsense About Prayer*,[1] Lewis Maclachlan has explained:

> Many people imagine that they are serving God when they are doing far too much and working far too hard. . . . People who work themselves to death, or very near it, for the sake of God have surely misunderstood what God requires of them. This passion for overwork, when it is not caused by conditions that call for the help of a psychiatrist, is usually due to an unconscious desire to expiate unworthiness and obtain merit and distinction. . . . Overwork continues to do so much harm largely because it is considered the mark of

---

[1] Lewis Maclachlan, *Commonsense About Prayer* (London, England: James Clarke & Co., Ltd., 1962).

devoted and saintly character. . . . Overwork is usually a failure both in faith and in self-discipline. It deserves more blame than praise. Far from being heroic it is often quite selfish and instead of being encouraged as a virtue, it should be reproved as a fault.

The worst feature of excessive *busy-ness* is that it deprives us of that calm and unhurried waiting upon God which is one of the means that He uses to communicate His mind to us. Many people in their prayers, as in their whole attitude to life, are far more conscious of what they are doing for God than of what God is doing for them. . . . Prayer is not so much something that we do as something that God does in us. Our excited self-importance must subside before God can use us. It is not as though we were labouring in prayer to produce some result. We are quietly putting the matter into the hands of God and leaving Him to do what we cannot do ourselves. *It is in rest that we receive much of God's answer to our prayers.*

It has been estimated that a person who practices the silence can accomplish more in thirty minutes than the average person accomplishes in eight or nine hours. Though this may be an overestimation, one thing is sure:

Too much talk, too much action, often wastes your powers and scatters your forces, whereas, through concentration and meditation on holy things, your mind is cleansed and becomes un crowded. It can then listen, hear, and follow the guidance given it in the silence. Just as in the silence the tiny sapling gathers strength to become a mighty oak, so do you gather immense strength to carry forward into your daily life. Carlyle advised:

> Hold thy tongue for one day; on the morrow see how clearer are thy purposes and duties. What rubbish within thee has been swept away.

Achievement is not always the result of struggle and strife. Sometimes the greatest rewards are won by the leisurely expectant. Strife does not win anything but temporary results. Knowing how to wait is always more permanently effective.

WHAT HAPPENS IN THE PRAYERFUL SILENCE

In the prayerful silence, you are not trying to rest the mind on a single idea, as in the prayer of concentration. You are not trying to consider freely many ideas and let them unfold their meaning to you, as in meditation. In the prayer of silence, you cease trying to think, be, do, get or have anything.

You simply become still and quiet mentally and physically, and make contact with your own indwelling Lord. Prayer has been described as communion with God. In the practice of the silence, you make common union with your indwelling Lord.

In the silence you may hear or receive new ideas and guidance or you may not. *Nothing may seem to happen in the silence.* Yet you are always helped through practicing the silence, because it feeds your inner being.

In the silence you are not reaching out. You are turning within; then resting, listening, waiting, trusting. In this "do nothing" state of mind, you become completely open and receptive to the flow of divine power from deep within. You become an empty vessel which the Holy Spirit is then able to fill anew.

When you first begin to practice the silence, you may feel a bit like George Bernard Shaw felt when asked his opinion of prayer: "Many people have prayed for me and I have not been any worse for it."

You may not feel that anything is happening when you first begin to practice the silence, but you will find that you are not any worse for having done it! As you continue the practice, you will begin to enjoy it and may finally find yourself looking forward to its "sweet stillness."

How One Little Boy Grew Up to "Sit in the Silence"

Once upon a time there was a lively little boy who accompanied his parents to the midweek prayer service at their church, though he personally considered it a waste of time. His objection was that nothing seemed to happen at these services: There would be a prayer, a few songs, and the minister would say a few words about prayer and healing. But most of the hour would be spent by the minister and congregation "sitting in the silence."

This little boy thought it foolish for his parents to come so far and sit for an hour with these people doing nothing. After everyone had been in silent prayer for a long time one night, this child jumped up and yelled: "Wake up, everybody! It's time to go home!"

Years later, this man realized the great power that had been generated in those prayer periods in his childhood, and he seriously took up the practice of the prayerful silence. He became so fascinated with its power that he finally became a minister. The day even came when he, too, conducted prayer meetings in his church which consisted of "sitting in the silence"—where nobody seemed to do anything!

HOW TO BE SPIRITUALLY READY FOR THE SILENCE

Prayer is effort; then becomes effortlessness. The silence is the effortless phase of prayer.

These "do nothing" prayer times can be among the most fruitful and rewarding of your life, once you are ready for them spiritually. Too many people try to be "advanced" in prayer, scoffing at the prayers of relaxation, denial, affirmation, concentration, and even meditation.

They state that they have gone "beyond" these types of prayer, and that they practice the silence only. *The prayer of silence, however, is creative, satisfying, productive only for those people who are ready for it spiritually, for those who have already worked their way through the other phases of prayer, and for those who readily use the other types of prayer.*

The average person has many old negative memories and psychological blocks that must be cleared up through prayers of relaxation, denial and affirmation, before he can possibly practice concentration, meditation, and the silence. *If one attempts to practice the silence before mastering the other types of prayer first, he will only meet with frustration.* He has not cleared the way to make contact with the innermost part of his being, out of which the silence comes.

In due time, as you practice the other types of prayer, you come to a period in which you are ready to practice the silence. When you reach that point in your spiritual unfoldment, you will know it because you will find that other forms of prayer no longer satisfy you or meet your spiritual needs. There will be an inner longing that turns your attention within in a waiting, receptive manner.

When you reach this point in your prayer development, you may find that your prayers are no longer being answered. No lesser method of prayer than the silence satisfies. It is then you are ready to launch forth into the prayer of silence.

In his book entitled *The Silence*,[2] E. V. Ingraham has written about its rewards:

> In the silence, man brings himself to a realization of the good for which he has long sought in vain.

ALL THE TRULY GREAT PEOPLE PRACTICE THE PRAYERFUL SILENCE

Practice of the silence clears away trivial thought and opens an inner channel through which results can then flow forth from infinite mind within. This method has been used by every genius, inventor, and philosopher of note throughout the ages: Buddha, Moses, Jesus, Mohammed, St. Benedict, Spinoza, Thoreau, Carlyle, Emerson—all of them knew that the power of solitude was among the most important practices in the art of fulfilled living.

The mystics of old described it as the art of "holy indifference." Brother Lawrence regarded the silence as a "holy inactivity."

Plotinus, the greatest philosopher of the Neoplatonist school, wrote in the 3rd Century: "We can pray only when we come

---

[2] E. V. Ingraham, *The Silence* (Lee's Summit, Mo.: Unity School of Christianity, 1922).

alone to the Alone." St. John of Damascus described solitude as "the mother of prayer." The individual nature of the prayer of great religious souls expressed itself in this solitariness.

There is a theory that great people often have a "period of obscurity" and that those "lost years" are times in which they gain wisdom, strength, and emotional stamina for the periods of intense activity and great achievement that lie ahead.

Jesus apparently observed an eighteen-year period of silence and obscurity prior to beginning his public ministry. His greatest works in his public ministry were always performed after He went up into the mountains and observed creative periods of silence.

Moses spent forty years in the silence of the Midian Desert tending sheep, in creative preparation for leading two million people out of bondage. Both David and Paul went into periods of obscurity after realizing they had divine missions to accomplish— David into the wilderness of Southern Judah, and Paul into Arabia. Those obscure periods prepared them for the work that lay ahead. Both later wrote of the importance of the silence: David, when he said, "My soul wait thou (in silence) for God only, for my expectation is from him" (Psalms 62:5). Paul, when he advised the early Christians, "Abound more and more, study to be quiet" (I Thess. 4:11).

It was in the silence of the temple that little Samuel first heard Jehovah's call. He responded, "Speak, for thy servant heareth" (I Samuel 3:10). Out of the silence Samuel soared forth to become the foremost figure of his age.

Many of the prophets and leaders of Israel were prepared for their work by the discipline of fasting from speech. The voice in the wilderness was felt to be a clearer revelation of God than earthquake, fire or storm to the prophet Elijah, who described God as "a still, small voice" (I Kings 19:12).

In almost all periods of religious history, in every part of the world, silence has been suggested as a preparation of the soul for spiritual contact. A 14th Century A.D. Chinese philosopher put it succinctly: "If a man keeps his mouth shut, his words become powerful."

The Greek essayist, Plutarch, stated: "In sacrifices, religious mysteries, and ceremonies of divine science we receive by tradition the command to keep silent. Silence is a mythical secret and a divine virtue."

The unspoken word was both center and circumference of the ancient Hindu religions and philosophies, as it was also of Buddhism. *Persian, Arabian, Greek, Hebrew and Christian mystics have all preached the discipline of silence as a way to find God.* Egyptian mystical worship called God "the Lord of the Silent."

The ancient Hebrews substituted the vowels of "Adonai" (Lord) and "Elohim" (God) for those of the sacred name Jahweh (Jehovah), so as to avoid uttering carelessly the name of the Almighty. The tradition among the ancient Druids of Wales, known as "the All-Knowing Ones," was to guard in silence the things that they had learned about their God who was "forever sacred and secret."

Socrates practiced silence as a means of inner culture, while the Greek philosopher, Pythagoras, required that his disciples observe an absolute silence for as much as from one to five years.

A number of the early Christian mystics spent several years alone practicing the silence, before ministering in powerful ways to the people of their era. Among the Christian Fathers, St. Augustine in particular insisted upon solitude and silence for one who would find God, and this practice descended to the various monastic orders. St. Catherine of Sienna spent three years alone in her house practicing the silence, and then went forth to pour out her spiritual power to the world. Her tremendous influence was felt among the heads of state as well as among the leading priests, soldiers, artists, merchants, lawyers and politicians of her day. They were all attracted to the serenity and wisdom she had gained from her years alone in the silence.

A well-known sect in modern times which practices the silence is the Quakers. To them God is an "inner light." It is interesting to note that, during the two hundred years of our early Colonial history when thousands of our colonists were attacked and killed by the Indians, the Quakers, who numbered more than any other group of outlying pioneers and who differed from the rest in an outer way only in that they never pulled in their latch strings at

night and never carried a gun by day, were always left un-
touched. Not a child, man or woman of the Quaker faith was hurt
by the Indians! Of course, their secret weapon was their knowledge and practice of the silence.

In his booklet *The Lord's Prayer*,[3] Glenn Clark reminds us that
20th Century religion needs to rediscover the power of the
silence:

> When one experiences a thing, he does not talk about it.
> He grows still and rests in it. The bane of our churches today
> is their much talking. A Chinese philosopher was once asked
> what he thought of the Christian religion. "Well," he said
> slowly, "it is a very talky religion."
>
> The first thing required, then, for a deeper outpouring of
> the spirit, first in our individual lives, and then in the lives
> of the world, is for us to *get still*. American churches cannot
> Christianize the world until they themselves have learned
> how to be still.

SILENCE IS IN EVERY ELEMENT OF DYNAMIC NATURE

We see the principle of the silence operating in every element
of nature: The night quiet after the day; the quiet going out of
the tide after it has noisily come in; the bare silent winter after
the profuse and bustling harvest beginning with spring, summer, and then fall; the creation story of six days of activity followed by the spiritual silence of the Sabbath.

Fishermen have a saying: "There is a time to fish and a time to
dry the nets." We all need to "dry our nets" occasionally. Periods
of silence are periods of "drying the nets."

Have you ever watched a ship going through a lock? When it
moves into the lock, it cuts off its own power, it rests, it stands
still. If the ship is going upsteam, the water in the lock slowly
rises and lifts it to a higher level, and then, when the gate is
opened, it moves forward again at that higher level. Just so with
man, when he "cuts off his engine" and dares to be silent.

The farmer knows about the power of silence in connection

---

[3] Glenn Clark, *The Lord's Prayer* (St. Paul, Minn.: Macalester Park Publishing
Company, 1932).

with the soil. He calls it "soil conservation" or "crop rotation." A good farmer refuses to plant any piece of land with the same crop year after year. He knows this depletes the soil. He will often plant that area with rye, then plow it under to enrich the soil. He knows *there must be an "inworking" before there can be an "out-working."*

Philosophers of all ages have taught that a person of no silence is like a tree with no roots, which is turned to leaves and boughs, and must eventually wither and die. The Chinese philosophers have a saying: "In returning to the root is rest."

THE HEALING POWER OF THE SILENCE

The silence is to the soul what food is to the body. Incessant talk, incessant activity, give the soul no chance to express normally and stifle it, whereas the silence is a healing balm. Carlyle said, "The highest melody dwells only in silence—the melody of health."

Incessant talk and incessant activity cause the most marvelous of all mechanisms, the body, to get thrown out of balance, fly off at a tangent, and cause all its delicate organs to set up war against each other. On the other hand, in quietness the soul is given a chance to inaugurate its recuperative powers and send its vital, regenerative influences flowing through the complex system of nerves, veins, and arteries of the body.

When you give yourself up to the practice of the silence, the soul comes into its own again, and channels are opened for its rhythmic vibrations to restore hurried, discordant nerves to normal action.

It is then that this health jingle seems appropriate:

> Joy and temperance and repose,
> Slam the door on the doctor's nose!

How Silence Healed in a Hospital

A busy woman found herself in the hospital. She mentally resisted thinking, "What have I done to cause this? I have too much to do to be here. I just cannot waste my time in this way."

Since she worried, fretted, and remained in an agitated state, she did not get well. Then a minister came to visit her and in a quiet moment he said, "It is so restful to sit here. Just to be still, to be very, very still, and to know that God is here healing."

After the minister's visit, this lady meditated on the idea of stillness. She practiced the silence by stilling her mind with the words of the Psalmist, "Be still and know that I am God" (Psalms 46:10). When thoughts of agitation tried to take over, she said to them, "Peace, be still."

In this stillness, her mind and body began to relax, and a great sense of peace finally came, followed later by a sense of joy. She "let go" every care. In relaxed stillness, she slept without medication that night. When she went home two days later, she realized it was only in stillness and silence that her healing had come.

There is an Oriental proverb: "The flower of Truth blooms in the stillness, after the storm and stress of effort."

Another woman once went to a hospital for just the opposite reason—not because she was sick, but to keep from getting sick by getting away from her noisy family!

During the hospital stay, she was freed from c ntact with an embittered relative who had had an unhappy love affair. This relative had poured out her bitterness upon this woman, who then entered the hospital to get peace, quiet, and freedom from the poisoned emotions of her unhappy relative. As she quietly relaxed, rested more physically, and calmed her mind emotionally, doing inspirational reading and spending long periods in quiet meditation and silence, she realized the value of Longfellow's healing formula:

> Let us labor for an inward stillness,
> An inward stillness and an inward healing.

INFORMAL METHODS OF PRACTICING THE SILENCE

Informally there are several simple ways you can begin to practice the silence and reap its unlimited benefits:

First; by being still, quiet, listening in prayer.

Second; through the act of self-control as you keep quiet in daily living.

Third; through the act of withholding criticism, condemnation, judgment of others.

Fourth; through the act of refusing to talk idly, to chatter needlessly.

Fifth; through the act of saying in prayer, "It is done," when you have prayed for a season and perhaps have witnessed no visible results. This should be a time of "letting go and letting God."

The following stories relate how others have used these simple methods of practicing the silence in daily living with rewarding results.

HOW A MAN IN ADVERTISING BUSINESS REAPED REWARDS OF SILENCE

You can take up the practice of the silence informally by making a practice of being still, quiet, listening in prayer.

A man in the advertising business said he used to sit down at his typewriter in the morning and try to turn out so many ideas in so many hours. He often strenuously produced the ideas, but felt dissatisfied about their content.

Then he learned to sit for about fifteen minutes each morning, waiting in the silence, before starting his work. He thought of God as the source of all ideas and as the creator of everything, and he asked that divine ideas be expressed in his work. As he quietly waited, out of the silence feelings, ideas, and phrases would come to him and he found himself eager to put them on paper. Practicing the silence each morning before beginning his work proved to be the turning point to his success.

The practice of the silence leads to power and increased productivity. Whatever you have to do, whether it be housework, farmwork, factory work, office work, handwork, or brainwork, you can get much more done in far less time if you take time out every day to do nothing but sit in silent communion for a time.

As you daily practice the silence, you will find confusion leaving your mind; you will feel a sense of inner peace and power, and you may even hear the "still small voice" of God as did Elijah.

I have found that my greatest inspirations and clearest guidance about personal and professional matters come when I have seasons of just being silent, open, receptive, listening.

First comes a sense of peace, followed by a sense of power. Next, a flow of ideas is often followed by a flow of energy which wells up from deep within. Isaiah had doubtless had this same experience when he wrote: "They that wait for Jehovah shall renew their strength" (Isaiah 40:31).

Edward Everett Hale tells a story about the little girl who had a habit of running into a chapel near the field where she played to talk to God. After she talked a bit she would get perfectly still for a few minutes, "waiting," she said, "to see if God wanted to say anything" to her. Though she did not hear literal words, often a great happiness welled up within her, and her life always seemed richer and fuller after these waiting periods.

HOW THE PRACTICE OF THE SILENCE CAN BRING MORE FRIENDS

The second way you may informally begin to practice the silence in daily living is through the act of self-control, of keeping quiet in daily activities.

A housewife recently said:

> I used to pride myself on being what I like to call "frank." But I was always in "hot water" with relatives and friends because I never hesitated to give them my honest opinion, which wasn't always complimentary. People seldom appreciate that kind of frankness because it is usually a form of disapproval or criticism. I finally learned if I cannot say something kind and constructive, I had better hold my tongue. Now I get along better and have more friends.

James Watt, Scottish engineer and inventor, is said to have conceived the idea of harnessing the power of steam through watching the rise and fall of the lid above the boiling water in his mother's teakettle. *Uncontrolled, steam is only a noisemaker.* Under control, it can drive trains across the continent, propel great liners across the ocean, generate electricity to light homes and cities and to run the wheels of industry.

When you are tempted to listen to the futile chatter around you, or to dissipate your own mental and spiritual forces in idle talk, remember the proverb: "Whosoever keepeth his mouth and his tongue, keepeth his soul from troubles" (Proverbs 21:23).

THE TRIUMPH THAT ONLY SILENCE CAN BRING

The third way mentioned that you can informally practice the silence is through the act of withholding criticism, condemnation and judgment of others.

There once was a housewife who was noted for her sharp tongue and scolding, nagging personality. Her husband tried to escape from it by drinking, and her children retaliated with very bad behavior. There was no harmony or cooperation in this home.

Finally this woman's health was affected, and she sought medical relief, to no avail. In desperation she sought out a spiritual counselor, who quickly informed her that her own sharp tongue was the cause of all her problems, both in her health and in her home. The counselor further said she would be helped only if she bridled her tongue, practiced harmonious thinking, and became silent in her speech.

With effort, this desperate woman became quiet and stayed quiet. When her husband arrived home drunk at night, she reacted only with silence. As she refrained from endlessly reprimanding him and the children an amazing thing happened: Gradually her husband's drinking diminished and finally ceased. One by one the children became more cooperative. Finally order and harmony were restored to the home. Peace and joy came into the atmosphere, and even the health problems disappeared.

One day when they could finally communicate again, her husband asked what had brought about all these pleasant changes.

This formerly "nagging wife" quietly replied, "Practicing the silence has transformed me and our lives."

In his book, *Honey and Salt*,[4] Carl Sandburg wrote:

> By the gong of time you live.
> Listen and you hear time saying you were silent long before
> you came to life and you will again be silent long after you
> leave it.
> *Why not be a little silent now?*
> *Hush yourself, noisy little man.*

THE INFINITELY PROSPERING POWER
OF THE SILENCE

The fourth method mentioned for informally practicing the silence in daily living was through the act of refusing to talk idly, to chatter needlessly.

"I was struggling and striving like mad, running in circles, and talking my head off, trying to make a go of my trucking business," a young man said, "until my nerves went to pieces and I was in an accident. Flat on my back, I had to be quiet for a while. I had time to think and got on the beam. Since then, I no longer struggle.

"I have learned to relax and listen to the voice of God within. *I never dreamed there could be such power in quietness! I have found that it is only when I'm still that God gives me the answer to my problems and shows me what to do.* He runs the universe without a lot of fussing and fuming and He knows how I should run my business better than I ever did. I have a bank balance to prove it. But I have something even better: satisfied customers, appreciative employees, and inner peace."

This man had discovered what the athletes meant by "pressing." When athletes try too hard they call it "pressing." They lose rhythm and fall short of peak performance.

He also discovered that if you do not willingly practice the

---

4 Carl Sandburg, *Honey and Salt* (New York: Harcourt, Brace & World, Inc., 1963).

silence, you may be forced to do so through negative circumstances that result from lack of quietness. When this happens it can be a blessing in disguise. There is an old mystical saying: "Darkness is but the mantle which closes round about to bring stillness to the soul."

HOW TO KNOW WHEN TO REST YOUR CASE!

The fifth method of informally practicing the silence in daily living is that of "letting go and letting God" after you have tried in inner and outer ways to make things right in your life. Just get silent with God and man. *Let go and let God.*

This method of the silence is very much like a lawyer "resting his case," after he has presented it to the judge and jury. It is in this state of "resting his case" that he awaits the decision of the judge. *It is only after he "rests his case" that the processes of law begin to operate.* At this point, all concerned withdraw their efforts and wait to learn in what manner the law itself will move.

How do you let go and let God at this point? How do you rest your case?

One woman had remarkable answers to prayer only after she released her prayers to God saying, "Father, I'm trusting." Whenever fear or doubt would try to creep in she would reaffirm, "Father, I'm trusting!" Her prayers were always answered.

A very discouraged woman had spent five years running a boardinghouse. It was a job of long, hard hours and strenuous work which she had been forced to take after her husband's death. One day, feeling she could stand it no longer, she sought out a spiritual counselor and poured out her unhappiness.

The counselor quietly replied, "Nothing was ever gained by fighting. What you fight always fights back. Before you can be free of this distasteful job, you must learn to love the place where you are and know that you are doing God's work, even if it is only washing pots and pans in a boardinghouse. Then you must pray and trust God to lead you to something better."

The prayer she was given to use was this: "I PLACE MYSELF AND ALL MY AFFAIRS LOVINGLY IN THE HANDS OF THE FATHER, WITH A

CHILDLIKE TRUST. THAT WHICH IS FOR MY HIGHEST GOOD SHALL COME TO ME."

During the long hours of the days and nights that followed, this previously embittered woman declared over and over amid the pots and pans, mops and cleaning utensils, "LOVINGLY IN THE HANDS OF THE FATHER."

At first nothing happened, nothing changed in an outer way, though much was changing within this woman's thoughts and feelings. Then two real estate men appeared one day and said they were looking for someone to manage a large, luxury hotel nearby.

This woman's heart sang because this had been her dream—to work amid beautiful surroundings where she could be meeting interesting people. As she continued affirming "LOVINGLY IN THE HANDS OF THE FATHER," she was offered the job and took it.

These words then became her secret text for success in her new assignment. Many times a day she declared, "LOVINGLY IN THE HANDS OF THE FATHER." One day the owner of the hotel said, "The whole atmosphere has changed since you took over managing the hotel. It is what I have always desired it to be. Now we never have an empty room and the class of people we are attracting are the kind I've always wanted here." She thanked him and as she walked away she said again, "IT IS LOVINGLY IN THE HANDS OF THE FATHER."

If there is some challenge in your life that has not been resolved after diligent prayer, like this woman you may need to "rest your case." Try practicing the silence. *Stop talking about the problem.* Place it "lovingly in the hands of the Father." Declare, "FATHER, I AM TRUSTING." Then do so! Let go and let God.

Many people's prayers are not answered because they do not practice the silence. Did you ever notice how impossible it is for you to help the person who loves to rehearse his difficulties? He cannot receive the answers to his prayers until he gets quiet and listens, because his mind is too crowded with the problem to receive the answer. Quiet listening is the only assured way one can receive answers.

HOW TO FORMALLY PRACTICE THE SILENCE

In order to experience fully the results of the silence, there comes a time when it is wise to have daily periods of practicing the silence in a more formal way than heretofore described.

Indeed, there comes a time in your prayer development when you must learn to let the mental, reasoning side of your nature alone. You must learn how to be still and listen to that which a loving Father would say to you through the intuitional side of your nature. The guidance you crave will come out of the deep silence within you, if you will get still and listen for it there.

Most people do not realize that they have this powerfully silent area within them, that this silence is nothing new or foreign, but a part of them. When they turn within and become attuned to it, they find it their greatest power.

The steps in practicing the prayer of the silence are these:

1. Relax your mind and body. "I RELAX AND LET GO. I LET GO AND LET GOD."

2. Turn your attention within, closing the eyes and quieting the mind. "I AM RELAXED IN MIND AND BODY."

3. Dwell upon the nature and presence of God, thereby establishing contact: "THERE IS ONLY ONE PRESENCE AND ONE POWER, GOD THE GOOD. GOD'S GOODNESS IS RIGHT HERE WITHIN ME AND AROUND ME NOW."

4. Continue to still your random thoughts by saying to them: "PEACE, BE STILL."

5. Then listen. If no conscious revelation or impression comes, give thanks for perfect results, and when you have experienced an inner feeling of peace, satisfaction, serenity, and a sense of well being, conclude your silence period. Inspiration and fulfillment may come later, since you have made inner contact.

6. Conclude your silence periods with a word of thanks for divine fulfillment: "FATHER, I THANK THEE THAT THOU HEARDEST ME, AND I KNOW THAT THOU HEAREST ME ALWAYS." Or, "IT IS DONE. THE PERFECT FINISHED RESULTS NOW MANIFEST." Or, "NOT BY

POWER, NOR BY MIGHT, BUT BY GOD'S SPIRIT, IT IS DONE." "THIS IS A TIME OF DIVINE FULFILLMENT."

Then get busy in an outer way, with your daily activities. You will carry with you into your world of activity the stored up energy, inspiration, and sense of tranquillity gained from the silence, thereby having achieved your purpose. Achievement will follow.

7. Make your beginning silence periods short—only two or three minutes.

Practice the silence more and more often: early in the morning, last thing at night, at odd moments during the day. The silence is not a spectacular time for seeing lights, hearing voices, or having unusual experiences. It is simply a time of quiet, peaceful, inner renewal.

8. Do not be discouraged if your silence periods do not yield anything in particular. Only by practice can you develop a consciousness of spiritual power that you seek in the silence. Practice makes perfect.

Often you will discover that it is after these silence periods that your greatest revelations come—through thoughts that flow into your mind, through words you read in a book, through something someone says that seems to contain special significance for you, or perhaps through dreams. In countless ways, the fruits of the silence will be gradually revealed to you.

THE FRUITS OF THE SILENCE

Though nothing definite or spectacular may happen in your silence periods, you will find some quietly rewarding results taking place within you after practicing the silence.

You will develop a strange new consciousness of serenity and quiet, a feeling that something has been done, that some new power to overcome is yours. The hard things in life become easier, the troublesome things will no longer have as much power to worry you, the rasping people and conditions of the world will lose their power to annoy you.

When you have learned how to abandon yourself to infinite

spirit and have sessions of doing this daily, you will be surprised at the marvelous change that will be wrought in you without any conscious effort on your part. It will search far below your conscious mind and root out things in your nature of which you had scarcely been conscious.

As you continue practicing the silence daily, you will stop being so humanly strenuous. (There is an Arab proverb: "*Hurry is the devil.*") The feeling of being so important, of having so much to do, will leave you.

The petty personality problems will begin to fall away from you: anger, fear, jealousy, impatience, depression. You will let go trivial things, activities, people. You will learn to say "no" to the lesser. You will have clearer insight about everything and will dare to follow that insight unhesitatingly. You will clear the clutter out of your life.

Previously, through intensity and hurry you have shut off the divine power within you. Through practicing the silence you will now find yourself rising out of this state of tension, into one of living trust. It is in this new state of quiet trust that the highest work is done in prayer. *There are some things which you are to do for yourself in your prayer experiences, but there are others which God does not expect you to do!*

For instance, with your conscious mind you are to speak the word of life, truth, abundance, health, peace, and you are to act as though the words are true. But the bringing of them to pass is the work of that Higher Power. *Its ability to work depends on your trusting by getting very still inside. It is when you get beyond the point where you try to do it all yourself and let God do His part, that you get the desires of your heart.*

There are ten direct references in the Bible to "stand still" in the face of challenging circumstances, beginning with Moses who instructed the children of Israel concerning how they were to escape from Egyptian bondage:

> Fear ye not, stand still, and see the salvation of Jehovah which he will work for you today; for the Egyptians whom ye have seen today, ye shall see them again no more forever.

Jehovah will fight for you, and ye shall hold your peace (Exodus 14:13, 14).

Just prior to being anointed king, Saul was instructed by Samuel to "stand thou still first, that I may cause thee to hear the word of God" (I Samuel 9:27).

The turning point from destruction to restoration of all God's blessings came in Job's life only after he followed the instructions: "Hearken unto this, O Job. Stand still, and consider the wondrous works of God" (Job 37:14).

These promises clearly reveal that one of the rewards of the silence is that the Lord can produce perfect results in your life, too, but only after you learn to hold your peace.

The anonymous 14th Century mystic who wrote *The Cloud of Unknowing* explained that there are two kinds of "life in the spirit": One is the active life and the other is the contemplative life. He states that the active life is lower, and the contemplative life is higher.

Dr. Robert Russell has explained in his book, *God Works Through the Silence*,[5] that "the way to immunize ourselves from the lesser things of life and to open ourselves to the greater ones is the way of the silence."

I trust that something in this chapter has helped you realize the great possibilities and rewards of practicing the prayer of silence, thereby developing the contemplative life, which *is* the highest phase of the spiritual way of life, and which will bring the most satisfying results in both the inner and outer phases of your world.

SUMMARY OF CHAPTER 9

1. The prayer of silence brings vast improvement in one's life because the silence is creative and prosperous.
2. Whatever your heart craves, or your life needs, may be contacted in the silence which is the source of all creative and prospering power.

---

[5] Robert Russell, *God Works Through the Silence* (Denver, Colo.: The Shrine of the Healing Presence, 1956)

3. Achievement is not always the result of struggle and strife. Sometimes the greatest rewards are won by the leisurely expectant. Strife does not win anything but temporary results. Knowing how to wait is always more permanently effective.

4. The prayers of the silence can be the most fruitful and rewarding of your life, once you are ready for them spiritually. The prayer of silence is creative, satisfying, productive, financially rewarding only for those people who are ready for it spiritually, for those who have already worked through the other phases of prayer, and for those who readily use the other types of prayer.

5. Practice of the silence clears away trivial thought and opens an inner channel through which rich results can flow forth from infinite mind within.

6. Informal methods of practicing the silence include:
   (1) Being still, quiet, listening in prayer.
   (2) The act of self-control as you keep quiet in daily living.
   (3) The act of withholding criticism, condemnation, judgment of others.
   (4) The act of refusing to talk idly, to chatter needlessly.
   (5) The act of saying in prayer "It is done," when you have prayed, yet have witnessed no results.

7. The steps in formal practice of the prayer of silence are these:
   (1) Relax your mind and body.
   (2) Turn your attention within.
   (3) Dwell upon the nature of God, decreeing some sacred name, text or affirmation.
   (4) Still your random thoughts with "peace."
   (5) Listen.
   (6) Conclude your silence with words of thanks.
   (7) Externalize your attention.
   (8) Make your silence periods short at first.

8. The fruits of the silence include a strange new consciousness of serenity and quiet, and all grace of richness in spiritual and material things.

10

The Prayer for Realization
That Gets Results

The prayer that gets results is the prayer of realization. The word "realization" means "a feeling." To realize is to feel, make real, accomplish, to acquire as a result, to conceive vividly as real.

This is what you are trying to accomplish as you study the various phases of prayer described in this book. You have sought to get the feeling of inner contact, the feeling of accomplishing results, or just a vivid feeling of peace, serenity, and that all is well.

Many people's prayers are not answered because they never get such an inner realization. *They do not work in prayer long enough or often enough to attain the feeling of answered prayer.* They observe short periods of verbal prayer or the silence, and then rush off wondering why their prayers have not been answered.

How a Complex Human Relations
Problem Was Cleared Up

A businessman faced complex human relations problems. To outer appearances there was nothing he could do. The power to produce satisfactory results seemed to be controlled by other people, who were hostile to him. In spite of this, he realized that if he could gain a realization of answered prayer, the good would manifest regardless of what others were doing or saying.

He began to declare with authority: "WITH GOD THERE IS ALWAYS A WAY. GOD IS NOW OPENING THE WAY TO PERFECT RESULTS IN THIS SITUATION. I AM IN RIGHT RELATIONSHIP WITH ALL PEOPLE AND ALL SITUATIONS NOW. THE GOOD IS NOW VICTORIOUS!"

He persisted in this declaration until he gained an inner realization of peace, and a vivid feeling that all was well. When he got that realization, he gave thanks for perfect results, dismissed the matter, and kept re-releasing it every time the troublesome subject entered his mind.

Suddenly the tide turned and his good began to work through the very people and conditions who had seemed hostile to him. Without knowing or caring what his desires in the matter were, these people began unconsciously to fulfill them anyway! His own prayer of vivid realization had opened the way.

HOW TO IDENTIFY WITH THE PRAYER OF REALIZATION

The prayer of realization is the prayer that gives you a good feeling. That good feeling may come as a sense of peace or it may come as one of electric excitement. But it produces a vivid feeling that all is well.

Charles Fillmore has explained the prayer of realization in his book, *Atom Smashing Power of the Mind:*[1]

> Spiritual realization changes things. In scientific prayer, realization is the high point of attainment.

HEALING OF BREAST ACCOMPLISHED THROUGH REALIZATION IN PRAYER

Many more people would experience answered prayer if they would just persist in prayer long enough to attain that vivid feeling of realization. Prayer can only do for you what it can first do through your thoughts and feelings. *Effective prayer works from the inside out.*

You do not have to get a spiritual realization in order for your

---

[1] Charles Fillmore, *Atom Smashing Power of the Mind* (Lee's Summit, Mo.: Unity School of Christianity, 1949).

prayers to have power, but realization is a sure indication that you have made inner contact, and that your prayers *will* be answered. Even though you can be helped—things can improve through prayer without your experiencing realization—usually the matter is not completely cleared up until you get a vivid feeling about it. Therefore, *realization is worth working for in prayer, because it produces completed results.*

A young businesswoman feared cancer of the breast. She had been under doctor's care for some time but meditation had rendered no improvement. Finally the doctor informed her that she should go to the hospital within a week for a biopsy and further tests. He tried to prepare her for the worst.

After returning from the doctor's office, this young woman wrote two letters: The first was to *Silent Unity* requesting their prayers for her healing. The second was to a friend who had proved a powerful prayer partner in the past.

There was no noticeable improvement until the day before she was scheduled to go to the hospital for tests. Then she noticed that some activity was occurring in the troubled area. By the next morning the lump that had been the size of a pecan was no larger than a pea. When the doctor examined it, he explained that what remained was nothing more than harmless scar tissue that probably would remain indefinitely. (It later disappeared too.)

Her prayer partner later wrote a letter saying:

"I usually sit in my big chair and pray for about fifteen minutes each night just before retiring. Last Thursday night (the night before you were to go to the hospital), I started to pray but somehow all I could think about was your healing, that it had begun and would continue. I knew then that our prayers for your health were being answered."

SPIRITUAL PREDICTION FOR THIS CENTURY COMING TRUE

Perhaps you think such experiences are "unusual" in these modern times when we hear so much about poverty, war, crime, and disease. They are not unusual, as reported in my book *The*

Dynamic Laws of Healing. But such good news is rarely shouted from the housetops nor does it get headlines in the press.

In the late 1890's the English medical doctor Richard Bucke predicted that the spiritual consciousness in man, which he called "cosmic consciousness" (also the title of his book), would soon become common thinking for everyone.

When Dr. Bucke spoke to the British Medical Association in Montreal in 1894, he told those physicians that this divine phase of man's being known as "cosmic consciousness" was even then becoming increasingly common and that it would eventually become general. Dr. Bucke also predicted that the development of the spiritual phase of the mind would soon lift the whole of human life to a higher level.

Dr. Bucke was a medical doctor who had had a spiritual awakening and dared to tell the world about it. He even dared to predict the spiritual evolution of mankind. He stated that the human race was in the process of developing a new kind of consciousness, far in advance of the present one, and that this new kind of consciousness would lift the race above and beyond the fears, ignorance and brutalities that beset it.

Certainly in this century, Dr. Bucke's predictions have been coming true. More and more people have quietly taken up a spiritual quest and have begun to develop their innate spiritual powers.

You don't hear much about them. You hear just the opposite—that the world is "going to the dogs." But in spite of all you hear, more people are quietly seeking spiritually in this century than at any time since the 1st or 2nd Century after Christ! They are doing so through a private search and they are keeping quiet about it. But the inner world of spirit is being discovered, explored and contacted as Dr. Bucke predicted it would be.

This is not unusual but follows a pattern:

History reveals that the great periods of mystical activity tend to correspond with the great periods of artistic, material, and intellectual civilization. As a rule, great periods of spiritual activity come immediately after and seem to complete such other periods. When science, politics, literature, and the arts have risen to their height and produced their greatest works, the mystics have then appeared and carried on, as though to give spiritual balance to these various areas of achievement!

Between the 1st Century A.D. and the 19th Century, this curve exhibited three great waves of mystical activity, besides many minor fluctuations. They came at the close of the Classical, the Medieval, and the Renaissance Periods in history, reaching their highest points in the 3rd, 14th, and 17th Centuries.

We can see why there has been so much spiritual searching in this 20th Century, which has also been a century of much scientific and intellectual discovery. Dr. Bucke's heartening prediction about man's spiritual evolution is in the process of quietly coming true!

HOLY TELEPATHY: HOW TO GET TRUE REALIZATION THROUGH PRAYER

Prayer has been described as "holy telepathy." *Surely the prayer of realization is the prayer of holy telepathy.*

You have heard much in recent years about "mental telepathy," where you become attuned in thought to some other person. But holy telepathy is an even higher activity of the mind, because in holy telepathy you become attuned in thought to a divine power and its indwelling presence within you.

That is the main purpose of prayer anyway. Not to get something but to be something, to find and express your indwelling divinity. Through the prayer of realization you make contact with the God power within you. This results in "holy telepathy" which, in turn, always brings appropriate results.

How does one get a realization in prayer that will assure results? Sometimes just by (1) asking for an inner assurance of answered prayer. (2) Sometimes just by dwelling upon the subject you need guidance about. (3) Sometimes just by affirming guidance and a realization of answered prayer. Any of these acts may result in a flash of "holy telepathy" that will reveal the answer to you. The following will indicate how you can develop the foregoing three methods.

How to Ask for Inner Assurance of Answered Prayer

Ten years ago I was overworked and underpaid in my first ministry and was suffering from near exhaustion from which there seemed no relief. One night while working late in my study, in a moment of despair I placed my head wearily on my desk and thought: "If this is what the ministry is all about, I won't last. I cannot believe that working so hard for so little and reaching so few people can be a loving Father's will. Surely there is a larger plan for my life and for my ministry than this."

Finally, I remembered to ask, "Father, what is the truth about this? What is the divine plan of my life? What is it that I am supposed to be doing in the ministry?"

Quick as a flash, on the inner plane I saw a stack of books, placed one on top of the other in a rather casual way. The stack was high. The books were big. Just as suddenly the vision was gone, though I can still see it mentally.

At that time I was writing magazine articles, but had no plans for writing books, nor any idea of what I would write books about. At first I was puzzled, then overwhelmed, because I realized how much work goes into writing. Nevertheless, within a year, through an orderly sequence of events, I was busy on my first book. Later, through another orderly sequence of events, a change in ministries gave me much more time to devote to writing. A far more balanced way of life with adequate time for rest and relaxation unfolded too.

That first book and others of mine are now beginning to stack up on my coffee table, just as they did in that inner flash ten years ago. There is still a large stack of books on the inner plane, though. I often see them. They are like unruly children, all clamoring to get my attention, impatient to be "born."

Often our prayers are answered in flashes of realization similar to this one, after we ask for guidance.

How to Receive Guidance by Dwelling on Subject

Sometimes a realization of answered prayer comes just by dwelling casually upon the subject you need guidance about and then by releasing it.

Last spring when I was planning to fly to Canada to lecture, one night late I was thinking that I must get my lecture notes made for that trip within the next few days. That night after turning out the light and relaxing, the main lecture for that trip, a banquet talk, came to me in three parts. The first part of the lecture started flowing in ideas to me so strongly that I turned on my light and made several pages of notes. Again the light went out and I prepared to sleep. Again, a flow of ideas started, which was the second part of the banquet talk. And the third part flowed forth an hour later, after I had again attempted to sleep. This time, the banquet talk was complete—at least in rough form. Thereafter, making final notes was a simple matter.

One spring during a yearbook deadline, an editor prayed for guidance about how she could have more time in her personal and professional life. Two mornings later, after dwelling for several days upon the truth that there should be time for everything, she awakened at 5 A.M. and a complete and workable plan for the next year's yearbook unfolded as rapidly as she could write it down. Exactly what to do in each section of the book was revealed. The end result would be a saving of time, energy, supplies, printing, and it would be a far better book, which it later proved to be.

How to Affirm Guidance Most Effectively

Sometimes just by affirming guidance and a realization of answered prayer, it comes.

It is wise to assert, decree, and declare it. Then you should stand fast in the vivid feeling that there is a right solution to every problem, a right answer to every prayer.

One lady often had amazing answers to prayer just by asserting over and over in the face of challenging experiences: "Prayer works!"

If you will begin to declare, affirm, decree this, you will find it coming true. For any situation that concerns you, begin now to declare, "THERE IS A RIGHT SOLUTION TO THIS SITUATION. THERE IS A RIGHT ANSWER TO THIS PRAYER."

Decreeing it over and over will give you a sense of peace and that is what you want. When you get that, the problem is well on the way to being resolved.

Repetition of truth has a tendency to open up the inner recesses of your mind to infinite power, and to allow it to flow forth as perfect, complete results.

YOUR INNER SENSING AND FEELING IS THE SECRET OF EFFECTIVE PRAYER

There was a period in the history of religion when there arose a division of thought as to the use of verbal prayers. Some said that prayer should be expressed silently, and, in the 17th Century, there grew up those groups called the Pietists and the Quietists who believed in quiet communion with God as the only method of prayer. But the former school of thought proclaimed that prayer was not prayer unless it was put into oral form and spoken. The majority of mankind was led to believe that prayer should and must be uttered aloud in definite words. So fixed prayers were formulated and people were taught to recite them. They were instructed to "say" their prayers.

The problem with just "saying" prayers was that the act of prayer became automatic with no feeling in it. *When the feeling was gone out of prayer so was its power, because only prayers with feeling or inner sensing have the necessary power in them to produce permanent, satisfying answers.*

Both schools of thought were right. Silent prayer and verbal prayer are both necessary. *The prayer method that helps you induce feeling is the one to use. The prayer with feeling is the prayer that brings realization, and realization produces results.*

You have often tried to solve your problems when you had not first gotten the right thought and the right feeling about those problems. The good works from within your God-nature outward. The answers come from the inside out.

When you have tried to master your problems without having first mastered your own thoughts and feelings about them, nothing much happened and frustration set in.

The creative activity of good must first take place within you before it can work for you, through you or round about you.

Knowing this, you stop trying to make things right in an outer way. Instead you get down to business spiritually within your own thoughts and feelings. You begin to work within yourself until you get a realization, a feeling, that all is well within. When you have mastered the problem there, the good manifests.

When you learn of the power of realization, you stop fighting your problems. You stop trying to force your good. You know that the only place you ever have to work out anything is on the inner plane of your own thoughts and feelings. When you have worked it out there, it is done. You can then let it alone and watch it come about in an outer way.

This kind of realization in prayer changes things. This kind of vivid feeling of well-being in prayer is result-getting. Such realizations are the high point of attainment in prayer. The famous lecturer and writer known only as "Neville" has written that "feeling is the secret," that a good feeling that comes in prayer is an inner assurance of outer results.

Regardless of how your realization comes, it is priceless. During the 17th Century, George Fox, founder of the Quakers, had a tremendous realization at the age of 24. He described it as an "opening" and stated: "In one quarter of an hour, I saw and knew more than if I had been many years at a university."

MANY PRAYER METHODS CAN BRING REALIZATION

Any of the prayer methods described in this book can give you a realization or feeling of answered prayer. Sometimes one prayer method will give you that feeling; sometimes another.

First: The Prayer of Relaxation, where you relax your mind and body and turn your attention within, often brings a realization of God's indwelling presence and power. Often realization comes as you breathe deeply and relax into this prayer: "I AM RELAXED IN MIND AND BODY. I AM OPEN AND RECEPTIVE TO MY HIGHEST GOOD WITHIN AND WITHOUT NOW."

Sometimes it is the relaxed attitude toward a problem that brings the realization of answered prayer.

A man recently wrote from England: "Not long ago I had a flat to let. It had been occupied for some time by a charming couple, and my wife and I were reluctant to advertise the vacancy lest we get tenants who would disappoint us. We decided to relax and leave the matter 'lovingly in the hands of the Father,' to let Him bring the right tenant knocking at the door.

"A week or so after we made this decision the telephone rang. It proved to be a wrong number, but before I could ring off, the voice on the other end of the wire said, 'I'm looking for a flat.' I asked him to come to see me, and he proved to be the tenant we were waiting for." How seemingly "indirect" was this prayer answered!

Second: The Prayer of Cleansing may be the one that brings a realization of answered prayer, as you dissolve negative appearances with the thought, "NO, no, no. I do not believe this." Or "No, no, no. I do not accept this," or such outright denials as "MY GOOD CANNOT BE LIMITED!" Also the prayers of forgiveness and release dissolve fear and bring a realization of peace and power.

One woman had so much trouble that she felt she was losing her mind. Then she began to declare over and over, "I DO NOT BELIEVE IT IS GOD'S WILL THAT I SHOULD BE IN TROUBLE, AND SO I DO NOT ACCEPT TROUBLE AS NECESSARY OR REAL IN MY LIFE." Over and over when troublesome thoughts or situations tried to take over her feelings she would declare Isaiah's promise: "THOU WILT KEEP HIM IN PERFECT PEACE WHOSE MIND IS STAYED ON THEE" (Isaiah 26:3). She was saved from her troubles, not only mentally and emotionally, but literally as conditions adjusted themselves.

Third: The Prayer of Decree for many people is the one that brings realization. Positively asserting words of truth releases tremendous spiritual power.

A lady who was sitting by her husband's sick bed suddenly realized that he appeared to be dying. Knowing that he was needed and wanted to remain on this earth plane, she began declaring over and over, "GOD IS LOVE, GOD IS LOVE, GOD IS LOVE!" That was the only prayer she could think of at the moment. It worked, as it gave her a sense of peace and harmony. Soon her husband rallied and he later completely recovered.

Another woman and her family were in great trouble. She knew that they could not endure much more strain. She could think of no words to decree except the name, "JESUS CHRIST." That became her secret text. As she used it many times daily, her family came through to safety.

Both of these women had proved the words of E. V. Ingrahm in his booklet, *The Silence:*[2]

> To be true to the fact that there is but one Presence and One Power is to be possessed of the key to a correct solution of life's problems.

Fourth: Sometimes it is *the Prayer of Concentration* that gives you the feeling of answered prayer. In concentration, you keep resting your mind on an idea; often by holding to one idea, that idea opens up its secrets to you. Then you find yourself suddenly realizing the truth about that idea, which you had not been able to see before. That is the quiet power of concentration. A marvelous prayer statement to use for this purpose is this: "TRUTH, TRUTH, TRUTH, MANIFEST THYSELF IN THIS SITUATION NOW. THAT WHICH IS HIDDEN SHALL BE REVEALED."

How the Author Attained Realization in Prayer of Concentration and Meditation

Once when I had been trying for many weeks to gain a realization of answered prayer about a troublesome human relations problem, it finally dawned on me that I needed to invoke the prayer of concentration; to get very emphatic in prayer about the situation because all lesser methods had failed.

---

[2] E. V. Ingrahm, *The Silence* (Lee's Summit, Mo.: Unity School of Christianity, 1922).

I asked a prayer partner who knew of this troublesome situation to join me in an afternoon session in the prayer room at the church. We spent an entire afternoon trying to gain a realization of answered prayer. Finally when all lesser prayers had not given us a sense of peace and well-being that we sought, we asked in a sense of quiet concentration: "TRUTH, TRUTH, TRUTH, MANIFEST THYSELF IN THIS SITUATION NOW. THAT WHICH IS HIDDEN SHALL BE REVEALED."

As we kept our minds on this idea, the thing that was revealed was that we should pray over and over the Lord's Prayer. We realized that the Lord's Prayer was filled with power from on high, having been given by Jesus as a result of His own strong spiritual realizations. We also realized that this prayer, perhaps above all others, was all-powerful because it had been used by praying people for twenty centuries.

We decided to boldly assert over and over in a loud voice the Lord's Prayer in an effort to gain a realization of victory in the face of this troublesome problem. The ancient people often spoke their prayer decrees over and over fifteen times when trying to gain a feeling of answered prayer. They believed that the number fifteen had a mystical power for breaking up hard conditions. Jesus had effectively spoken forth in a loud voice the decree, "Lazarus, come forth!" with amazing results (John 11:43).

As we slowly but loudly decreed each phrase from the Lord's Prayer over and over with authority, the troubled feeling within us began to diminish. Then as we said the Lord's Prayer the ninth time, we both stopped right in the middle of it as we gained a tremendous feeling that the problem had just been "broken up" within our thoughts and feelings. It was in great relief and thanksgiving that we continued decreeing the Lord's Prayer and concluded it after fifteen times.

Our realization proved right. When the block was resolved inwardly, the outer block was gone too. All involved quickly responded with right action. The hard condition had been dissolved. However, the turning point had not come until we had gained a vivid realization of peace about it. In this instance, it had taken an emphatic prayer method to bring that about.

The prayer through which realization comes is not the prayer that begs or beseeches God to do anything. The prayer that brings results is the one that asserts the truth positively, confidently.

Fifth: The Prayer of Meditation may bring your realization of answered prayer, as you take one basic idea, hold it in mind, let it begin to come alive, giving you other ideas or feelings related to it.

I have found it particularly powerful to meditate upon the name "JESUS CHRIST," when I am trying to get a realization of answered prayer. When you take the name "JESUS CHRIST," breathing it in and out a number of times with your eyes closed, and then begin to meditate upon that name, it will come alive within you and go to work for you in any situation or condition that concerns you. Often you can feel when the Christ consciousness has completed its work in your thoughts and feelings, because it subsides and that inner activity is terminated. All sense of hurt, confusion and concerns dissolves and subsides too, and peace returns. You know then that the work is done, you feel at peace, and all is well.

On one occasion I encountered a difficult situation that did not seem to clear up. There was one troublesome personality involved, who was causing many unnecessary problems for himself and countless other people.

I had prayed and blessed the situation and the person decreeing that "THIS PERSON IS A DIVINE IDEA IN THE MIND OF GOD AND IS NOW GUIDED INTO HIS TRUE PLACE," but I had not been able to get any clear feeling that this was actually happening. Things remained troubled; this person did not fade out of the picture nor conform to it.

One night when the situation had come to my attention again and something obviously needed to be done I thought, "If I can just get the right feeling about this situation, it will begin to clear up. The feeling is the thing. No one has gotten the right feeling about it yet."

I went to the church chapel and sat there alone in the dark for a long time trying to get into a peaceful, prayerful state of mind.

Finally I decreed aloud that "JESUS CHRIST IS IN CONTROL OF THIS SITUATION. NOT PEOPLE OR CONDITIONS, BUT JESUS CHRIST." And that "JESUS CHRIST IS HEALING THE MATTER IN HIS OWN WAY." After that I relaxed and meditated on the name "JESUS CHRIST," over and over breathing it in and out.

In a little while there was an inner click and it was as though the Christ consciousness had come alive within me. There was a feeling of vibrating power at work, as I kept meditating upon that name.

Previously there had been a sense of burden about the problem; it felt like a lump of hurt, concern, anxiety. But now as I meditated upon the name "JESUS CHRIST" and it came alive within my feeling nature in the area of the lungs and breath, it was as though the hurt, concern, anxiety and the pulsating power of the Christ consciousness suddenly met there in consciousness. Later in my meditation it felt as though that Christ consciousness had begun to surround, enfold and dissolve the burdensome problem, right there within me.

Finally the problem of hurt and concern seemed to have been completely dissolved by the tremendous vibration of the Christ consciousness as it worked deep within my meditation. Then the meditation gradually subsided, so that there was only a feeling of peace and quiet remaining. I knew then that the work was done in consciousness.

Very soon the outer picture changed. The troublesome personality found his true place in life, to everyone's relief and satisfaction.

Sixth: it may be through *the Prayer of Silence* that your realization comes, as you join the prophet in knowing that "in quietness and confidence shall be your strength" (Isaiah 30:15). In the prayer of the silence, you stop, look and listen.

Some of the world's greatest spiritual realizations came to those who went into the solitude of the silence. Every new creation in the sphere of religion had its origin in the prayer of silence. The silence has been the birthplace of most of the world religions, as well as the source from which have come great religious reformations.

It was on the lonely mountain of Sinai that Jehovah revealed Himself to Moses. It was in the stillness of prayer at the baptism by the Jordan that this same spirit came upon Jesus of Nazareth and revealed to Him the secret of His divinity and messianic task. It was in the lonely sojourn in the desert that Paul, who had been laid hold of by Christ at Damascus, realized he was to become an apostle to the Gentiles, an unheard-of thing in those days.

It was on a solitary mount near Mecca that Mohammed was called to be the messenger of Allah. It was on the remote crags of the highlands of Alverno that Francis of Assisi was visited by the resurrected Christ as he was in the solitude of prayer. It was in private struggles in prayer that Luther won at Worms that unshakable strength and assurance with which he became the great reformer. Even the gentle, self-renouncing sage of India, whose message of salvation to Asia became a world religion, through the prayer of silence became the founder of a religion.

Everything that has been great, new and creative in the history of religion rose out of the depths of silent prayer. And everything that is great, new and creative in the life of man began sometime somewhere in the silence. It was to such creative periods of the silence that Paul might have been referring when he advised, "Be ye transformed by the renewing of your mind, that ye may prove what is the good and acceptable and perfect will of God" (Romans 12:2).

REALIZATION THROUGH GROUP PARTICIPATION

Realization may not come through the formal act of prayer.
Sometimes in a more casual way—on the golf course or while driving your car, or just before dropping off to sleep at night, or early in the morning before arising, as you are in a relaxed, receptive mood—realization may come. However, the formal act of prayer usually induces that realization and starts it on its way into your conscious mind where you can recognize it.

Realization may come while you are reading a book, studying the Bible, attending an inspirational class or lecture, in a church service, or while you are talking with others along inspirational lines. There is something powerful about getting into a group of like-minded people when you are trying to get a realization of answered prayer. (For twenty years I have had prayer partners for this purpose, and highly recommend such an arrangement.)

How Prayer Was Tested in Scientific Experiments

Several years ago, Dr. William R. Parker, director of the speech clinic at the University of Redlands, California, conducted a scientific experiment in prayer which he later wrote about in his book entitled *Prayer Can Change Your Life*.[3]

The experiment was conducted as a test by psychologists to determine what part prayer might play in improving a person's life. The usual psychological tests were given. Then those tests were separated into three groups:

Group I were those receiving individual psychotherapy with no mention of prayer or religion.

Group II were the random pray-ers, those who prayed on their own every night at home without benefit of psychological insight or group prayer support of others.

Group III were the prayer therapy group, which met once a week for a two-hour session of psychological therapy and group prayer.

Two significant things came out of these experiments:

The first group, which received individual psychotherapy with no mention of prayer or religion, made some progress.

The second group of random pray-ers who prayed at home on their own made no progress.

The third group, the prayer therapy group, made the greatest progress!

Dr. Parker concluded from these experiments that *prayer is the most important tool in the reconstruction of a man's personality and way of life.*

---

[3] William R. Parker, *Prayer Can Change Your Life* (Englewood Cliffs, N.J.: Prentice-Hall, Inc., 1957).

The thing that interested me in Dr. Parker's experiments was the power of group therapy in prayer.

You are a part of a similar technique every time you attend a church service, or an inspirational class or lecture. You pray together and sit together considering uplifting ideas. There is tremendous power released in this procedure, because *two agreed tune in on a third power.* There is multiplied power in group therapy along spiritual lines. Psychology has placed much emphasis upon this method.

SOME EXAMPLES OF HOW REALIZATION WAS RECEIVED THROUGH PRAYER TELEPATHY

Often you will get a realization by sitting in a group of people who are considering uplifting ideas, when nothing else has given you that realization. Because there is a multiplied spiritual consciousness being generated by the group, you tune in on that multiplied power and get a realization.

A lady who always attended the midweek services at her church was in trouble one Wednesday. The bookkeeper could not find an item of thousands of dollars, which had been wrongly entered on the ledger so that nothing balanced. All day they looked for the mistake. As the time drew near to attend church that night, she considered breaking her rule of never missing a service, but decided against it.

When she entered the church chapel and relaxed for the first time that day, a sense of peace and relief enveloped her and she went into a deep meditation that renewed her mind and body. Suddenly she "saw" in a flash the bookkeeping entry and where it had been posted on the wrong ledger sheet. In an instant her problem was solved; but only after she got to church and joined in the uplifted unified consciousness she found there, and then got quiet, still, and listened.

To please his wife, a young bridegroom attended a lecture on healing that his father-in-law, a prominent church layman, was giving. The young son-in-law, who had never been interested in spiritual subjects, became fascinated with his father-in-law's talk.

On the way home from the lecture he was non-committal, but spent the night awake, considering all he had heard. Later he made a plane trip to a distant state to talk with a minister he had once met and admired. From that point on he was on his way spiritually. But his awakening had come at his father-in-law's lecture.

A woman was in much pain. Though medical aid had helped, it had not healed her. One day she attended the midday healing service at her church. She wondered if she would be able to sit through the service because of the pain. But as the congregation rose to sing, "I'm healed! Praise God, I'm healed!" her whole body responded to that idea. By the conclusion of the service her pain was gone and never returned. She had gotten a realization of healing by hearing others sing about it in church.

AFTER REALIZATION, THEN WHAT?

Regardless of how your realization comes, remember this:

First, Keep quiet about it so that you do not dissipate it.

Second, Remember that you may get a realization on the inner plane long before it works out as a visible result. (In some instances, I have waited years for my realizations of answered prayer to manifest, but always they have at the right time in the right way, when all the pieces of the puzzle were ready to fit together for the good of everyone involved.)

Once you get that vivid feeling, or that inner flash of answered prayer, just hold to it mentally. Do not disturb yourself if it is a long time in coming forth as a visible result. That realization came to encourage, inspire and assure you of further good. It will manifest as a result at the right time in the right way, if you keep quiet about it.

As Stella Terrill Mann has explained in her book, *How to Live in the Circle of Prayer:*[4]

> There is a spiritual law which says, "Tell no one," when you are working in prayer for anything.

---

[4] Stella Terrill Mann, *How to Live in the Circle of Prayer* (New York: Dodd, Mead & Co., 1959).

Perhaps the hardest part of the assignment is to keep quiet after you have gotten a realization of how things are to be, far in advance. The realization that I was to enter the ministry came a number of years before it actually happened. That realization was made clear to me one day when I opened my Bible asking for guidance and these words stood out "For to this end have I appeared unto thee, to appoint thee a minister and a witness" (Acts 26:16). For several years thereafter I would open my Bible, look at those words and then quickly shut my Bible again. This had been the call into the ministry to Paul from the Christ Himself. With Paul I later found that I, too, could not be "disobedient unto the heavenly vision" (Acts 26:19).

Third, be sure to recognize your realization when it comes:

It may appear as an excited, electrifying, uplifting feeling; or it may come as a quiet, peaceful feeling of power, harmony, bliss. It may come in a flash of ideas, or you may suddenly "see" the pictured result. To receive a realization is an exciting, satisfying experience usually. But later when its vividness and the assured feeling of results that usually accompanies it has faded, you may doubt that what you experienced had power.

Once when I was trying to get a realization concerning ministering to more people in the first church I served, in a flash I saw hundreds of people and assumed my prayer had been answered. All those people never appeared in that ministry, but I was soon traveling around the country lecturing to hundreds of people in church and convention groups.

A realization makes real. It accomplishes results on the spiritual and mental planes first. You conceive vividly as real a feeling or a flashed mental picture. That is your realization that makes real. It is the highest form of prayer.

Such a realization will banish every ill. It is the light that reduces darkness to nothingness. Prayer expands the mind to receive. Realization is receiving. Realization is answered prayer. You can help bring about more such realizations by declaring often:

"THERE IS A RIGHT SOLUTION TO EVERY SITUATION. THERE IS A RIGHT ANSWER TO EVERY PROBLEM. I HAVE FAITH THAT EVERY NEED

IS FULFILLED NOW. THERE IS DIVINE FULFILLMENT FOR EVERY NEED. I GIVE THANKS FOR DIVINE REALIZATION NOW!"

Realization changes things, people, situations and events for the better. The prayer of realization is the one worth working for, because it is all-powerful in its assurance of answered prayer.

SUMMARY OF CHAPTER 10

1. The prayer that gets results is the prayer of realization.
2. Spiritual realization changes things. In scientific prayer realization is the high point of attainment. Realization is worth working for in prayer because it produces completed results.
3. One may obtain realization by:
   1) Asking for an inner assurance of answered prayer.
   2) By dwelling upon the subject you need guidance about.
   3) By affirming guidance and a realization of answered prayer.
4. The prayer with feeling is the prayer that brings realization and produces results.
5. Any of the prayer methods heretofore described in this book can give you a realization or feeling of answered prayer.
6. Realization may not come through the formal act of prayer but in some informal way. It may also come through group participation that is spiritually uplifting, such as a prayer group, or a church service.
7. After you experience realization:
   1) Keep quiet about it so as not to dissipate it.
   2) Remind yourself that you may get a realization on the inner plane long before it works out as a visible result. Quietness and patience bring it to pass.
8. Realization changes things, people, situations, all for the better. The prayer of realization is worth working for because it assures answered prayer.

Epilogue—
After Prayer, Then What?

A sage once said: "He who rises from his prayer a better man, his prayer is answered."

For twenty years I have been searching out the mystical laws of prayer. The more I probed into the power of prayer, the more intrigued I became with its force for producing riches in both the little and big experiences in life, including financial supply to an overflowing degree.

But I soon discovered something:

You start out to get a problem of life solved. That's how you usually get "hooked on prayer." And you discover, if you stick with it, that prayer power *is* problem-solving power, in its own time and way. Sometimes there are immediate results. At other times the answers are slow—very slow—in coming.

But in that exasperating slowness, something else happens.

You find yourself contacting an inner world you never dreamed was there before. Even if you touch its mystical power only occasionally and briefly, that supernatural contact is enough to keep you going back for more.

It is only after the sweetness of prayer fades that you discover with a jolt that from the mountaintop of prayer you must descend again into the valley of outworking. First there must be the inworking, through the act of prayer. Then there must be the outworking, through the time after prayer when its sweetness may have faded and nothing seems to be happening.

Dr Evelyn Underhill, in writing of the prayer process in man, explained that the mystics of old did not stand aside wrapped in delightful prayers, feeling pure and agreeable to God. Instead, they got "right down in the mess, and there, right down in the mess, they were able to radiate God."

So don't feel badly if the same thing happens to you, and after prayer you find yourself back down in the mess of living, trying to radiate God. Instead, just consider yourself a modern mystic— one who has the mystic keys of prayer that can unfold the richness of life as described in this book.

HOW TO PREPARE RATHER THAN DESPAIR

A college professor recently observed: "I always get what I pray for, but it invariably involves more work than I had anticipated."

So after prayer, dare to work and prepare for the answer.

Prepare rather than *despair*.

How?

Remember that God withholds the next step until order is established in the present situation. Like the ancient Greeks, observe purification rites: Clean up and clean out the old to make way for the new.

You can do so easily as you follow some of the techniques suggested in this book. Try forgiving and releasing people and situations of the past or present that are no longer for your good by decreeing:

"CHRIST IN ME NOW FREES ME FROM ALL RESENTMENT OR ATTACHMENT TOWARD PEOPLE, PLACES OR THINGS OF THE PAST OR PRESENT. CHRIST IN ME NOW FREES ME FROM ALL RESENTMENT OR ATTACHMENT *FROM* PEOPLE, PLACES OR THINGS OF THE PAST OR PRESENT. I MANIFEST MY TRUE PLACE WITH THE TRUE PEOPLE AND WITH THE TRUE WAY OF LIFE NOW."

Next, form a vacuum literally. Get rid of what you do not want to make way for what you do want in your life. Throw out and pass on old possessions to which are attached old memories and emotional ties that are no longer of value.

Then make a success covenant with God.

In part I of that success covenant, tell God what you want Him to do for you:

(1) List what you want Him to help you *eliminate* from your life.

(2) List what you want Him to help you *manifest* in your life.

(3) List what you now have to be *thankful* for.

Then in part II of that success covenant, write out what you are going to do for God, such as:

(1) Spending half an hour or an hour daily in prayer, meditation and inspirational study.

(2) Putting God first financially by tithing a tenth of your income to His work at the point or points where you are receiving spiritual help and inspiration.

(3) List other things you plan to do for God.

Next, get busy invoking your part of that success covenant, part II. Since thanksgiving is the price of answered prayer, pay as well as pray! Observe the Old Testament custom of giving a "faith offering" *before* answered prayer and of giving a "thank offering" *after* answered prayer. Giving thanks beforehand connects you with the source of power. Giving thanks afterward keeps you connected with the source of power.

There is something about the mental act of thanksgiving that carries the human mind far beyond the region of doubt into the clear atmosphere of faith and trust where all things are possible. To praise and give thanks before there is anything to be thankful for invariably opens the way to answered prayer. Indeed, giving thanks beforehand gets your prayers answered. Giving thanks afterward keeps them answered!

As mentioned in my book, *The Prosperity Secret of the Ages*, Jacob made a success covenant with God at the lowest point in his life, when he was out of favor with God and man. He then got busy invoking his part of that covenant, trusting God to do the rest. All that he asked for—wealth, peace of mind, reconciliation with his family, and increased spiritual understanding—was given him. Jehovah finally renamed him "Israel" meaning "prince of God" (Genesis 28:20–22).

There is an inner discipline that brings answer to prayer and nobody places that discipline upon you but yourself.

Are you willing to follow through by making a prayer wheel on which you place pictures of your prayers as though they were already answered? Remember the promise of Jehovah to the Bible's first millionaire, Abraham: "All the land that thou seest, to thee will I give it" (Genesis 13:14). That same promise applies to you as you invoke the picturing power of the mind on your prayer wheel.

You can claim your good, and press your claim, by picturing your prayers as already answered. As you look at your prayer wheel declare often: "FATHER, I'M TRUSTING. THANK YOU GOD FOR ANSWERED PRAYER. THIS OR SOMETHING BETTER. LET THINE UNLIMITED GOOD WILL BE DONE IN MY LIFE HERE AND NOW."

Then give thanks for "divine results" coming forth under "divine timing." Place your desires "lovingly in the hands of the Father" and go on your way.

How far are you willing to go to get your prayers answered? In the process of preparing for answered prayer, are you willing to pay your emotional debts?

There are doubtless people in your life who have helped you along the way. You probably took them for granted at the time or felt there was little you could do to show appreciation. But you can show your appreciation now by doing something special and specific for them. Show them you are grateful. Show them you care. Do so in both tangible and intangible ways that are so obvious they cannot discount your gratitude. Whether they respond to your gratitude or not is totally unimportant. The important thing is that you express it, deliberately and definitely, and then let results be what they may.

If those people are no longer available, having either passed from your life so completely that it would be unwise to recall them, or having passed from this earth plane beyond recall, then do something for someone else who needs it, in memory of them. Wherever they are, in this sphere or some other, they will unconsciously know and rejoice.

While waiting for your own prayers to be answered, prepare by helping someone else's prayers to be answered. Make this your "magnificent obsession."

After prayer, as you get busy doing for others what you hope and pray God will do for you, this act pays old karmic debts, clears away old emotional blocks, and puts you on the receiving end of answered prayer.

Often along the way remind yourself: "I AM PUTTING MY TRUST IN GOD FOR MY ANSWERS TO PRAYER. I AM NOT DEPENDING UPON PERSONS OR CONDITIONS."

GET READY FOR SURPRISES!

After prayer, get ready for surprises. Prayer may change your answers, or your life, so that the right answers can come. Prayer may even reverse results on you. If so, can you take it? If the highest and best answer to your prayer is at variance with the answer you wanted, will you recognize and accept it as answered prayer?

The last half of this book got delayed in writing for six months because during that time a special prayer project came up that required my full attention. For a time it looked as though my prayers were going to be answered the way I thought I wanted them answered at that point. God seemed to be cooperating with me beautifully. But as I kept praying, an uneasy, unsettled feeling came that things weren't really the way they appeared, so I got busy praying the prayer of guidance: "FATHER, WHAT IS THE TRUTH ABOUT THIS SITUATION? MAKE IT SO PLAIN AND CLEAR THAT I CANNOT MISTAKE IT OR YOUR GOOD FOR ME."

My prayer partners were also praying a prayer of protection for me: "YOUR LIFE IS SURROUNDED BY THE PURE WHITE LIGHT OF THE CHRIST INTO WHICH NOTHING NEGATIVE CAN PENETRATE AND OUT OF WHICH ONLY GOOD CAN COME."

Gradually what at first had seemed an answer to prayer did an about-face.

When the truth about the situation manifested and hidden factors revealed themselves, I realized that my own humanly conceived answer would have been a disaster. It was then I affirmed:

`I RELEASE THIS SITUATION TO THE PERFECT OUTWORKING OF THE CHRIST CONSCIOUSNESS NOW." Everything changed. Soon all involved realized that what we originally thought would have been answered prayer would have only been a tragedy had it come to pass.

Prayers for guidance, protection and release brought the true answer to prayer for all concerned, though it proved a reverse result from that which I had originally had in mind.

Thus it is from fresh experience in the arena of prayer that I say to you, "When you pray and after you pray, be ready for God's divine answer (which is the sublime answer), rather than your humanly conceived one, even if His answer for you is a reversal of what you thought you wanted. It will later prove to be heavenly guidance, even when he says, 'No, No, No. This isn't it. Wait a while, honey.'"

As you relax, let go, and nonresistantly follow His will and His way to your answered prayer; it is then that you will walk in paths of "pleasantness and peace" of which Solomon wrote (Proverbs 3:17).

Along the way, you may wish to declare, "FATHER, SHOW ME HOW TO DIVINELY ADJUST MYSELF TO RECEIVE THE ANSWER TO MY PRAYERS AND HELP ME TO DIVINELY ACCEPT IT WHEN IT COMES."

AFTER PRAYER COMES THE NEVER-FAILING LIGHT

By now I am sure you have discovered that *prayer isn't just for people with problems. Prayer also makes happy people happier and healthy people healthier. It even makes rich people richer!*

Perhaps after you pray is the most important time, because that's the time to trust God and follow the very first guidance that comes. Sometimes your prayers begin to get answered in bits and pieces.

Rich or poor, old or young, happy or lonely, there is a need for developing your prayer consciousness. And developing a prayer consciousness is like developing any other ability or talent: Practice makes perfect. Every time you try again, it gets easier and the results are more gratifying.

Some of the prayers I have prayed have been fifteen, even twenty years, in getting answered, and even then the answers came in bits and pieces. Some are yet to be answered. I've known how David must have felt when he had to wait twenty years to become king of Israel, though he had received that spiritual assignment as a youth when Samuel anointed him. I have discovered what he must have realized when he was waiting for the good he knew was his: That I was having to grow big enough to receive some of the answers to my prayers; that our good comes as fast as we are ready to receive it and maintain it.

Such growing is usually done in the darkness, especially the struggle connected with that growth. Such darkness is good. Learn to give thanks for the darkness that accompanies growth and to rest in it so that new energies of the soul may gather there and mount within.

After the darkness finally comes the light. In that light you will agree with the man who once said, "I believe we always get answers. We get what we ask for, or something better, in prayer."

So after prayer, continue praying, and continue growing to receive the answer, even if that growth contains darkness. Meanwhile *do the things that need to be done in your present circumstances, rather than trying to force and strain for good you are not yet ready to receive. What comes easily goes easily.* Be willing to grow and then grow some more. Be willing to change and then change some more. Be willing to let prayer change you first, so that it can later change the situations about which you pray. Give both yourself and the power of prayer time to work until the leaven can permeate every recess of your being with its expanding, balancing power.

Declare for people and conditions about you: "I LOVE YOU, I BLESS YOU, I HAVE FAITH IN YOU." Or "I AM IN RIGHT RELATION WITH ALL PEOPLE AND ALL SITUATIONS NOW." For your own prayer projects declare: "I RELEASE THIS PRAYER TO BE ANSWERED IN THE FAITH THAT THE ANSWER SHALL BE RELEASED TO ME."

Remember—you were divine before you were human and to that divinity you must return. I pray that something in this book will help you make that "return trip" in triumph, garnering all the rich blessings of life along the way.

Be assured that you go accompanied by my love and blessing. Indeed, I am but one of many fellow travelers silently journeying with you toward a rich destiny of health, wealth and happiness. Prayer makes easier our journey, every step of the way.

And now, at the end of this book as you journey forth, I invite you to take with you the lavish promise that was given by the prophet Malachi at the end of another book—the Old Testament:

". . . Prove me now herewith saith the Lord, if I will not open you the windows of heaven and pour you out a blessing that there shall not be room enough to receive it." (Malachi 3:10)

In other words, pray and grow rich!